Fund-raising,
Grants, and Foundations

Fund-raising,
Grants, and Foundations
A Comprehensive Bibliography

Charlotte Georgi
Librarian for Management Bibliography
University of California, Los Angeles

and

Terry Fate
Research Coordinator

Libraries Unlimited, Inc.
Littleton, Colorado

1985

LIBRARIES UNLIMITED, INC.
P.O. Box 263
Littleton, Colorado 80160-0263

Library of Congress Cataloging in Publication Data

Georgi, Charlotte.
  Fund-raising, grants, and foundations.

    Includes index.
    1. Fund raising—United States—Bibliography.
I. Fate, Terry. II. Title.
Z7164.F5G46 1985 [HG177] 016.6581'522 84-21821
ISBN 0-87287-441-9

Libraries Unlimited books are bound with Type II nonwoven material that
meets and exceeds National Association of State Textbook Administrators'
Type II nonwoven material specifications Class A through E.

Table of Contents _____

Foreword. . . . . ? vii

Introduction. ix

Section I:
Reference Information Sources 1

Associations and Centers. 3
Bibliographies. 20
Directories: National 24
Directories: State and Local 32
Government Publications 39
Handbooks and Manuals. 47
Online Databases. 54
    General Works 54
    Directories. 55
    Journals and Looseleaf Services 56
    Individual Databases 56
    Database Vendors 57
Periodical Indexes, Journals, and Newsletters 58
    Periodical Indexes 58
    Journals and Newsletters. 60

Section II:
Subject Information Sources 69

Accounting, Business Methods, and Management. 71
Computers and the Automated Office. 82
    Computers: General Works 82
    Computers: Reference Sources. 83
    Computers: Directories. 84
    Computers: Buying a Computer. 85
    Computers: Journals and Looseleaf Services 85
    The Automated Office: General Works 86

Computers and the Automated Office (cont'd)
    The Automated Office: Guides and Handbooks. 87
    The Automated Office: Journals and Looseleaf Services 88
Corporate Social Responsibility and Philanthropy 89
Foundations and Foundation Grants. 100
Fund-raising. 105
Grantsmanship and Proposal Writing. 118
Law and Taxation 126
Not-for-Profit Organizations and Agencies 130
Publicity and Public Relations 147
Volunteerism 151

Section III:
A Basic Fund-raising Library 159

    Index 169

Foreword _____

A novice can't be in the fund-raising business long before asking what the priorities are. Should two nineteenth century concrete lions be accepted just because a prospective donor wants to give them?

This question reflects the realization of how important it is to consider donors' needs and to satisfy their interests. It also requires an understanding of the fund-raiser's role. The professional must motivate the officers of the organization seeking fund support to define what they need and want, in both general and specific terms. Then, and only then, can the needs of the donor be matched with those of the institution.

Meanwhile, the fund-raiser's primary goal is to bring in money—with no strings attached, if possible. These overlapping objectives require skills in dealing with people, skills in communication, and skills in business management.

The fund-raiser's job is always changing. Because of the importance of having a focus, it is frequently given the classification of "development officer." The job requires the development of a plan, the development of the organization's aims and objectives, the development of a volunteer program, and the development of staff personnel. The goals are never static, nor are the people involved: donors, volunteers, staff, and directors. Development is always fluid and changing, yet it must be secured on a solid base.

A primary characteristic of a development officer is the willingness to promote a cause. Commitment to an organization requires a knowledge of what its mission is and a belief in the people who will make it work. It is salesmanship for a dream, not for a product.

In the short term, an honest and enthusiastic spirit can make up for lack of staff leadership, lack of a development plan, and lack of sound financial control. The commitment of a volunteer can do the selling that the executive director or a staff member cannot do. Volunteers can ask friends for financial support of a cause they are already committed to and have given to themselves. The friend will want to jump on the bandwagon.

In the long term, however, the fund-raising staff must take the responsibility for reporting on the use of the money raised. They must present well thought-out plans, to be implemented within a definite time frame. They must demonstrate a genuine spirit of cooperation with the volunteers, who have every right to ask about the use of the funds they have helped to raise.

Development can take a variety of forms. Money can be raised by direct mail solicitation, by telephone campaigns, or by organized personal visits to donors. Money can also be obtained by program planning and proposal writing for grants-in-aid from corporate, community, and independent foundations. This necessitates developing an understanding with a foundation whose interests are congenial to the purposes of one's own institution. It can mean an ongoing, long-term relationship with a foundation or corporation with whom there are these mutual ties.

To accomplish all this, the development officer must spend a great deal of time in a variety of activities and tasks. The director of a program needs to perfect the coding system of a computerized mailing list; to develop plans to organize larger and larger circles of volunteers, advisers, and friends; to edit leaflets, letters, and other publications for distribution to potential donors; to plan and organize meetings with vital agendas and visual presentations.

The fund-raiser may have to spend as much as three years or more developing a major campaign to bring in the funds that will solve the institution's financial problems. This means a specific timetable, programmed charts, schedules to track progress, and a word processor capable of producing thank-you letters within the week that the checks have been deposited in the bank.

It all comes down to the most important advice of all: *Ask!* The key to fund-raising success is to be willing to run the risk of being told no—and to go right on taking the chance of asking again and again. The encouraging experience is that so often the response is *yes.*

Fund-raising is a developing American institution, a multibillion dollar business. An amazing amount of published material—books, journals, newsletters, newspapers, looseleaf services, even online databases—has grown up around this phenomenon. The investigative reader can choose from among many experts the ones who have the best advice and information.

Whether you are a public administrator trying to make up a deficit with outside funds, a volunteer working for battered women, a missionary helping the people of the Third World, or a long-term professional development officer, *Fund-raising, Grants, and Foundations* provides a comprehensive collection of source materials for information seekers with a wide range of fund-raising interests.

This bibliography serves the serious researcher with an up-to-date assemblage of sources of information about an exciting new profession—fund-raising. Fund-raising is 90 percent information and 10 percent luck. If you can find the right persons at the right times, for the right projects and the right amounts, your campaign will be successful. And, the odds can be significantly reduced by having the right information at hand, whether your prospective donor is an individual, a corporation, a foundation, a government agency, or a political action committee.

This bibliography can start you on your way.

Susan F. Rice
Alumni and Development Director
Graduate School of Management
UCLA Public Affairs

Introduction

Americans donated over sixty billion dollars to thousands of charitable causes even in the recession year 1982. Nearly 81 percent of that total, almost forty billion dollars, was contributed by individuals, while the other 19 percent came from corporations, bequests, and foundations. Total giving has tripled over the past 15 years (1968-1982) from 17.56 to 60.39 billions of dollars as reported in *Giving USA* (1983), the annual report of the American Association of Fund Raising Counsel.

What are the causes of this philanthropic phenomenon? Inflation, unemployment, changes in the philosophy of governmental aid to the less fortunate, business recession, the weather, spots on the moon? Whatever the reasons, fund-raising has become big business.

Dozens of associations, centers, and publishers have sprung up—among the most prestigious of these are the Foundation Center, the Taft Corporation, and the Grantsmanship Center. The Artists Foundation has recently published a directory of grants and awards for creative artists with the explicitly mercenary title, *Money Business.*

Not-for-profit management courses are appearing in business school curricula. The UCLA Graduate School of Management (GSM), for example, now offers an MBA degree in Arts Management. There are workshops, seminars, extension courses, even certificate programs now being offered in the field of fund-raising.

The UCLA Graduate School of Management Library noted this trend in the early 1970s. Development of the library collection on the subject resulted in a 76-page bibliography which was published in 1976 by the GSM School Publications Department. It was reprinted several times until it went out of print in 1981. The popularity of that bibliography was one of several reasons for this greatly expanded, commercially published book.

This is an extensive and, we hope, virtually complete bibliography of signficant titles in the fields of fund-raising, grants, and foundations. A variety of related subjects is included, with the intention of enhancing the book's practical value. The intended audience is librarians, fund-raisers, entrepreneurs, arts managers, not-for-profit businesses, social welfare agencies, creative artists, students, hospital administrators, volunteer organizations, colleges and universities, research specialists, environmentalists, symphony orchestras, civic groups, private and public schools, churches—the list goes on and on.

This volume is a comprehensive bibliography of 1,500 titles. The materials cited are, for the most part, recent imprints (from 1970 on) and are English language, primarily U.S. publications. Exceptions to these general guidelines have been made for especially significant landmark works.

The material has been organized into three sections. Section I, Reference Information Sources, is subdivided by "form"—associations, directories, government publications, databases, and so on. Section II, Subject Information Sources, is organized into 10 subject categories—accounting, proposal writing, public relations, volunteerism, and so forth. Section III is a basic fund-raising library of the very best titles available.

The bibliographic form used is unorthodox; it is designed to be useful rather than academically impressive. Entries give the full title first, then the author's name, followed by the publisher's address and the date of publication. This form of citation is used in the Gale Research Company directories and in the Scarecrow Press's *The Arts and the World of Business,* second edition, 1979.

There are few annotations. The contents of the books are fairly clearly indicated by their title, their classification in one or another category of the book and, in many cases, by their publishers' reputations. If a title fits into more than one category, it has been listed in each area where it is relevant.

No specific periodical articles are listed per se. Instead, the chapter on "Periodical Indexes, Journals, and Newsletters" suggests various indexes which provide access to the enormous amount of such materials available. It also lists selected basic journals, newsletters, and newspapers. The chapter, "Online Databases" opens up even greater bibliographic possibilities.

In conclusion, our special thanks are due to the continuous interest and substantial help of Susan Rice, UCLA GSM Director of Alumni and Development, and to Kunin Professor of Business and Society, George Steiner.

Section I:
Reference
Information
Sources

This first of three sections comprises reference sources of information on the subjects involved. The entries are subdivided by "form," namely professional associations, centers, institutes, et al.; bibliographies; national, state, and local directories of organizations and agencies; United States government publications; handbooks and manuals; computerized databases; and, finally, the vast resources of periodical literature, journals, magazines, newsletters, and newspapers.

ASSOCIATIONS AND CENTERS

Writing to professional associations, centers, committees, councils, foundations, societies, government agencies, and other organizations can be a very simple and rewarding way of getting information. Most of these organizations publish newsletters, bulletins, journals, annual reports, or monographs that may be worth acquiring. In general, membership fees and prices of publications are quite low.

For further reference to such sources, use the Gale Research Company's *Encyclopedia of Associations.* See also the entries under **Directories: National** in this section.

American Association for State and Local History (1940)

708 Berry Road, Nashville, Tennessee 37204.

Telephone: (615) 383-5991.

Membership: 8,000 state and local historical societies, educators, historians, writers.

Geographic Scope: United States and Canada.

Purpose: To improve the study of state and local history. Holds seminars, workshops, and other training courses to help members improve their public services.

Special Services: Consulting. Placement. Awards. Internships.

Publications: *A Bibliography on Historical Organization Practices,* six volumes; *Directory of Historical Societies and Agencies in the U.S. and Canada,* biennial; *Funding Sources and Technical Assistance for Museums and Historical Agencies: A Guide to Public Programs* (1979); *History News,* monthly.

American Association of Fund Raising Counsel (1935)

25 West 43rd Street, New York, New York 10036.

Telephone: (212) 354-5799.

Membership:	30 fund-raising counseling firms.
Geographic Scope:	International.
Purpose:	To assist nonprofit institutions with their fund-raising programs.
Special Services:	Consulting.
Publications:	*Fund Raising Review*, bimonthly; *Giving USA: Annual Report.*

American Council for the Arts (1960)

570 Seventh Avenue, New York, New York 10018.

Telephone: (212) 354-6655.

Membership:	Arts councils, community leaders, arts patrons, universities, libraries, and performing arts organizations.
Geographic Scope:	United States.
Purpose:	To address significant issues in the arts by promoting communication, management improvement, and problem solving among those who shape and implement arts policy.
Special Services:	Seminars and conferences. Information service. Referral service. Maintains statistical information on corporate giving practices.
Publications:	*ACA Update*, monthly; *American Arts*, bimonthly; *Arts in Education Sourcebook*; *The Cultural Wasteland*; *Guide to Corporate Giving in the Arts*, biennial; *Survey of Arts Administration Training in the U.S.*

American Council on Education (1918)

One Dupont Circle, Washington, D.C. 20036.

Telephone: (202) 833-4700.

Membership:	1,632 colleges, universities, and educational organizations.
Geographic Scope:	United States.
Purpose:	To improve education through volunteerism by educational groups.
Special Services:	Library.
Publications:	*Educational Record*, quarterly; *Factbook on Higher Education*; *Higher Education and National Affairs*, weekly.

American Society of Directors of Volunteer Services (1968)

American Hospital Association, 840 North Lakeshore Drive, Chicago, Illinois 60611.

Telephone: (312) 260-6000.

Membership:	1,600 individuals with responsibility at a professional level for the management or coordination of the volunteer services department/program of a hospital; the individual and the institution must be eligible for membership in the American Hospital Association.
Geographic Scope:	United States and Canada.
Purpose:	To provide an organized structure to advance and develop effective volunteer services management, and to encourage and assist members to develop their knowledge and increase their competence; to provide consultation and guidance; to establish and maintain professional standards and ethics; to cooperate with organizations and institutions of higher education in volunteer services management activities and in developing programs in the field of volunteer services mangement.
Special Services:	Provides resources and materials developed by the society for purchase and distribution to members only.
Publications:	*Hospitals*; *Membership Roster*, annual (available to members only); *Volunteer Leader*; *Volunteer Services Administration*, quarterly.

Artists Foundation, Inc. (1973)

110 Broad Street, Boston, Massachusetts 02110.

Telephone: (617) 482-8100.

Membership:	Public nonprofit organization to enhance the professional careers of creative artists.
Purpose:	To help create an environment in which artists have more time to pursue their careers; to assist artists in the public presentation of their works; to assist artists to acquire proper living/working space; to offer artists professional training and support services; to foster a sense of community and collegiality among artists.
Special Services:	Fellowships. Artists-in-Residence Program. Workshops. Referral service. Art competitions.
Publications:	*Money Business: Grants and Awards for Creative Artists* (1982)

Arts and Business Council (1973)

130 East 40th Street, New York, New York 10016.

Telephone: (212) 683-5555.

Membership:	140 business and nonprofit arts organizations.
Geographic Scope:	United States.
Purpose:	To establish and manage programs of benefit to the arts and business communities; to promote business involvement in the arts; to help arts organizations develop proposals in line with corporate needs. Recruits and trains corporate executives to provide pro bono business assistance to arts groups.
Special Services:	Training seminars.
Publications:	*Business Volunteers for the Arts*, quarterly; *Highlights* (booklet series); *Winterfare* (directory).

Association for Volunteer Administration (1960)

Box 4584, Boulder, Colorado 80406.

Telephone: (303) 497-0238.

Membership: 900 educators, researchers, students, and administrators of volunteer programs.

Geographic Scope: International.

Purpose: To develop professional standards and ethics; to develop degree and nondegree professional training courses with educational institutions. Sponsors meetings, workshops, forums, and conferences to aid cooperation and communication among community volunteer services.

Special Services: National Service Award. Distinguished Member Service Award.

Publications: *AVA in the Marketplace*, annual; *Journal of Volunteer Administration*, quarterly; *Membership Directory*, annual; *Newsletter/Bulletin*, monthly.

Association of Voluntary Action Scholars (1971)

S-203 Human Development Building, Pennsylvania State University, University Park, Pennsylvania 16802.

Telephone: (814) 863-2944.

Membership: 450 individuals involved in research, study, and programs concerned with better understanding of citizen involvement and volunteer participation.

Geographic Scope: United States.

Purpose: To make available to scholars and administrators of volunteer service programs information and research on voluntary action topics.

Special Services: Sponsors research proposals and projects on voluntary action topics.

Publications: *Citizen Participation and Voluntary Action Abstracts*, quarterly; *Journal of Voluntary Action Research*, quarterly; *Newsletter*, quarterly.

Association of Volunteer Centers (1951)

c/o Mary Louise Gilkes, 812 W. Paseo del Prado, Green Valley, Arizona 85614.

Telephone: (602) 625-5117.

Membership:	300 volunteer bureaus and centers concerned with health and welfare concerns.
Geographic Scope:	International.
Purpose:	Members assume community responsibility for developing standards for, placement of, and training of citizen volunteers.
Special Services:	Accreditation of member bureaus, centers, and other central clearinghouses.
Publications:	*Directory of Volunteer Bureaus and Voluntary Action Centers*, annual; *Model Volunteer Program*, annual; *Notebook* (newsletter), monthly. *Salary Study and Surveys*, annual.

Business Committee for the Arts (1967)

1775 Broadway, New York, New York 10019.

Telephone: (212) 921-0700.

Membership:	160 leaders of U.S. businesses and corporations, distributed evenly by industry and geographic location. Membership is by invitation.
Geographic Scope:	United States.
Purpose:	To encourage business support of the arts; to provide information to the business and artistic communities relating to support available to the arts from industry.
Special Services:	Research and analysis. Advertising. With *Forbes* magazine, sponsors awards for outstanding corporate programs in the arts.
Publications:	*BCA News*, monthly; *5,123 Examples of How BCA Companies Supported the Arts.*

Center for Non-Profit Organizations, Inc. (1980)

203 West 25th Street, Third Floor, New York, New York 10001.

Telephone: (212) 989-9026.

Membership:	Nonprofit organizations.
Geographic Scope:	United States.
Purpose:	To provide assistance to new and existing nonprofit organizations in administration, public relations and advertising, fund raising, publications, and legal matters.
Special Services:	Consulting. Seminars. Speakers bureau. Resource Center.
Publications:	*Laws and Regulations Concerning Nonprofit Organizations Explained for Laymen* (1983).

Committee for Full Funding of Education Programs (1969)

1707 H Street, N.W., Fifth Floor, Washington, D.C. 20006.

Telephone: (202) 547-4434.

Membership:	300 institutions and individuals in elementary, secondary, and higher education.
Geographic Scope:	United States.
Purpose:	To promote full government funding of education by analyzing budgets and appropriations and lobbying members of the federal government.
Publications:	*Effort* (Education Full Funding Report), 6-10 times per year.

Council for Advancement and Support of Education (1974)

11 Dupont Circle, N.W., Suite 400, Washington, D.C. 20036.

Telephone: (202) 328-5900.

Membership:	11,200 educational institutions and individuals involved in fund-raising, public relations, publications, alumni groups, and government relations in colleges, universities, community colleges, elementary and secondary schools.

Council for Advancement and Support of Education (cont'd)

Purpose: To aid education through training programs, publica-
                    tions, research projects. Monitors federal legislation
                    of interest to education.

Publications: *Case Currents*, monthly; *Directory*, annual; *Guide to
                    the Administration of Charitable Remainder Trusts*
                    (1984).

Council for Financial Aid to Education (1952)

680 Fifth Avenue, New York, New York 10019.

Telephone: (212) 541-4050.

Membership: 30 businessmen and educators.

Geographic Scope: United States.

Purpose: To promote and maintain financial aid to higher
                    education from the public and from business, indus-
                    try, labor, and service organizations.

Special Services: Library of materials concerning aid to education.

Publications: *Corporate Support of Higher Education, 1979*
                    (1980); *Corporate Social Responsibility: Policies,
                    Programs, and Publications* (1982); *Profile of
                    Corporate Contributions* (1983).

Council on Foundations (1949)

1828 L Street, N.W., Washington, D.C. 20036.

Telephone: (202) 466-6512.

Membership: Approximately 950 foundations, grantmakers, and
                    corporations having charitable giving programs.

Geographic Scope: Primarily United States.

Purpose: To keep its members aware of developments and
                    trends in philanthropy; to increase public under-
                    standing of philanthropy; and to serve as a legislative
                    liaison for grantmakers.

Special Services: Consulting. Sponsors meetings.

Publications: *Annual Report*, annual; *Corporate Philanthropy*
                   (1982); *Foundation News*, bimonthly; *The Handbook*
                   on Private Foundations (1981); *Memorandum on*
                   Corporate Giving (1981); *Opportunities for Philan-*
                   thropy–1976 (1977); *Philanthropy in the 70's: An*
                   Anglo-American Discussion (1973); *Private and*
                   Foreign Aid (1982); *Public Information Handbook*
                   for Foundations (1973).

Direct Mail Fundraisers Association (1972)

151 Lexington Avenue, New York, New York 10016.

Telephone: (212) 679-0553.

Membership: 180 direct mail fund-raisers and those providing ser-
                   vices to these fund-raisers.

Geographic Scope: United States.

Purpose: To improve direct mail fund-raising by aiding com-
                   munication among members and by establishing
                   ethical standards and guidelines.

Special Services: Placement.

Publications: *Membership Directory*; *Newsletter*, quarterly.

Federation of Protestant Welfare Agencies (1922)

281 Park Avenue South, New York, New York 10010.

Telephone: (212) 777-4800.

Membership: 250 human welfare agencies.

Geographic Scope: New York City Greater Metropolitan area.

Purpose: To provide consultation, planning and support,
                   training in management, and recruitment of volun-
                   teers for member groups.

Special Services: Referral Service. Camping program for disadvantaged
                   children. Scholarships. Program grants for member
                   agencies in the New York City Small Metropolitan
                   Area.

Publications: *Annual Report*; *Deferred Giving Newsletter*,
                   quarterly; *Newsletter*, 3 times per year.

Four-One-One (1979)

7304 Beverly Street, Annandale, Virginia 22003.

Telephone: (703) 354-6270.

Membership: National clearinghouse composed of educational institutions, volunteer programs, and other human service agencies.

Geographic Scope: United States.

Purpose: To provide information necessary to maintain volunteer programs in community and human services areas.

Special Services: Library.

Publications: *Community Resource Tie Line* (includes *Green Sheets, Training Blue Book*, and *Program Profiles*), annual; *Federal Funding Forum*, annual; *Mirror-on-Volunteerism,* quarterly.

Foundation Center (1956)

888 Seventh Avenue, New York, New York 10106.

Telephone: (212) 975-1120.

Membership: 200 sponsoring foundations.

Geographic Scope: United States.

Purpose: To provide information, conduct research, and publish materials about foundations and their grants.

Special Services: National collections of source materials and regional collections in public or university and college libraries throughout the United States.

Publications: For a list of publications of the Foundation Center, see **A Basic Fund-raising Library**, in Section III of this volume.

Independent Sector (1980)

1828 L Street, N.W., Washington, D.C. 20036.

Telephone: (202) 223-8100.

Membership:	500 voluntary organizations, businesses, and foundations.
Geographic Scope:	United States.
Purpose:	To promote charitable giving, volunteerism, and not-for-profit initiative by informing the public, conducting research, and emphasizing effective management of volunteer and not-for-profit organizations.
Publications:	*Americans Volunteer–1981* (1981); *Update*, monthly.

International Council on United Fund Raising (1974)

United Way Plaza, Alexandria, Virginia 22314.

Telephone: (703) 836-7100.

Membership:	19 associations of the United Way International.
Geographic Scope:	Multinational.
Purpose:	To increase volunteerism and understanding among nations; to provide effective delivery of services to the needy.
Publications:	*United for Service*, 1-2 times per year.

International Fund Raising Association (1957)

One Lincoln Center, Suite 999, 5400 LBJ Freeway, Dallas, Texas 75240.

Telephone: (214) 960-1717.

Membership:	78 businesses and individuals involved in fund-raising for religious and charitable groups.
Geographic Scope:	International.

National Assistance Management Association (1978)

> Box 57051, Washington, D.C. 20037.
>
> Telephone: (202) 223-1448.
>
> Membership: Individuals involved in government and private foundation grants management.
>
> Geographic Scope: United States.
>
> Purpose: To improve training, education, administration, management, communication in grants and assistance management.
>
> Special Services: Surveys. Seminars. Workshops.
>
> Publications: *Grants and Assistance News*, monthly; *Journal*, semi-annual; *Membership Directory*, annual.

National Association of Student Financial Aid Administrators (1968)

> 1776 Massachusetts Avenue, N.W., Suite 100, Washington, D.C., 20036.
>
> Telephone: (202) 785-0453.
>
> Membership: 2,800 institutions of higher education, financial aid administrators, and interested others.
>
> Geographic Scope: United States.
>
> Purpose: To serve administrators, students, and faculty in matters concerning student financial aid.
>
> Publications: *Journal of Student Financial Aid*, 3 times per year; *Newsletter*, monthly.

National Catholic Development Conference (1968)

> 119 North Park Avenue, Suite 409, Rockville Centre, New York 11570.
>
> Telephone: (516) 764-6700.
>
> Membership: 400 fund-raising organizations, development officers, and fund-raisers of religious institutions.
>
> Geographic Scope: United States.

Purpose: To promote an ethical code for fund-raisers; to assist its members to develop effective methods of fund-raising; to enable members to discuss and exchange ideas and information.

Special Services: Seminars.

Publications: *Bibliography of Fund Raising and Philanthropy* (1982); *Dimensions* (newsletter), monthly, *Fund Raising Forum*, monthly; *A Guide for Preparing a Statement of Accountability* (1982).

National Foundation on the Arts and the Humanities (1965)

Washington, D.C. 20506.

Membership: Consists of the National Endowment for the Arts and the National Endowment for the Humanities.

Geographic Scope: United States.

Purpose: To encourage and support national progress in the humanities and the arts.

National Endowment for the Arts

Washington, D.C. 20506.

Telephone: (202) 634-6369.

Membership: Council composed of the Endowment Chairman and 26 members appointed by the President.

Geographic Scope: United States.

Purpose: To foster professional excellence of the arts in the United States by awarding grants to individuals, arts agencies, and nonprofit organizations in the fields of design arts, dance, expansion arts, folk arts, literature, film, radio, television, museums, theater, and visual arts.

Publications: *Annual Report*; *Cultural Post*, bimonthly; *Guide to Programs*, annual.

National Foundation on the Arts and the Humanities (cont'd)

National Endowment for the Humanities

Washington, D.C. 20506.

Telephone: (202) 724-0386.

Membership:	Council composed of the Endowment Chairman and 26 members appointed by the President.
Geographic Scope:	United States.
Purpose:	To promote and support knowledge in the humanities, in particular as it applies to contemporary values and public issues, by making grants to individuals, groups, or institutions.
Publications:	*Annual Report*; *Program Announcement*, annual.

National Society of Fund Raising Executives (1960)

Investment Building, Suite 1000, 1511 K Street, N.W., Washington, D.C. 20005.

Telephone: (202) 638-1393.

Membership:	4,000 individuals involved in managing fund-raising programs for all types of not-for-profit organizations.
Geographic Scope:	United States and Canada.
Purpose:	To promote research and teaching in fund-raising through workshops and seminars.
Special Services:	Awards. Hall of Fame. Speakers Bureau. Placement.
Publications:	*Journal*, semi-annual; *Membership Directory* (available to members only); *Newsletter*, monthly.

Public Relations Society of America (1948)

845 Third Avenue, New York, New York 10022.

Telephone: (212) 826-1750.

Membership:	10,000 public relations professionals in business, industry, government, health and welfare, and education.
Geographic Scope:	United States.
Purpose:	To aid public relations professionals by sponsoring development programs, referral services, speakers bureaus, and accreditation programs.
Publications:	*Public Relations Journal*, monthly; *Public Relations Register*, annual.

United Way International (1974)

801 North Fairfax Street, Alexandria, Virginia 22314.

Telephone: (703) 836-7100.

Membership:	20 United Way agencies.
Geographic Scope:	International.
Purpose:	To provide assistance to nations and communities with United Way federated, communitywide fundraising organizations or those wishing to begin them, through training, information exchange, and philanthropic programs.

United Way of America (1918)

801 North Fairfax Street, Alexandria, Virginia 22314.

Telephone: (703) 836-7100.

Membership:	1,264 local United Ways and planning councils.
Geographic Scope:	United States.
Purpose:	To supply support to local United Ways in fundraising, budgeting, management, allocation of funds, planning, and communications.

United Way of America (cont'd)

Special Services:	National Corporate Development Program (to increase corporate giving). National Academy of Volunteerism (training for staff and volunteers). Internships. National media support. Library. Competitions. Awards.
Publications:	*Accounting and Financial Reporting: A Guide for United Ways and Not-for-Profit Human Service Organizations* (1974); *Budgeting*; *Community Focus*, 10 times per year; *Digest of Selected Reports*, semi-annual; *Executive Newsletter*, 40 times per year; *International Directory*, annual; *Quarterly Newsletter*, quarterly.

Volunteer: The National Center for Citizen Involvement (1979)

Box 4179, Boulder, Colorado 80306.

Telephone: (303) 447-0492.

Membership:	300 voluntary action centers.
Geographic Scope:	United States.
Purpose:	To act as a clearinghouse for information on volunteer programs; to encourage citizens to volunteer.
Special Services:	Sponsors National Volunteer Week. Workshops. Training courses.
Publications:	*Catalog of Publications*, annual; *Clearinghouse Greensheets*, annual; *Helping the Volunteer Get Started* (1972); *Planning, Implementing, Evaluating a Workshop for Directors of Volunteers* (1973); *Voluntary Action Leadership*, quarterly; *Volunteering* (newsletter), monthly.

Volunteers of America (1896).

3813 North Causeway Boulevard, Metairie, Louisiana 70002.

Telephone: (504) 837-2652.

Membership:	3,800 paid staff; 44 state groups, commissioned members and volunteers.
Geographic Scope:	United States.

Purpose:	To give aid to those in need regardless of race or creed.
Special Services:	Many service centers nationwide. Adoption services. Aid to the handicapped, the elderly, the homeless, prisoners and their families, the emotionally disturbed, families, unwed mothers, alcoholics. Day care. Disaster relief. Nutrition programs. Half-way houses. Nursing homes. Summer camps. Sunday schools.
Publications:	*The Volunteer Gazette*, monthly.

Women and Foundations/Corporate Philanthropy (1977)

70 West 40th Street, New York, New York 10018.

Telephone: (212) 759-7712.

Membership:	400 staff and trustees of grantmaking organizations.
Geographic Scope:	United States.
Purpose:	To increase grant money available to women's and girl's programs; to improve women's status within philanthropic organizations.
Special Services:	Networks of men and women in philanthropy. Research.
Publications:	*Newsletter*, quarterly.

BIBLIOGRAPHIES

For the most part, the bibliographies cited in this section are English language, primarily from American, publications. They are recent imprints, the majority from 1970-1982. Exceptions have been made for significant landmark works.

There are few annotations, the assumption being made that intelligent judgment will recognize content sufficiently from the title and its classification into one of the 10 subject categories or eight formal reference divisions. Evaluations can be made as well by way of authors' and publishers' reputations. Inferences can also be drawn from dates and pagination. The basic library on fund-raising that concludes this work will possibly confirm conclusions the reader has already reached.

In short, the bibliographies listed below are meant to augment, enhance, and offer more guidelines to selection.

Action in the Action Grants: A Select Bibliography on the Urban Development Action Grant Program. John P. Worsham. Vance Bibliographies, Box 229, Monticello, Illinois 61856. 1981. 12p.

Administration in the Arts: An Annotated Bibliography of Selected References. E. Arthur Prieve and Daniel J. Schmidt. Center for Arts Administration, Graduate School of Business, University of Wisconsin, Madison, Wisconsin 53706. 1977. 127p.

The Arts and the World of Business: A Selected Bibliography. Second edition. Charlotte Georgi. Scarecrow Press, 52 Liberty Street, Box 656, Metuchen, New Jersey 08840. 1979. 188p.

Arts Management: An Annotated Bibliography. Revised edition. Stephen Benedict and Linda C. Coe. Center for Arts Information, 625 Broadway, New York, New York 10012. 1980. 47p.

Bibliography of Fund Raising and Philanthropy. Second edition. George T. Holloway, executive editor; Rosy B. Gonzales, editor and director of research. National Catholic Development Conference, 119 North Park Avenue, Suite 409, Rockville Centre, New York 11570. 1982. 76p.

Bibliography of U.S. Government Documents Pertaining to Government Support of the Arts, 1963-1972. M. Gladstone. Drama Book Publishers, 821 Broadway, New York, New York 10003. 1977. n.p.

A Bibliography on Arts Administration. Victoria E. Levene and William J. Buckley. School of Management, School of Arts and Sciences, State University of New York at Binghamton, Binghamton, New York 13901. 1977. 30p.

A Bibliography on Fundraising. Alfreda Doyle, editor. Bibliotheca Press, Box 98378, Atlanta, Georgia 30359. 1982. 50p.

Comsearch Printouts. Foundation Center, 888 Seventh Avenue, New York, New York. 10106. (Computer-produced subject guides to foundation grants.) Annual.

SUBJECTS: Films, Documentaries and Audiovisuals; Television, Radio and Communications; Language, Literature, and Journalism; Publications; Adult and Continuing Education; Public Elementary and Secondary Education; Private Elementary and Secondary Education; Higher Education—Capital Support; Higher Education—Endowments; Junior and Community Colleges; Scholarships, Fellowships, Student Aid, and Loans; Library and Information Services; Educational Research; Vocational Education, Career Development and Employment; Medical and Health Education; Medical Research; Dentistry and Nursing; Mental Health; Public Health; Alcohol and Drug Abuse; Cancer Care and Research; Hospices; Abortion, Birth Control and Family Planning; Children and Youth—Health Care; Children and Youth—Medical Research; Theater; Music Schools and Music Education; Orchestras and Musical Performances; Architecture, Historical Preservation and Historical Societies; Aged; Handicapped; Mentally Retarded and Mentally Disabled; Boys; Blacks; Hispanics; Biology and Genetics; Agriculture and Farming; Chemistry; Environmental Law, Education, and Protection; Computer Systems and Services; Energy; Engineering; Business Education; Economics; Political Science; Law Schools and Legal Education; Public Policy and Consumer Affairs; Housing and Transportation; Community Funds; Crime and Law Enforcement; Child Abuse; Family Services and Parent Education; Community Centers; Young Men's and Women's Associations; Food and Nutrition; Animal Welfare and Wildlife; Rural Development; Athletics, Physical Fitness and Recreation; Camps and Camperships; Parks, Gardens, and Zoos; Refugee and Relief Services; Volunteer Programs; Community and Urban Development; Religion; Religious Education; Governmental Agencies; Matching and Challenge Grants; Conferences and Seminars.

Comsearch Printouts (cont'd)

Geographic: Washington, D.C.; New York City; California; Illinois; Massachusetts; Michigan; Minnesota; New Jersey; New York (except New York City); North Carolina; Ohio; Pennyslvania; Texas; Northeast (Maine, New Hampshire, Rhode Island, Vermont, Connecticut); Southeast (Florida, Georgia, Alabama, Mississippi, Louisiana, South Carolina); Northwest (Washington, Oregon); Rocky Mountains (Arizona, New Mexico, Colorado, Utah, Nevada, Idaho, Montana, Wyoming).

Special Topics: The 1,000 Largest Foundations in the U.S. by Asset Size; The 1,000 Largest Foundations in the U.S. by Annual Grant Totals; 1,300 Operating Foundations Which Administer Their Own Projects or Programs.

Corporate Responsibility for Social Problems: A Bibliography. Bank of America, Editorial Services Department 3124, Box 37000, San Francisco, California 94137. 1975. 78p.

Foundations and Fund Raising: A Bibliography of Books to 1980. John J. Miletich. Vance Bibliographies, Box 229, Monticello, Illinois 61856. 1981. 10p.

Grant and Contract Funding Newsletters, Journals, Periodicals and Newspapers: An Annotated Buyer's and Researcher's Bibliography. Tony Ott. Grant Administration Consultants, Box 234, Chesterfield, Missouri 63017. 1980. 125p.

Grants-in-Aid: A Bibliography of Selective References, 1861-1960. U.S. Department of Health, Education and Welfare, Washington, D.C. 20201. 1962. 91p.

The Grants Resource Manual. Donald Levitan and Daniel F. Donahue. Government Research Publications, Box 122, Newton Center, Massachusetts 02159. 1980. 108p.

Grants Survival Library—1980. Donald Levitan and Daniel F. Donahue. Vance Bibliographies, Box 229, Monticello, Illinois 61856. 1980. 13p.

Grantsmanship and Proposal Development Publications: An Annotated Buyer's and Researcher's Bibliography. Tony Ott. Grant Administration Consultants, Box 234, Chesterfield, Missouri 63017. 1980. 125p.

A Guide to Grants: Governmental and Nongovernmental. Donald Levitan and Daniel F. Donahue. Government Research Publications, Box 122, Newton Center, Massachusetts 02159. 1979. n.p.

Major Sources of Grant and Contract Program Information: An Annotated Buyer's and Researcher's Bibliography. Tony Ott. Grant Administration Consultants, Box 234, Chesterfield, Missouri 63017. 1980. 500p.

Management of Visual Arts, Museums and Galleries: A Selected Bibliography. Anthony G. White. Vance Bibliographies, Box 229, Monticello, Illinois 61856. 1979. 8p.

Marketing the Arts: A Selected and Annotated Bibliography. Kent Nakamoto and Kathi Levin. Association of College, University and Community Arts Administrators, Box 2137, Madison, Wisconsin 53701. 1978. 18p.

A Resource Guide of State and Philanthropic Grants Information. Donald Levitan and Clara A. Bonney. Council of Planning Librarians. Available from Vance Bibliographies, Box 229, Monticello, Illinois 61856. 1978. 25p.

Selected Bibliography on Grantsmanship. Donald Levitan. Council of Planning Librarians, CPL Bibliographies, 1313 East 60th Street, Merriam Center, Chicago, Illinois 60637. 1974. 15p.

Selected Information Resources on Scholarships, Fellowships, Grants and Loans. John Henry Hass, compiler. U.S. Library of Congress, Science and Technology Division, National Referral Center, Washington, D.C. 20540. 1977. 17p.

Voluntary Associations in Change and Conflict–A Bibliography. James Nwannukwu Kerri. CPL Bibliographies, 1313 East 60th Street, Merriam Center, Chicago, Illinois 60637. 1974. 13p.

Volunteer Workers: A Bibliography. Mary A. Vance. Vance Bibliographies, Box 229, Monticello, Illinois 61856. 1982. 27p.

While You're Up, Get Me a Grant: A Basic Bibliography on Grants. Bay Area Social Responsibilities Round Table, 2745 Stuart, #3, Berkeley, California 94705. 1976. 10p.

DIRECTORIES: NATIONAL

National directories are one of the best places to go for names, addresses, officers, telephone numbers, descriptions of programs and publications, membership, dues, et al. The investment of a 20 cent stamp can bring rich rewards not only in the way of expert suggestions but also in the confidence of a knowledge of collegiality of interests.

The Advisory Panels of the National Endowment for the Arts. Washington International Arts Letter, Box 9005, Washington, D.C. 20003. 1983. 22p.

Annual Register of Grant Support. Marquis Academic Media, 200 East Ohio Street, Chicago, Illinois 60611. Annual.

The A-V Connection: The Guide to Federal Funds for Audio-Visual Programs. American Library Association, 50 East Huron Street, Chicago, Illinois 60611. 1981. 248p.

Awards, Honors and Prizes: An International Directory of Awards and Their Donors. Fifth edition. Paul Wasserman, editor. Gale Research Company, Book Tower, Detroit, Michigan 48226. 1982. Volume 1: U.S. and Canada. Volume 2: International and Foreign. Supplemented by *New Awards, Honors and Prizes.* Two volumes.

A Catalog of Federal Grant-in-Aid Programs to State and Local Governments. Advisory Commission on Intergovernmental Relations, Washington, D.C. 20575. Annual.

Complete Grants Sourcebook for Higher Education. Public Management Institute. Available from American Council on Education, One Dupont Circle, Suite 20, Washington, D.C. 20036. 1980. 605p.

Computer Resource Guide for Nonprofits. Second edition. Kenneth Gilman. Public Management Institute, 358 Brannan Street, San Francisco, California 94107. 1984. 691p.

Comsearch Printouts. Foundation Center, 888 Seventh Avenue, New York, New York 10106. Annual. (Computer-produced subject guides to foundation grants.) Available in the following categories: Subjects, Geographic, and Special Topics. For full subjects covered, see the *Comsearch Printouts* entry in the **Bibliographies** section.

Corporate 500: The Directory of Corporate Philanthropy. Second edition. Stephen Hitchcock, executive editor. Public Management Institute, 358 Brannan Street, San Francisco, California 94107. 1983. 1,000p.

Corporate Foundation Profiles. Revised edition. Foundation Center, 888 Seventh Avenue, New York, New York 10106. 1980. 512p.

Corporate Fund Raising Directory. Public Service Materials Center, 111 North Central Avenue, Hartsdale, New York, 10530. Annual.

Cultural Directory II: Federal Funds and Services for the Arts and Humanities. Linda C. Coe, Rebecca Denny, and Anne Rogers. Prepared for the Federal Council on the Arts and Humanities. Smithsonian Institution Press, Room 2280, Arts and Industries Building, Washington, D.C. 20560. 1980. 270p.

Cumulative List of Organizations Described in Section 170 (c) of the Internal Revenue Code of 1954. Internal Revenue Service, U.S. Department of the Treasury. Available from U.S. Government Printing Office, Washington, D.C. 20402. Annual with three quarterly supplements.

Directory of Associations in Canada. Micromedia Ltd., 144 Front Street West, Toronto, Ontario, M5J 2L7, Canada. Annual.

Directory of California Non-Profit Associations. Judith Yung and Mary Kasik. Staff Association, San Francisco Public Library, Civic Center, San Francisco, California 94102. 1970. 217p.

Directory of Directories: An Annotated Guide to Business and Industrial Directories, Professional and Scientific Rosters, and Other Lists and Guides of All Kinds. James M. Ethridge, editor. Information Enterprises. Available from Gale Research Company, Book Tower, Detroit, Michigan 48226. Biennial.

Directory of Grants for Children and Youth Programs. Christopher Vail, editor. Public Management Institute. Available from Gale Research Company, Book Tower, Detroit, Michigan 48226. 1980. 1,020p.

Directory of Grants for Crime and Delinquency Prevention. Cynthia Forster, editor. Public Management Institute. Available from Gale Research Company, Book Tower, Detroit, Michigan 48226. 1981. 500p.

Directory of Grants for Energy and the Environment. Cynthia Forster, editor. Public Management Institute. Available from Gale Research Company, Book Tower, Detroit, Michigan, 48226. 1981. n.p.

Directory of Grants for Health. Public Management Institute. Available from Gale Research Company, Book Tower, Detroit, Michigan 48226. 1981. 1,200p.

Directory of Grants for Law and Advocacy. Cynthia Forster, editor. Public Management Institute. Available from Gale Research Company, Book Tower, Detroit, Michigan 48226. 1981. 500p.

Directory of Grants for Nonprofit Management Support. Audrey Richards, editor. Public Management Institute. Available from Gale Research Company, Book Tower, Detroit, Michigan 48226. 1980. 142p.

Directory of Grants for the Disabled. Cynthia Forster, editor. Public Management Institute. Available from Gale Research Company, Book Tower, Detroit, Michigan 48226. 1981. 700p.

Directory of Research Grants. Oryx Press, 2214 North Central at Encanto, Phoenix, Arizona 85004. Annual.

Directory of Volunteer Bureaus and Voluntary Action Centers. Association of Volunteer Centers, c/o Mary Louise Gilkes, 812 West Paseo del Prado, Green Valley, Arizona 85614. Annual.

Encyclopedia of Associations. Denise Akey, editor. Gale Research Company, Book Tower, Detroit, Michigan 48226. Annual. Volume 1: National Organizations of the U.S. Volume 2: Geographic and Executive Index. Volume 3: New Associations and Projects. Volume 4: International Organizations. Volume 5: Research Activities and Funding Programs.

Encyclopedia of U.S. Government Benefits. Roy A. Grisham, Jr. and Paul D. McConaughy, editors. William H. Wise and Company, 336 Mountain Road, Union City, New Jersey 07087. 1974. 1,013p.

Federal Funds for Research, Development, and Other Scientific Activities. U.S. National Science Foundation. Available from U.S. Government Printing Office, Washington, D.C. 20402. Annual.

Federal Grants: Where in the Bureaucracy to Find Them. Second edition. Sara Case. American Library Association, Washington Office, 110 Maryland Avenue, N.E., Box 54, Washington, D.C. 20002. 1977. 27p.

Foundation Center National Data Book. Foundation Center, 888 Seventh Avenue, New York, New York 10106. Annual.

Foundation Center Source Book Profiles. Foundation Center, 888 Seventh Avenue, New York, New York 10106. Quarterly.

Foundation Directory. Foundation Center, 888 Seventh Avenue, New York, New York 10106. Biennial.

Foundation 500. Douglas M. Lawson Associates, 39 East 51st Street, Third Floor, New York, New York 10022. Annual.

Foundation Grants to Individuals. Carol Kurzig, general editor. Foundation Center, 888 Seventh Avenue, New York, New York 10106. Biennial.

Foundations That Send Their Annual Report. Public Service Materials Center, 111 North Central Avenue, Hartsdale, New York 10530. 1982. n.p.

Grants: How to Find Out About Them and What to Do Next. Virginia P. White. Plenum Publishing Corporation, 233 Spring Street, New York, New York 10013. 1975. 354p.

Grants and Awards Available to American Writers. PEN, 47 Fifth Avenue, New York, New York 10003. Biennial.

Grants for Libraries: A Guide to Public and Private Funding Programs and Proposal Writing Techniques. Emmett Corry. Libraries Unlimited, Box 263, Littleton, Colorado 80160. 1982. 240p.

Grants in the Humanities: A Scholar's Guide to Funding Sources. William Coleman. Neal-Schuman Publishers, Inc., 23 Cornelia Street, New York, New York 10014. 1980. 152p.

Grants Register. Craig Alan Lerner, editor. Gale Research Company, Book Tower, Detroit, Michigan 48226. Biennial.

Grantseekers Guide: A Directory for Social and Economic Justice Projects. Jill R. Shellow. National Network of Grantmakers, 919 North Michigan Avenue, Fifth Floor, Chicago, Illinois 60611. 1981. 313p.

Guide to Corporate Giving in the Arts. Robert Porter. American Council for the Arts, 570 Seventh Avenue, New York, New York 10018. Biennial.

Guide to European Foundations. Giovanni Agnelli Foundation. Distributed by Columbia University Press, 562 West 113th Street, New York, New York 10025. 1973. 401p.

Guide to Federal Assistance. Wellborn Associates, 5791 Beaumont Avenue, La Jolla, California 92037. Basic volume with monthly updates.

Guide to Federal Funding for Education. Education Funding Research Council, 1611 North Kent Street, Suite 508, Arlington, Virginia 22209. Annual.

Guide to Government Resources for Economic Development—A Handbook for Non-Profit Agencies and Municipalities. Compiled by Northeast Midwest Institute. Public Service Materials Center, 111 North Central Avenue, Hartsdale, New York 10530. Annual.

Guide to the National Endowment for the Arts. Office of Public Affairs, National Endowment for the Arts, Washington, D.C. 20506. 1983. 40p.

Handicapped Funding Directory. Burton J. Eckstein. Research Grant Guides, Box 357, Oceanside, New York 11572. Biennial.

International Awards in the Arts: For Graduate and Professional Study. Institute of International Education, 809 United Nations Plaza, New York, New York 10017. 1969. 105p.

International Foundation Directory. Second edition. H. V. Hodson, consultant editor. Gale Research Company, Book Tower, Detroit, Michigan 48226. 1979. 378p.

International Philanthropy: A Compilation of Grants by U.S. Foundations. Martha R. Keens. Foundation Center, 888 Seventh Avenue, New York, New York 10106. 1981. 240p.

KRC Guide to Direct Mail Fund Raising. Mitchell Keller, editor. KRC Development Council. Available from Public Service Materials Center, 111 North Central Avenue, Hartsdale, New York 10530. 1977. 205p.

List of Organizations Filing as Private Foundations. Foundation Center. Distributed by Columbia University Press, 562 West 113th Street, New York, New York 10025. 1973. 167p.

Minority Organizations: A National Directory. Second edition. Katherine W. Cole, editor. Garrett Park Press, Garrett Park, Maryland 20766. 1982. 814p.

National Directory of Arts and Education Support by Business Corporations. Second edition. Daniel Millsaps, editor. Washington International Arts Letter, Box 9005, Washington, D.C. 20003. 1982. 229p.

National Directory of Arts Support by Private Foundations. Fifth edition. Daniel Millsaps, editor. Washington International Arts Letter, Box 9005, Washington, D.C. 20003. 1983. 336p.

National Directory of Grants and Aid to Individuals in the Arts, International. Fifth edition. Daniel Millsaps, editor. Washington International Arts Letter, Box 9005, Washington, D.C. 20003. 1983. 246p.

National Directory of Nonprofit Management Support Organizations. Support Center, 1709 New Hampshire Avenue, N.W., Washington, D.C. 20009. Biennial.

National Society of Fund Raising Executives—Directory of Membership. National Society of Fund Raising Executives, 1511 K Street, N.W. Suite 1000, Washington, D.C. 2005. Annual. Available to members only.

NSF Factbook. Guide to National Science Foundation Programs and Activities. Second edition. Marquis Academic Media, 200 East Ohio Street, Chicago, Illinois 60611. 1975. 561p.

Resource Directory for the Funding and Managing of Non-Profit Organizations. Ingrid Lemaire. The Edna McConnel Clark Foundation, 250 Park Avenue, Room 900, New York, New York 10017. 1977. 127p.

Source Guide to Government Technology and Financial Assistance. Harry Greenwald, editor. Prentice-Hall, Inc., Englewood Cliffs, New Jersey 07632. 1981. 213p.

State and Local Grant Awards. U.S. Environmental Protection Agency, Grants Administration Division, Washington, D.C. 20460. Semi-annual.

Survey of Arts Administration Training in the United States and Canada. Revised edition. Ellen S. Daniels, editor. Center for Arts Administration, Graduate School of Business, University of Wisconsin, Madison, Wisconsin 53706. 1977. 69p.

Survey of Grant-Making Foundations, 1983-84 edition. Public Service Materials Center, 111 North Central Avenue, Hartsdale, New York 10530. 1983.

Taft Corporate Directory: Profiles and Analyses of America's Corporate Foundations and Giving Committees. Taft Group, 5125 MacArthur Boulevard, N.W., Suite 300, Washington, D.C., 20016. Annual. Includes *Corporate Updates*, monthly, and *Corporate Giving Watch*, monthly.

The Taft Trustees of Wealth: A Biographical Directory of Private Foundations and Corporate Foundation Officers. Fifth edition. Taft Group, 5125 MacArthur Boulevard, N.W., Suite 300, Washington, D.C. 20016. 1979. 565p.

Training and Development Organizations Directory. Second edition. Paul Wasserman, editor. Gale Research Company, Book Tower, Detroit, Michigan 48226. 1980. 95pp.

Washington and the Arts: A Guide and Directory to Federal Programs and Dollars for the Arts. Janet English Gracey and Sally Gardner, special editors. American Council for the Arts, 570 Seventh Avenue, New York, New York 10018. 1971. 176p.

Where America's Large Foundations Make Their Grants. Fifth edition. Joseph Dermer. Public Service Materials Center, 111 North Central Avenue, Hartsdale, New York 10530. 1983. 253p.

World Dictionary of Awards and Prizes. Gale Research Company, Book Tower, Detroit, Michigan 48226. 1979. 380p.

DIRECTORIES: STATE AND LOCAL

State and local organizations can be very helpful in that they are accessible geographically. A telephone call or a half-hour drive might bring just the information that is needed. One might even make the acquaintance of a colleague with mutual interests.

ARKANSAS

A Guide to Arkansas Private Foundations. Independent Community Consultants, Inc., Box 141, Hampton, Arkansas 71744. 1983. 92p.

CALIFORNIA

Guide to California Foundations. Fifth edition. Shelley Barclay, editor. Northern California Grantmakers, 210 Post Street, #814, San Francisco, California 94108. 1983. 493p.

National Directory of Corporate Charity (California edition). Sam Sternberg, compiler. Regional Young Adult Project, 330 Ellis Street, Room 506, San Francisco, California 94102. 1981. 512p.

The San Diego County Foundation Directory. Community Congress of San Diego, 1172 Morena Boulevard, San Diego, California 92110. 1980. 71p.

Small Change from Big Bucks. Herb Allen and Sam Sternberg, editors. Bay Area Committee for Responsive Philanthropy, Regional Young Adult Project, 944 Market Street, #705, San Francisco, California 94102. 1979. 226p.

Where the Money's At. Irving Warner, editor. Irving Warner, 3235 Berry Drive, Studio City, California 91604. 1978. 536p.

COLORADO

Colorado Foundation Directory. Jennifer Mandelson, editor. The Junior League of Denver, Inc., 1805 South Bellaire Street, Suite 400, Denver, Colorado 80222. Biennial.

CONNECTICUT

Connecticut Foundation Directory. Michael Burns, editor. OUA/DATA. One State Street, New Haven, Connecticut 06511. Biennial.

Directory of Connecticut Foundations. Revised second edition. John P. Huber, editor. Eastern Connecticut State College Foundation, Box 431, Willimantic, Connecticut 06226. 1974. 276p.

Guide to Corporate Giving in Connecticut. OUA/DATA, 81 Saltonstall Avenue, New Haven, Connecticut 06513. 1982. 374p.

DELAWARE

Delaware Foundations. Revised edition. United Way of Delaware, Inc., 701 Shipley Street, Wilmington, Delaware 19801. 1983. 120p.

FLORIDA

Guide to Foundations in Florida. Susan M. Cook. Department of Community Affairs, 2571 Executive Center Circle East, Tallahassee, Florida 32301. 1980. 146p.

GEORGIA

Georgia Foundation Directory. Foundation Collection, Atlanta Public Library. One Margaret Mitchell Square, Atlanta, Georgia 30303. 1982. n.p.

Guide to Foundations in Georgia. State Economic Opportunity Unit, Office of District Programs. Georgia Department of Human Resources, 618 Ponce de Leon Avenue, N.E., Atlanta, Georgia 30308. 1978. 145p. Supplement, 1981.

HAWAII

A Guide to Charitable Trusts and Foundations in the State of Hawaii. Alu Like, Inc., 2828 Paa Street, Suite 3035, Honolulu, Hawaii 96819. Biennial.

IDAHO

Directory of Idaho Foundations. Caldwell Public Library, 1010 Dearborn Street, Caldwell, Idaho 83605. 1980. 12p.

ILLINOIS

The Chicago Corporate Connection: A Directory of Chicago Area Corporate Contributions. Donors Forum of Chicago, 208 South LaSalle Street, Chicago, Illinois 60604. Biennial.

Corporate Giving in Chicago. Kenneth Cmiel and Susan Levy. Donors Forum of Chicago, 208 South LaSalle Street, Chicago, Illinois 60604. 1980. 32p.

INDIANA

Indiana Foundations: A Directory. Paula Reading Spear, editor. Central Research Systems, 320 North Meridian Street, Suite 1011, Indianapolis, Indiana 46204. Biennial.

KANSAS

Directory of Kansas Foundations. Molly Wiseman, editor. Association of Community Arts Councils of Kansas, 112 West Sixth Street, Fourth Floor, Topeka, Kansas 66603. 1979. Biennial updates.

MAINE

A Directory of Maine Foundations. Fifth edition. Janet F. Brysh, compiler. Center for Research and Advanced Study, University of Southern Maine, 246 Deering Avenue, Portland, Maine 04102. 1983. 39p.

MARYLAND

Annual Index Foundation Reports. Sharon Smith, editor. Maryland Attorney General, One South Calvert Street, Baltimore, Maryland 21202. Annual.

MASSACHUSETTS

Directory of Foundations in Massachusetts. Carol Fubini, editor. Division of Public Charities, Massachusetts Department of the Attorney General, One Ashburton Place, Boston, Massachusetts 02108. 1982. 135p. Place orders with Associated Grantmakers of Greater Boston, 294 Washington Street, Suite 501, Boston, Massachusetts 02108.

Directory of Massachusetts Foundations. Second edition. John P. Huber, editor. Eastern Connecticut State College Foundation, Box 431, Willimantic, Connecticut 06226. 1976. 161p.

Grants Resource Manual. Don Levitan and Daniel F. Donahue, editors. Government Research Publications, Box 122, Newton Center, Massachusetts 02159. 1979. 108p.

Massachusetts Foundation Directory. Associated Grantmakers of Massachusetts, Inc., 294 Washington Street, Suite 501, Boston, Massachusetts 02108. 1983. 136p.

MICHIGAN

The Michigan Foundation Directory. Michigan League for Human Services, 300 North Washington Square, Suite 311, Lansing, Michigan 48933. Biennial.

MINNESOTA

Guide to Minnesota Foundations. Minnesota Council on Foundations, 413 Foshay Tower, Minneapolis, Minnesota 55402. Biennial.

MONTANA

Directory of Montana and Wyoming Foundations. Eastern Montana College Foundation, 1500 North 30th Street, Billings, Montana 59101. 1981. 16p.

NEW HAMPSHIRE

Directory of Charitable Funds in New Hampshire. Third edition. Division of Charitable Trusts, New Hampshire Attorney General's Office, State House Annex, Concord, New Hampshire 03301. 1976. 107p. Annual supplement.

NEW JERSEY

Foundations in New Jersey. Governmental Reference Office, Division of the State Library, Archives and History, New Jersey Department of Education, 185 West State Street, Trenton, New Jersey 08625. 1978. 45p.

Mitchell Guide to New Jersey Foundations, Corporations, and Their Managers. Janet A. Mitchell, editor. Mitchell Guides, Box 413, Princeton, New Jersey 08540. Biennial.

NEW YORK

Mitchell Guide to Long Island Foundations, Corporations, and Their Managers. Janet A. Mitchell, editor. Mitchell Guides, Box 413, Princeton, New Jersey 08540. Biennial.

Mitchell Guide to Upstate New York Foundations, Corporations, and Their Managers. Janet A. Mitchell, editor. Mitchell Guides, Box 413, Princeton, New Jersey 08540. Biennial.

New York City Resources for the Arts and Artists: A Listing of Services and Support Available through the Agencies and Institutions of New York City. Cultural Council Foundation, 175 Fifth Avenue, New York, New York 10010. 1973. 95p.

On TAP (Technical Assistance Programs): A Directory of Resources for New York City Nonprofit Organizations. Public Interest Public Relations, 225 West 34th Street, New York, New York 10001. 1979. 200p.

OHIO

Charitable Foundations Directory of Ohio. Fifth edition. Susan Boone, editor. Charitable Foundations Section, Attorney General's Office, 30 East Broad Street, 15th Floor, Columbus, Ohio 43215. 1982. 101p.

Guide to Charitable Foundations in the Greater Akron Area. United Way of Summit County, Box 1260, Akron, Ohio 44309. Biennial.

OKLAHOMA

Directory of Oklahoma Foundations. Second edition, revised and enlarged. Thomas E. Broce and Daniel P. Junkin. University of Oklahoma Press, 1005 Asp Avenue, Norman, Oklahoma 73019. 1982. 304p.

OREGON

The Guide to Oregon Foundations. Tri-County Community Council of Portland, 718 West Burnside Street, Portland, Oregon 97209. Biennial.

PENNSYLVANIA

Directory of Pennsylvania Foundations. Second edition. S. Damon Kletzien, editor. Friends of the Free Library, Logan Square at 19th Street, Philadelphia, Pennsylvania 19103. 1981. 280p.

The Metropolitan Philadelphia Philanthropy Study. Regional Science Department, University of Pennsylvania, Philadelphia, Pennsylvania 19104. 1980. n.p.

SOUTH CAROLINA

South Carolina Foundation Directory. Second edition. Reader Services Department, South Carolina State Library, Box 11469, Columbia, South Carolina 29211. 1983. 51p.

TEXAS

Directory of Texas Foundations. William T. Hooper, Jr., compiler. The Texas Foundations Research Center, Box 5494, Austin, Texas 78763. Annual.

Guide to Texas Foundations. Dallas Public Library, Publishing Services, 1954 Commerce Street, Dallas, Texas 75201. 1980. 103p.

WASHINGTON

Charitable Trust Directory. Jeanette Dieckman, editor. Washington Attorney General's Office, Temple of Justice, Olympia, Washington 98504. Annual.

WASHINGTON, D.C.

> The Guide to Washington, D.C. Foundations. Second edition. F. G. DeBettencourt. Guide Publishers, Box 5849, Washington, D.C. 20014. 1975. 58p.

> Washington, D.C. Metropolitan Area Foundation Directory. Julia M. Jacobsen and Kay Carter Courtade, editors. Management Publications, 4416 Edmunds Street, N.W., Washington, D.C. 20007. 1979. 80p.

WEST VIRGINIA

> West Virginia Foundation Directory. William Seeto, editor. West Virginia Foundation Directory, Box 96, Route 1, Terre Alta, West Virginia 26764. 1980. 49p.

WISCONSIN

> Foundations in Wisconsin: A Directory. Susan Hopwood, editor. The Foundation Collection, Marquette University Memorial Library, 1415 West Wisconsin Avenue, Milwaukee, Wisconsin 53233. Biennial.

WYOMING

> Directory of Montana and Wyoming Foundations. Eastern Montana College Foundation, 1500 North 30th Street, Billings, Montana 59101. 1981. 16p.

GOVERNMENT PUBLICATIONS

The U.S. Government Printing Office (GPO) is probably the largest publisher in the world. In the recession year 1982, sales produced an income of $55 million ($4.9 million net) from an inventory of some 16-21,000 titles. Its publications in this field are essential and reasonably priced.

See **A Basic Fund-raising Library** in Section III for indispensable titles, a list of local GPO bookstores, and ordering information.

Action Grants: Revitalizing and Conserving Cities. Wallace Katz. U.S. Department of Housing and Urban Development, Office of Community Planning and Development, Washington, D.C. 20460. Semi-annual.

Administrative Policies and Information Sources Relating to Federal Domestic Assistance Programs. Revised. U.S. Executive Office of the President, Office of Management and Budget, Intergovernmental Relations and Regional Operations Division. Available from U.S. Government Printing Office, Washington, D.C. 20402. 1977. n.p.

Alternatives in Public Service Delivery: Volunteers in Federal Agencies. Prepared for the Subcommittee on Intergovernmental Relations of the Committee on Government Affairs, U.S. Senate, by the U.S. Library of Congress, Congressional Research Service. Available from Committee on Government Affairs, U.S. Senate, Washington, D.C. 20570. 1982. 53p.

Annual Report. National Endowment for the Arts, Washington, D.C. 20506. Annual.

Awakening the Slumbering Giant: Intergovernmental Relations and Federal Law. Advisory Commission on Intergovernmental Relations, Washington, D.C. 20575. 1980. 103p.

Becoming a Volunteer: Resources for Individuals, Libraries and Organizations. U.S. Library of Congress, National Library Service for the Blind and Physically Handicapped, Washington, D.C. 20540. 1981. 17p.

Catalog of Federal Domestic Assistance. U.S. Executive Office of the President, Office of Management and Budget. Available from U.S. Government Printing Office, Washington, D.C. 20402. Annual.

A Catalog of Federal Grant-In-Aid Programs to State and Local Governments. Advisory Commission on Intergovernmental Relations, Washington, D.C. 20575. Annual.

Catalog of State Services. California Office of Planning and Research, 1400 Tenth, Sacramento, California 95814. 1976. various pagings.

Categorical Grants: Their Role and Design; The Intergovernmental Grant System: An Assessment and Proposed Policies. Advisory Commission on Intergovernmental Relations. Available from U.S. Government Printing Office, Washington, D.C. 20402. 1978. 319p.

Challenge Grant Recipient Study. Conducted for the National Endowment for the Arts by Leonard R. Vignola. National Foundation on the Arts and Humanities, National Endowment for the Arts, 1100 Pennsylvania Avenue, N.W., Washington, D.C. 20506. 1979. 74p.

Community Development: The Workings of a Federal-Local Block Grant: The Intergovernmental Grant System: An Assessment and Proposed Policies. Advisory Commission on Intergovernmental Relations. Available from U.S. Government Printing Office, Washington, D.C. 20402. 1977. 93p.

Cost Principles Applicable to Grants and Contracts with State and Local Governments. U.S. General Services Administration, Office of Federal Management Policy, Washington, D.C. 20405. 1974. 25p.

Cumulative List of Organizations Described in Section 170 (c) of the Internal Revenue Code of 1954. Internal Revenue Service. U.S. Department of the Treasury. Available from U.S. Government Printing Office, Washington, D.C. 20402. Annual with 3 quarterly supplements.

Directory of Funded Projects. U.S. Department of Health, Education and Welfare, Office of Education, Bureau of Higher and Continuing Education, Division of Student Services and Veterans Programs, Washington, D.C. 20202. 1978. 133p.

Educational Volunteerism: A State of the Art Summary with Implications for Vocational Education. U.S. Department of Education, Office of Vocational and Adult Education, Washington, D.C. 20202. 1980. 26p.

The Effective Coordination of Volunteers. Lorraine Lafota. National Clearinghouse on Domestic Violence, Box 2309, Rockville, Maryland 20852. 1980. 133p.

Federal Aid to States. U.S. Department of the Treasury, Fiscal Service, Bureau of Government Financial Operations, Division of Government Accounts and Reports, Washington, D.C. 20220. Annual.

Federal Funds for Research, Development, and Other Scientific Activities. U.S. National Science Foundation. Available from U.S. Government Printing Office, Washington, D.C. 20402. Annual.

Federal Grants, Their Effects on State-Local Expenditures, Employment Levels, Wage Rates: The Intergovernmental Grant System: An Assessment and Proposed Policies. Advisory Commission on Intergovernmental Relations, Washington, D.C. 20575. 1977. 75p.

Federal Procurement Data System. U.S. Executive Office of the President, Office of Management and Budget, Office of Federal Procurement Policy, Washington, D.C. 20503. Quarterly.

Federal Support to Universities, Colleges and Selected Nonprofit Institutions: Fiscal Year 1980. Available from U.S. Government Printing Office, Washington, D.C. 20402. 1982. 174p.

Financial Aspects of Administration of Grants-In-Aid, Loans and Contracts with Program Participants. U.S. Department of Housing and Urban Development, Office of Administration, 451 7th Street, N.W., Washington, D.C. 20410. Updated by continuing supplements and cumulated irregularly.

Financial Management of Federal Aid. U.S. Executive Office of the President, Office of Management and Budget. Available from U.S. Government Printing Office, Washington, D.C. 20402. 1981. 24p.

Geographic Distribution of Federal Funds: A Report of the Federal Government's Impact by State, County, and Large City. U.S. Executive Office of the President, Community Services Administration, Office of Operations, Division of State and Local Government. Available from National Technical Information Service, Springfield, Virginia 22161. Annual.

Grants Administration Manual. U.S. Environmental Protection Agency, Washington, D.C. 20460. Annual.

Grants Administration Policies. U.S. Social and Rehabilitation Service. Available from U.S. Government Printing Office, Washington, D.C. 20402. 1972. 53p.

Grants and Awards. U.S. Government Printing Office, Washington, D.C. 20402. Annual.

Grants Policy Statement. U.S. Department of Health and Human Services, Public Health Service. Available from U.S. Government Printing Office, Washington, D.C. 20402. 1982. 97p.

A Guide for State and Local Government Agencies: Cost Principles and Procedures for Establishing Cost Allocation Plans and Indirect Cost Rates for Grants and Contracts with the Federal Government. U.S. Department of Health, Education and Welfare, Division of Financial Management Standards and Procedures. Available from U.S. Goverment Printing Office, Washington, D.C. 20402. 1976. 88p.

Guide to Government Resources for Economic Development—A Handbook for Non-Profit Agencies and Municipalities. Available from Public Service Materials Center, 111 North Central Avenue, Hartsdale, New York 10530. Annual.

HEW Catalog of Assistance. U.S. Department of Health, Education and Welfare. Available from U.S. Government Printing Office, Washington, D.C. 20402. Irregular.

Improving Federal Grants Management: The Intergovernmental Grant System: An Assessment and Proposed Policies. Advisory Commission on Intergovernmental Relations, Washington, D.C. 20575. 1977. 287p.

Improving the Financial Management and Auditing of Federal Assistance Programs: The "Single Audit" Concept. U.S. Congress, House, Committee on Government Operations, Intergovernmental Relations and Human Resources Subcommittee. Available from House Documents Room, Washington, D.C. 20402. 1982. 38p.

The Intergovernmental Grant System: An Assessment and Proposed Policies. Advisory Commission on Intergovernmental Relations, Washington, D.C. 20575. 1978. 29p.

The Intergovernmental Grant System As Seen by Local, State, and Federal Officials: The Intergovernmental Grant System: An Assessment and Proposed Policies. Advisory Commission on Intergovernmental Relations. Available from U.S. Government Printing Office, Washington, D.C. 20402. 1977. 287p.

Managing Federal Assistance in the 1980's: A Report to the Congress of the United States, Pursuant to the Federal Grant and Cooperative Agreement Act of 1977. U.S. Executive Office of the President, Office of Management and Budget, Washington, D.C. 20503. 1980. 69p.

Managing Federal Assistance in the 1980's: A Report to the Congress of the United States, Pursuant to the Federal Grant and Cooperative Agreement Act of 1977: Working Papers. U.S. Executive Office of the President, Office of Management and Budget. Available from U.S. Government Printing Office, Washington, D.C. 20402. 1980. 2 volumes.

Managing Federal Assistance in the 1980's: A Study of Federal Assistance Management, Pursuant to the Federal Grant and Cooperative Agreement Act of 1977. U.S. Executive Office of the President, Office of Management and Budget, Washington, D.C. 20503. 1979. 9 volumes.

New Dimensions for the Arts: 1971-1972. National Foundation on the Arts and Humanities, National Endowment for the Arts, Washington, D.C. 20506. 1973. 135p.

Nonprofit Organization Participation in the Federal Aid System. U.S. Senate, Committee on Governmental Affairs, Washington, D.C. 20510. 1980. 2 volumes.

Opera Program. National Foundation on the Arts and Humanities, National Endowment for the Arts, Washington, D.C. 20506. 1975. 16p.

Profiles of Financial Assistance Programs. U.S. Department of Health, Education, and Welfare, Public Health Service. Available from U.S. Government Printing Office, Washington, D.C. 20402. Annual.

Program Announcement. National Foundation on the Arts and Humanities, National Endowment for the Humanities, 1100 Pennsylvania Avenue, N.W., Washington, D.C. 20506. Annual.

Proposal Preparation Manual. William F. Brown. U.S. Department of Transportation. Available from U.S. Government Printing Office, Washington, D.C. 20402. 1983. 87p.

Recent Trends in Federal and State Aid to Local Governments. Advisory Commission on Intergovernmental Relations, Washington, D.C. 20575. 1980. 95p.

Report. National Foundation on the Arts and Humanities, National Endowment for the Humanities, 1100 Pennsylvania Avenue, N.W., Washington, D.C. 20506. Annual.

Research, Demonstration, Training and Fellowship Awards. U.S. Environmental Protection Agency, Grants Administration Division, Washington, D.C. 20460. Semi-annual.

Research Program Guidelines. National Foundation on the Arts and Humanities, National Endowment for the Humanities, 1100 Pennsylvania Avenue, N.W., Washington, D.C. 20506. Annual.

Restructuring Federal Assistance: The Consolidation Approach. Advisory Commission on Intergovernmental Affairs, Washington, D.C. 20575. 1975. 26p.

Review Guide, Grantees Financial Management Systems. U.S. Executive Office of the President, Office of Management and Budget. Available from U.S. Government Printing Office, Washington, D.C. 20402. 1977. 32p.

Section 504 Resources Manual: A Guide for Small Institutions to Useful Sources, Services, and Procedures for Locating and Applying Funds to Meet Section 504 Mandates. U.S. Department of Health and Human Services, Washington, D.C. 20201. 1981. 48p.

Selected Information Resources on Scholarships, Fellowships, Grants and Loans. John Henry Hass, compiler. U.S. Library of Congress, Science and Technology Division, National Referral Center, Washington, D.C. 20540. 1977. 17p.

Significant Features of Fiscal Federalism. Advisory Commission on Intergovernmental Relations. Available from U.S. Government Printing Office, Washington, D.C. 20402. Annual.

SSA Grants Policy Handbook. U.S. Social Security Administration, Office of Management, Budget and Personnel, Baltimore, Maryland 21235. 1981. 19p.

State and Local Grant Awards. U.S. Environmental Protection Agency, Grants Administration Division, Washington, D.C. 20460. Semi-annual.

State Planning Agency Grants: Guideline Manual. U.S. Department of Justice, Law Enforcement Assistance Administration, Washington, D.C. 20530. 1977. 117p.

The States and Intergovernmental Aids: The Intergovernmental Grant System: An Assessment and Proposed Policies. Advisory Commission on Intergovernmental Relations, Washington, D.C. 20575. 1977. 83p.

Survey of United States and Foreign Government Support for Cultural Activities. U.S. Senate, Committee on Labor and Public Welfare, Special Subcommittee on Arts and Humanities. Available from U.S. Government Printing Office, Washington, D.C. 20402. 1971. 245p.

Symphony Orchestra Program: Application Guidelines. National Foundation on the Arts and Humanities, National Endowment for the Arts, 1100 Pennsylvania Avenue, N.W., Washington, D.C. 20506. Annual.

Theatre Program: Application Guidelines. National Foundation on the Arts and Humanities, National Endowment for the Arts, 1100 Pennsylvania Avenue, N.W., Washington, D.C. 20506. Annual.

Uniform Requirements for Assistance to State and Local Governments. Revised. U.S. Executive Office of the President, Office of Management and Budget, Washington, D.C. 20503. 1981. various pagings.

Visual Arts Program: Application Deadlines. National Foundation on the Arts and Humanities, National Endowment for the Arts, 1100 Pennsylvania Avenue, N.W., Washington, D.C. 20506. Annual.

Voluntarism in America: Promoting Individual and Corporate Responsibility: Hearing Before the Subcommittee on Aging, Family and Human Services of the Committee on Labor and Human Resources. U.S. Senate, Committee on Labor and Human Resources, Washington, D.C. 20510. 1982. 147p.

Volunteers in Human Services. U.S. Department of Health and Human Services, Washington, D.C. 20201. 1980. 31p.

HANDBOOKS AND MANUALS

Handbooks and manuals are just what they state they are, books that are easily handled manually and meant to be consulted quickly as ready desktop references.

When in doubt reach for your trusty handbook first. It may give you all the information you need, or background data of interest, or clues to resources for further information.

Accounting Handbook for Non-Accountants. Second edition. Clarence B. Nickerson. CBI Publishing Company, Inc., 51 Sleeper Street, Boston, Massachusetts 02210. 1979. 701p.

An Accounting Manual for Voluntary Social Welfare Organizations. Child Welfare League of America. Family Service Association of America, 44 East 23rd Street, New York, New York 10010. 1971. 67p.

The Art of Asking: A Handbook for Successful Fund Raising. Paul H. Schneiter. Walker and Company, 720 Fifth Avenue, New York, New York 10019. 1978. 198p.

The Basic Handbook of Grants Management. Robert Lefferts. Basic Books, Inc., 10 East 53rd Street, New York, New York 10022. 1983. 292p.

The California Nonprofit Corporation Handbook. Third edition. Ralph Warren, editor. Nolo Press, Box 544, Occidental, California 95465. 1983. 288p.

A Communications Manual for Nonprofit Corporations. Lucille A. Maddalena. American Management Association, Inc., 135 West 50th Street, New York, New York 10020. 1978. 73p.

Dollars and Sense: A Community Fundraising Manual for Women's Shelters and Other Non-Profit Organizations. Western States Shelter Network, 870 Market Street, Suite 1058, San Francisco, California 94102. 1982. 135p.

The **Effective Nonprofit Executive Handbook.** Stephen Hitchcock, editor. Public Management Institute, 358 Brannan Street, San Francisco, California 94107. 1983. 600p.

Evaluation Handbook. Public Management Institute, 358 Brannan Street, San Francisco, California 94107. 1980. 400p.

Federal Grants: Course Manual. Lawrence R. Sidman and Leonard A. Zax. Federal Publications, 1120 20th Street, N.W., Washington, D.C. 20036. 1982. 476p.

The **Foundation Handbook: A Private Foundation Approach to Fund Raising at State Colleges and Universities.** Donald L. Lemish. American Association of State Colleges and Universities Publications, One Dupont Circle, Suite 700, Washington, D.C. 20036. 1983. 36p.

The **FRI Annual Giving Book.** M. Jane Williams. The Fund Raising Institute, Box 365, Ambler, Pennsylvania 19002. Annual.

Fund-Raising: A Comprehensive Handbook. Hilary Blume. Routledge & Kegan Paul, Ltd., 9 Park Street, Boston, Massachusetts 02108. 1977. 188p.

The **Fund Raising Manual: Strategies for Non-Profit Organizations.** Thomas W. Tenbrunsel. Prentice-Hall, Inc., Englewood Cliffs, New Jersey 07632. 1982. 192p.

The **Fund Raising Resource Manual.** Thomas W. Tenbrunsel. Prentice-Hall, Inc., Englewood Cliffs, New Jersey 07632. 1982. 182p.

Grant Money and How to Get It: A Handbook for Librarians. Richard W. Boss. R. R. Bowker Company, 1180 Avenue of the Americas, New York, New York 10036. 1980. 138p.

Grant Writer's Handbook. Public Management Institute. Available from Gale Research Company, Book Tower, Detroit, Michigan 48226. 1980. 400p.

Grants Administration Manual. U.S. Environmental Protection Agency, Washington, D.C. 20460. Annual.

Handbook for Agency Coordinators for Volunteer Programs. Voluntary Action Center for New York City, Mayor's Office for Volunteers, 51 Chambers, New York, New York 10007. 1972. 20p.

Handbook for Development Officers at Independent Schools. Donald J. Whelan, editor. Council for Advancement and Support of Education, 11 Dupont Circle, Suite 400, Washington, D.C. 20036. 1982. 350p.

The Handbook for Direct Mail Fundraising. Direct Mail Fundraisers Association, 151 Lexington Avenue, New York, New York 10016. 1980. n.p.

Handbook for Educational Fund Raising: A Guide to Successful Principles and Practices for Colleges, Universities, and Schools. Francis C. Pray, editor. Jossey-Bass, Inc., 433 California Street, San Francisco, California 94104. 1981. 422p.

Handbook of Corporate Social Responsibility: Profiles of Involvement. Second edition. Human Resources Network. Chilton Book Company, Chilton Way, Radnor, Pennsylvania 19089. 1975. 629p.

Handbook of Federal Assistance: Financing, Grants, Technical Aids. C. Schaevitz, editor—with the assistance of Elizabeth A. Van. Warren, Gorham & Lamont, 210 South Street, Boston, Massachusetts 02111. 1979. 694p.

Handbook of Public Relations. Second edition. Howard Stephenson. McGraw-Hill Book Company, 1221 Avenue of the Americas, New York, New York 10020. 1971. 836p.

Handbook of Special Events for Nonprofit Organizations: Tested Ideas for Fund Raising and Public Relations. Edwin R. Leibert and Bernice E. Sheldon. Taft Group, 5125 MacArthur Boulevard, N.W., Suite 300, Washington, D.C. 20016. 1972. 224p.

Handbook of Successful Fund-Raising. Paul C. Carter. E. P. Dutton, Two Park Avenue, New York, New York 10016. 1970. various pagings.

The Handbook on Private Foundations. David F. Freeman. Published for the Council on Foundations by Seven Locks Press, Box 72, 6600 81st Street, Cabin John, Maryland 20731. 1981. 452p.

How to Write for Development. Henry Gayley. Council for Advancement and Support of Education, 11 Dupont Circle, Suite 400, Washington, D.C. 20036. 1981. 50p.

If You Want Air Time: A Publicity Handbook. National Association of Broadcasters, 1771 N Street, N.W., Washington, D.C. 20036. 1979. 18p.

Institute for Community Service Manual: A Process for Developing Agency-Based Volunteer Social Work Staff. Lutheran Social Services of Minnesota, 2414 Park Avenue, Minneapolis, Minnesota 55404. 1973. 122p.

The KRC Aide and Advisor for Fund Raising Copywriters. Mitchell Keller. KRC Development Council. Available from Public Service Materials Center, 111 North Central Avenue, Hartsdale, New York 10530. 1981. 60p.

The KRC Desk Book for Fund Raisers with Model Forms and Records. Lisa Pulling Semple. KRC Development Council. Available from Public Service Materials Center, 111 North Central Avenue, Hartsdale, New York 10530. 1980. 184p.

KRC Fund Raiser's Manual: A Guide to Personalized Fund Raising. Paul Blanshard, Jr. KRC Development Council, 431 Valley Road, New Canaan, Connecticut 06840. 1974. 246p.

KRC Handbook of Fund Raising Principles and Practices with Sample Forms and Records. KRC Development Council, 431 Valley Road, New Canaan, Connecticut 06840. 1982. 118p.

Legal Handbook for Non-Profit Organizations. Marc J. Lane. American Management Association, Inc., 135 West 50th Street, New York, New York 10020. 1981. 320p.

Lesly's Public Relations Handbook. Third edition. Philip Lesly, editor. Prentice-Hall, Inc., Englewood Cliffs, New Jersey 07632. 1983. 718p.

Media Handbook for the Arts. Richard M. Cottam and Martin Umansky. Association of Community Arts Councils of Kansas, 112 West Sixth Street, Topeka, Kansas 66603. 1979. 28p.

Models for Money: Obtaining Government and Foundation Grants and Assistance. Second edition. Louis Urgo. Suffolk University Management Education Center, 41 Temple Street, Boston, Massachusetts 02114. 1978. 187p.

Needs Assessment Handbook. Public Management Institute, 358 Brannan Street, San Francisco, California 94107. 1980. 400p.

Nonprofit Organization Handbook: A Guide to Fund Raising, Grants, Lobbying, Membership Building, Publicity and Public Relations. Patricia V. Gaby and Daniel M. Gaby. Prentice-Hall, Inc., Englewood Cliffs, New Jersey 07632. 1979. 333p.

Nonprofit Organization Handbook. Tracy D. Connors, editor. McGraw-Hill Book Company, 1221 Avenue of the Americas, New York, New York 10020. 1979. 740p.

The Nonprofit Secretary Handbook. Susan Fox and Stephen Hitchcock. Public Management Institute, 358 Brannan Street, San Franscisco, California 94107. 1983. v.p.

Printing and Promotion Handbook: How to Plan, Produce and Use Printing, Advertising and Direct Mail. Third edition. Daniel Melcher and Nancy Larrick. McGraw-Hill Book Company, 1221 Avenue of the Americas, New York, New York 10020. 1966. 451p.

Proposal Development Handbook. American Association of State Colleges and Universities, One Dupont Circle, N.W., Washington, D.C. 20036. 1982. 12p.

Proposal Preparation and Management Handbook. Roy J. Loring and Harold Kerzner. Van Nostrand Reinhold, 135 West 50th Street, New York, New York 10020. 1982. 416p.

Proposal Preparation Manual. William F. Brown. U.S. Department of Transportation. Available from U.S. Government Printing Office, Washington, D.C. 20402. 1983. 87p.

Public Information Handbook for Foundations. Saul Richman. Foreword by Robert F. Goheen. Council on Foundations, 1828 L Street, N.W., Washington, D.C. 20036. 1973. 95p.

Public Media Manual for Museums. John Anderson and Diana Sperberg. Texas Association of Museums, Box 13353, Capitol Station, Austin, Texas 78711. 1979. 79p.

Public Relations Handbook. Second edition, revised. Richard W. Darrow and Dan J. Forrestal. Dartnell Corporation, 4660 Ravenswood Avenue, Chicago, Illinois 60640. 1979. 1,115p.

Publicity for Volunteers: A Handbook. Virginia Borton. Walker and Company, 720 Fifth Avenue, New York, New York 10019. 1981. 128p.

Section 504 Resources Manual: A Guide for Small Institutions to Useful Sources, Services, and Procedures for Locating and Applying Funds to Meet Section 504 Mandates. U.S. Department of Health and Human Services, Washington, D.C. 20201. 1981. 48p.

The Small Theatre Handbook: A Guide to Management and Production. Joann Green. Harvard Common Press, 535 Albany Street, Boston, Massachusetts 02172. 1982. 163p.

SSA Grants Policy Handbook. U.S. Social Security Administration, Office of Management, Budget and Personnel, Baltimore, Maryland 21235. 1981. 19p.

Stalking the Large Green Grant: A Fundraising Manual for Youth Serving Agencies. Third edition. Publications Office, National Youth Work Alliance, 1346 Connecticut Avenue, N.W., Washington, D.C. 20036. 1980. 78p.

State Planning Agency Grants: Guideline Manual. U.S. Department of Justice, Law Enforcement Assistance Administration, Washington, D.C. 20530. 1977. 117p.

Successful Fundraising: A Handbook of Proven Strategies and Techniques. William K. Grasty and Kenneth G. Sheinkopf. Charles Scribner's Sons, 597 Fifth Avenue, New York, New York 10017. 1982. 318p.

Successful Resource Fairs: Guidelines for Planning. Jay W. Vogt. Associated Grantmakers of Massachusetts, 294 Washington Street, Suite 417, Boston, Massachusetts 02108. 1983. 75p.

Theatre Profiles/2: An Informational Handbook of Nonprofit Professional Theatres in the United States. Lindy Zesch, editor; Marsue Cumming, associate editor. Theatre Communications Group, Inc., 355 Lexington Avenue, New York, New York 10017. 1975. 219p.

Training Volunteer Leaders: A Handbook to Train Volunteers and Other Leaders of Program Groups. Research and Development Division, Young Men's Christian Associations of the United States, 101 North Wacker Drive, Chicago, Illinois 60606. 1974. 189p.

United Arts Fundraising Manual. Robert Porter, editor. American Council for the Arts, 570 Seventh Avenue, New York, New York 10018. 1980. 77p.

Volunteer Training and Development: A Manual for Community Groups. Revised edition. Anne K. Stenzel and Helen M. Feeney. Continuum Publishing Company, 575 Lexington Avenue, New York, New York 10017. 1976. 204p.

ONLINE DATABASES

No less an authority than the Librarian of Congress, Daniel Boorstin, in an address at the UCLA Graduate School of Library and Information Science on the occasion of its twenty-fifth anniversary, 19 April 1984, estimated that 20 percent of the books published in 1983 were about computers. And we are afraid that the book will become obsolete because of the computer!

Hardware, software, and databases are the bones, sinews, and beef of computerland. Books and articles are pouring out to explain what it's all about. Witness entire issues of *Publishers Weekly* which are now devoted to computer literature.

Since this publication is so voluminous and varied, the titles cited are divided into five sections to facilitate reference access: General Works; Directories; Journals and Looseleaf Services; Individual Databases; and Database Vendors. See also **Computers and the Automated Office** in Section II of this volume.

General Works

Data Processing Management. Andrew Parkin. Little, Brown and Company, 34 Beacon Street, Boston, Massachusetts 02106. 1982. 168p.

Fee-based Information Services: A Study of a Growing Industry. Richard W. Boss and Lorig Maranjian. R. R. Bowker Company, 1180 Avenue of the Americas, New York, New York 10036. 1980. 199p.

An Introduction to Automated Literature Searching. Elizabeth P. Hartner. Marcel Dekker, Inc., 270 Madison Avenue, New York, New York 10016. 1981. 168p.

Introduction to Online Information Systems. David Raitt, editor. Learned Information, 143 Old Marlton Pike, Medford, New Jersey 08055. 1983. n.p.

The Library and Information Manager's Guide to Online Services. Ryan E. Hoover, editor. Industry Publications, Inc., 2 Corporate Park Drive, White Plains, New York 10604. 1980. 269p.

Managing the Data Resource Function. Second edition. Richard L. Nolan. West Publishing Company, Box 3526, St. Paul, Minnesota 55165. 1982. 465p.

On Online: An Introduction to Online. Data Courier, Inc., 620 South 5th Street, Louisville, Kentucky 40202. 1982. (An excellent 16-page pamphlet. Free on request.)

Directories

Computer Readable Databases: A Directory and Data Sourcebook. Martha E. Williams, editor. American Society for Information Science. Knowledge Industry Publications, Inc., 701 Westchester Avenue, White Plains, New York 10604. 1982. 1,516p.

The Directory of Fee-based Information Services. Kelly Warnken, editor. Information Alternative, Box 5571, Chicago, Illinois 60680. 1982. 89p.

Directory of Information Management Software for Libraries, Information Centers and Record Centers. Cibbarelli and Associates, Inc., 11684 Ventura Boulevard, Suite 295, Studio City, California 91604. 1983. 133p.

Directory of Online Data Bases. Ruth N. Cuadra, David M. Abels, and Judith Wanger, compilers. Cuadra Associates, 2001 Wilshire Boulevard, Suite 305, Santa Monica, California 90403. Revised every six months; one supplement between revisions.

Directory of Online Information Resources. CSG Press, 11301 Rockville Pike, Kensington, Maryland 20895. Semi-annual.

Encyclopedia of Information Systems and Services. Fifth edition. Anthony T. Kruzas and John Schmittroth, Jr., editors. Gale Research Company, Book Tower, Detroit, Michigan 48226. 1982. 993p. Supplemented by *New Information Systems and Services.*

Information Industry Market Place: An International Directory of Information Products and Services. R. R. Bowker Company, 1180 Avenue of the Americas, New York, New York 10036. Annual.

International Directory of Data Bases Relating to Companies. United Nations, Centre on Transnational Corporations. United Nations, Sales Section, New York, New York 10017. 1979. 246p.

Online Bibliographic Databases. Third edition. James L. Hall and Marjorie J. Brown, editors. Published by ASLIB, London. Available from Gale Research Company, Book Tower, Detroit, Michigan 48226. 1983. 383p.

Journals and Looseleaf Services

Data Base Alert. Knowledge Industry Publications, Inc., 701 Westchester Avenue, White Plains, New York 10604. Monthly.

Datapro Directory of Online Services. Datapro Research Corporation, 1805 Underwood Boulevard, Delran, New Jersey 08075. Two looseleaf volumes updated monthly.

Datapro Directory of Software. Datapro Research Corporation, 1805 Underwood Boulevard, Delran, New Jersey 08075. Two looseleaf volumes updated monthly.

Online Review. Learned Information, 143 Old Marlton Pike, Medford, New Jersey 08055. Bimonthly.

Individual Databases

CompuServe. Information Services Division, 5000 Arlington Centre Boulevard, Columbus, Ohio 43220. A major nationwide network offering news services, electronic mail, financial reports, and special purpose programming. Inquire as to online cost and availability.

(Foundation Center Computer Databases.) The Foundation Center, 888 Seventh Avenue, New York, New York 10106. Information on nongovernmental and nonprofit foundations and on the grants they award; corresponds in form and context to printed volumes *Foundation Directory, Foundation Grants Index,* and *National Data Book*; updating varies by database. Inquire as to online cost and availability.

New York Times Information Bank. New York Times Information Service Company, 1719A Mount Pleasant Office Park, Route 10, Parsippany, New Jersey 07054. Indexing and abstracting of current affairs, primarily from the *New York Times*, 1969 to present. Inquire as to online cost and availability.

PAIS Bulletin. Public Affairs Information Service, Inc., 11 West 40th Street, New York, New York 10018. Literature of social and political science, 1976 to present. Worldwide coverage. Inquire as to online cost and availability.

SOURCE • Source Telecomputing Corporation. 1616 Anderson Road, McLean, Virginia 22102. A major nationwide network offering news services, electronic mail, financial reports, and special purpose programming. Inquire as to online cost and availability.

Database Vendors

Note: To get yourself started, contact the online vendors of information retrieval systems which access, via computer terminals, computerized databases. In addition, each database producer will identify the vendor(s) handling its database. Some of the large vendors are:

Bibliographic Retrieval Service (BRS). 1200 Route 7, Latham, New York 12110. Has fewer databases but does offer MEDLARS, the National Library of Medicine's online counterpart to *Index Medicus.* See *BRS Database Catalog.*

Lockheed Information Retrieval Service (DIALOG). Marketing Department, 3640 Hillview Avenue, Palo Alto, California 94304. Covers the largest number of databases, over 100, in a wide variety of subjects and includes government indexes such as the U.S. Government Printing Office's *Monthly Catalog* and the *National Technical Information Service.* Also can provide copies of documents cited. See *DIALOG Database Catalog.*

System Development Corporation (ORBIT). 2500 Colorado Avenue, Santa Monica, California 90406. ORBIT is a close competitor, having many of the same files and some exclusive ones. See *ORBIT Search Service Databases.*

PERIODICAL INDEXES, JOURNALS, AND NEWSLETTERS

There is unlimited information on all aspects of fund-raising, grants, and foundations to be found in periodical literature: journals, magazines, newsletters, newspapers, as well as proceedings, transactions, reports, yearbooks, et al. As a matter of policy, no individual serials articles are cited as such in this bibliography except as specifically noted.

However, a variety of indexes to periodical literature provide ready access to this material. The following 16 indexes are suggested as being most helpful. Look under entries related to the subject to be investigated.

Some 80 or more specially selected journals and newsletters are then listed in a following section.

Periodical Indexes

Art Index. H. W. Wilson Company, 950 University Avenue, Bronx, New York 10452. Quarterly with annual cumulations.

Business Index. Information Access Corporation, 404 Sixth Avenue, Menlo Park, California 94025. Monthly microfilm installments, cumulated and updated. Annual and quadrennial microfiche cumulations.

Business Periodicals Index. H. W. Wilson Company, 950 University Avenue, Bronx, New York 10452. Monthly with quarterly and annual cumulations. Service basis.

Business Publications Index and Abstracts. Gale Research Company, Book Tower, Detroit, Michigan 48226. Monthly. Subject/author citations cumulated month-by-month throughout each quarter. Quarterly cumulations are merged and published in hardback annual editions. Individual monthly abstracts are numbered and require no cumulation. These are also available in annual editions.

Current Contents/Arts and Humanities. Institute for Scientific Information, 3501 Market Street, University City Science Center, Philadelphia, Pennsylvania 19104. Weekly.

Current Index to Journals in Education. Oryx Press, 2214 North Central at Encanto, Phoenix, Arizona 85004. Monthly with semi-annual cumulations.

Digest of Selected Reports. United Way of America, Information Center, 801 North Fairfax Street, Alexandria, Virginia 22314. Twice per year.

Education Index. H. W. Wilson Company, 950 University Avenue, Bronx, New York 10452. Monthly with quarterly and annual cumulations. Service basis.

Foundation Grants Index Annual. Foundation Center, 888 Seventh Avenue, New York, New York 10106. Annual. Updated by *Foundations Grants Index Bimonthly*.

Index to Legal Periodicals. H. W. Wilson Company, 950 University Avenue, Bronx, New York 10452. Monthly, October-August, with quarterly and annual cumulations.

Monthly Catalog of United States Government Publications. U.S. Government Printing Office, Washington, D.C. 20402. Monthly with a semi-annual index published following the June issue, and an annual index in the December number.

Music Index. Information Coordinators, Inc., 1435 Randolph Street, Detroit, Michigan 48226. Monthly with annual cumulations.

New York Times Index. (New York Times Company.) Microfilming Corporation of America, 1620 Hawkins Avenue, Box 10, Sanford, North Carolina 27330. Semi-monthly.

Public Affairs Information Service Bulletin. PAIS, 11 West 40th Street, New York, New York 10018. Semi-monthly. Cumulated four times per year and annually. An index to publications (books, journals, pamphlets, and government documents) relating to economic and social affairs.

Social Sciences Citation Index. Institute for Scientific Information, 3501 Market Street, University City Science Center, Philadelphia, Pennsylvania 19104. Three times per year with annual cumulations.

Wall Street Journal Index. Dow Jones & Company, 22 Courtland Street, New York, New York 10007. Monthly with annual cumulations.

Journals and Newsletters

Ulrich's International Periodicals Directory, twenty-second edition, R. R. Bowker Company, 1180 Avenue of the Americas, New York, New York 10036, 1983, lists over 70,000 periodicals in 373 subject areas. The ninth edition of Bowker's *Irregular Serials and Annuals, 1983*, lists another 35,000 titles in 556 subjects. *Ulrich's International Periodicals Directory* and *Irregular Serials and Annuals* are available online from Bibliographic Retrieval Service (BRS), 1200 Route 7, Latham, New York 12110, or DIALOG Information Services, 3640 Hillview Avenue, Palo Alto, California 94304.

The Standard Periodical Directory, Oxbridge Publishing Company, Inc., 183 Madison Avenue, New York, New York 10016, published biennially, provides still more titles. For newsletters, see *The Oxbridge Directory of Newsletters*, Oxbridge Communications, Inc., 183 Madison Avenue, Room 1108, New York, New York 10016, a biennial publication, and *The National Directory of Newsletters and Reporting Services*, second edition, Gale Research Company, Book Tower, Detroit, Michigan 48226, 1981.

For the publications of various associations and centers, see the section so titled.

ACA Update. American Council for the Arts, 570 Seventh Avenue, New York, New York 10018. Monthly. Membership only. Circulation: 4,000.

Advancement Analysis. Box 994, Minneapolis, Minnesota 55440. Monthly.

American Artist Business Letter. Billboard Publications, Inc., 1515 Broadway, New York, New York 10036. 10 times per year. Looseleaf. Circulation: 4,000.

American Arts. American Council for the Arts, 570 Seventh Avenue, New York, New York 10018. Bimonthly. Advertising. Book reviews. Charts. Illustrations. Index. Circulation: 7,000.

American Association of Fund Raising Counsel Bulletin. American Association of Fund Raising Counsel, 500 Fifth Avenue, New York, New York 10036. Monthly. Circulation: 10,000.

Arts Business. Business Committee for the Arts, 1775 Broadway, New York, New York 10019. Monthly.

Arts Management. Radius Group, Inc., 408 West 57th Street, New York, New York 10019. 5 times per year. Book reviews. Statistics. Index. Circulation: 12,000.

Arts Reporting Service. 9214 Three Oaks Drive, Silver Spring, Maryland 20901. Fortnightly. Book reviews. Circulation: 1,500.

Association for Volunteer Administration Newsletter/Bulletin. Association for Volunteer Administration, Box 4584, Boulder, Colorado 80306. Monthly.

Association of Volunteer Centers Notebook. Association of Volunteer Centers, c/o Mary Louise Gilkes, 812 West Paseo del Prado, Green Valley, Arizona 85614. Monthly.

BCA News. Business Committee for the Arts, 1775 Broadway, New York, New York 10019. Monthly.

Business and Society Review. Warren, Gorham, and Lamont, Inc., 210 South Street, Boston, Massachusetts 02111. Quarterly. Indexed in *Computing Reviews, Personnel Management Abstracts, Social Sciences Index, Work Related Abstracts.*

Business Volunteers for the Arts. Arts and Business Council, 130 East 40th Street, New York, New York 10016. Quarterly.

Case Currents. Council for Advancement and Support of Education, 11 Dupont Circle, Suite 400, Washington, D.C. 20036. Monthly except August and December. Advertising. Book reviews. Abstracts. Illustrations. Index. Circulation: 10,500.

Case Placement Letter. Council for Advancement and Support of Education, 11 Dupont Circle, Suite 400, Washington, D.C. 20036. Monthly.

Citizen Participation and Voluntary Action Abstracts. Association of Voluntary Action Scholars, S-203 Human Development Building, Pennsylvania State University, University Park, Pennsylvania 16802. Quarterly.

Community Focus. United Way of America, 801 North Fairfax, Alexandria, Virginia 22314. Monthly. Charts. Illustrations. Circulation: 3,000.

CSFA News. Citizens' Scholarship Foundation of America, Box 636, Concord, New Hampshire 03301. Monthly.

Cultural Post. National Endowment for the Arts, Washington, D.C. 20506. Bimonthly. Bibliographies. Illustrations.

Daedalus. American Academy of Arts and Sciences, 136 Irving Street, Cambridge, Massachusetts 02138. Quarterly. Charts. Illustrations. Index. Circulation: 20,000. Indexed in *Public Affairs Information Service Bulletin.*

Deferred Giving Newsletter. Federation of Protestant Welfare Agencies, 281 Park Avenue South, New York, New York 10010. Quarterly.

Dimensions. National Catholic Development Conference, 119 North Park Avenue, New York, New York 11570. 10 times per year. 4-6 pages. Advertising. Circulation: 800.

Direct Mail Fundraisers Association Newsletter. Direct Mail Fundraisers Association, 151 Lexington Avenue, New York, New York 10016. Quarterly.

Educational Record: The Magazine of Higher Education. American Council on Education, One Dupont Circle, Washington, D.C. 20036. Quarterly. Book reviews. Charts. Index. Circulation: 12,000. Indexed in *Current Contents, Education Index, Public Affairs Information Service Bulletin, Current Index to Journals in Education.*

Effort: Education Full Funding Report. Committee for Full Funding of Education Programs, 148 Duddington Place, S.E., Washington, D.C. 20003. 6 to 10 times per year. 4-26 pages. Circulation: 310.

ELHI Funding Sources Newsletter. The Oryx Press, 2214 North Central at Encanto, Phoenix, Arizona 85004. Monthly.

Exempt Organizations Reports. Commerce Clearing House, 4025 West Petersen Avenue, Chicago, Illinois 60646. Biweekly.

Federal Grants and Contracts Weekly: Selected Project Opportunities for the Education Community. Capitol Publications, Inc., 1300 North 17th Street, Arlington, Virginia 22209. Weekly. Looseleaf.

Federation of Protestant Welfare Agencies Newsletter. Federation of Protestant Welfare Agencies, 281 Park Avenue South, New York, New York 10010. 3 times per year.

Foundation News: The Journal of Philanthropy. Council on Foundations, Inc., 1828 L Street, N.W., Washington, D.C. 20036. Bimonthly. Book reviews. Illustrations. Statistics. Index. Circulation: 15,200.

FRI Monthly Portfolio. Fund Raising Instititue, Box 365, Ambler, Pennsylvania 19002. Monthly. Book reviews. Circulation: 2,700.

FRM Weekly. Hoke Communications, Inc., 224 Seventh Street, Garden City, New York 11530. Weekly. Circulation: 800.

Fund Raiser's Exchange. 237 Brookfield Gulf Road, Randolph, Vermont 05060. 10 times per year. Book reviews, Circulation: 1,200.

The Fund Raiser's Guide. Central Florida Research Services, Inc., Box 1776, Maitland, Florida 32751. 8 times per year.

Fund Raising Forum. National Catholic Development Conference, 119 North Park Avenue, Rockville, New York 11570. 10 times per year. Available to members only. Four pages. Circulation: 500.

Fund Raising Management. Hoke Communications, Inc., 224 Seventh Street, Garden City, New York 11530. Monthly. Advertising. Book reviews. Illustrations. Circulation: 8,000.

Fund Raising Review. American Association of Fund Raising Counsel, Inc., 25 West 43rd Street, New York, New York 10036. Bimonthly.

Grant Information System. Oryx Press, 2214 North Central at Encanto, Phoenix, Arizona 85004. Monthly.

Grants and Assistance News. National Assistance Management Association, Box 57051, Washington, D.C. 20037. Monthly.

Grants Magazine: The Journal of Sponsored Research and Other Programs. Plenum Publishing Corporation, 233 Spring Street, New York, New York 10013. Quarterly. Advertising. Book Reviews. Charts. Illustrations.

The Grantsmanship Center News. Grantsmanship Center, 1031 South Grand Avenue, Los Angeles, California 90015. Bimonthly. Advertising. Book reviews. Index. Circulation: 15,000.

Grassroots Fundraising Journal. CRG Press, Box 42120, Northwest Station, Washington, D.C. 20015. Bimonthly.

Health Funds Development Letter. Health Resource Publishing, Box 1442, Brinley Plaza, Highway 38, Wall Township, New Jersey 07719. Monthly. Book reviews.

Higher Education and National Affairs. American Council on Education, One Dupont Circle, Washington, D.C. 20036. Weekly, 40 times per year. Circulation: 25,000.

Higher Education Management Newsletter. National Education Industry Group of Coopers and Lybrand, One Post Office Square, Boston, Massachusetts 02109. Irregular.

Hospital Fund Raising Newsletter. Health Resource Publishing, Box 1442, Brinley Plaza, Highway 38, Wall Township, New Jersey 07719. Bimonthly.

Humanities. National Endowment for the Humanities, Washington, D.C. 20506. Bimonthly.

Independent Sector Update. Independent Sector, 1828 L Street, N.W., Washington, D.C. 20036. Monthly.

Journal of Arts Management and Law. 4000 Albermarle Street, N.W., Washington, D.C. 20016. Quarterly.

Journal of Student Financial Aid. National Association of Student Financial Aid Administrators, 1776 Massachusetts Avenue, Suite 100, Washington, D.C. 20036. 3 times per year.

Journal of Voluntary Action Research. Association of Voluntary Action Scholars. Available from Transaction Periodicals Consortium, Rutgers University, New Brunswick, New Jersey 08903. Quarterly. Index. Circulation: 750. Indexed in *Current Contents, Social Sciences Citation Index.*

Journal of Volunteer Administration. Association for Volunteer Administration, Box 4584, Boulder, Colorado 80306. Quarterly.

Kennedy Center News. John F. Kennedy Center for the Performing Arts, Washington, D.C. 20566.

KRC Letter. KRC Development Council, 431 Valley Road, New Canaan, Connecticut 06840. 10 times per year. Book reviews. Index. Circulation: 500. Looseleaf.

Medical Research Funding Bulletin. Science Support Center, Box 587, Bronxville, New York 10708. 3 times per month. Looseleaf. Circulation: 1,500 (controlled).

Mirror-On-Volunteerism. Four-One-One, 7304 Beverly Street, Annandale, Virginia 22003. Quarterly.

NASFAA Newsletter. National Association of Student Financial Aid Administrators, 910 17th Street, N.W., Suite 228, Washington, D.C. 20006. Monthly. 8 pages. Circulation: 3,200.

National Assistance Management Association Journal. National Assistance Management Association, Box 57051, Washington, D.C. 20037. Semi-annual.

National Society of Fund Raising Executives Newsletter. National Society of Fund Raising Executives, Investment Building, Suite 831, 1511 K Street, N.W., Washington, D.C. 20005. Monthly.

National Society of Fund Raising Executives Journal. National Society of Fund Raising Executives, Investment Building, Suite 831, 1511 K Street, N.W., Washington, D.C. 20005. Semi-annual.

New Jersey Notes. Box 413, Princeton, New Jersey 08540. Bimonthly.

New York Notes. Box 413, Princeton, New Jersey 08540. Bimonthly.

The Nonprofit Executive/NPO Careers/Taft Report. Taft Group, 5125 MacArthur Boulevard, N.W., Suite 300, Washington, D.C. 20016. Monthly. Index. Looseleaf. Circulation: 2,000.

NPO Resource Review. (Non-profit Organizations). Caller Box A-6, Cathedral Station, New York, New York 10025. Bimonthly.

Partners for Progress. Pan American Development Foundation, 19th and Constitution Avenue, N.W., Washington, D.C. 20006. Quarterly. Circulation: 50,000.

Philanthropic Digest. Brakeley, John Price Jones, Inc., 1100 17th Street, N.W., Washington, D.C. 20036. Monthly. Circulation: 1,000.

Philanthropy Monthly. 2 Bennitt Street, Box 989, New Milford, Connecticut 06776. Monthly.

PR Reporter: Weekly Newsletter of Public Relations, Public Affairs and Communication. PR Publishing Company, Inc., Box 600, Dudley House, Exeter, New Hampshire 03833. Weekly.

Public Relations Journal. Public Relations Society of America, Inc., 845 Third Avenue, New York, New York 10022. Monthly. Advertising. Book reviews. Charts. Illustrations. Index. Circulation: 2,000. Indexed in *Business Periodicals Index, Public Affairs Information Service Bulletin.*

Public Relations News. Public Relations Information Services, 127 East 80th Street, New York, New York 10021. Weekly.

Public Relations Quarterly. Newsletter Clearinghouse, 44 West Market Street, Rhinebeck, New York 12572. Quarterly. Advertising. Book reviews. Charts. Illustrations. Statistics. Index. Circulation: 5,000.

RF Illustrated. Rockefeller Foundation, 1133 Avenue of the Americas, New York, New York 10036. Quarterly.

The School Fund Raiser. Sedgewood Publishing Corporation, 1426 La Honda Drive, Escondido, California 92026. 3 times per year. Circulation: 152,860.

Taft Foundation Reporter. Taft Group, 5125 MacArthur Boulevard, N.W., Suite 300, Washington, D.C. 20016. Annual. Includes *Foundation Giving Watch,* monthly, and *Foundation Updates,* monthly.

Tax-Exempt News. Capitol Publications, Inc., 1300 North 17th Street, Arlington, Virginia 22209. Monthly. Looseleaf.

Taxwise Giving. 13 Arcadia Road, Old Greenwich, Connecticut 06870. Monthly.

United for Service. International Council on United Fund Raising, United Way Plaza, Alexandria, Virginia 22314. 1 or 2 times per year.

United Way of America Executive Newsletter. United Way of America, 801 North Fairfax Street, Alexandria, Virginia 22314. 40 times per year.

United Way of America Quarterly Newsletter. United Way of America, 801 North Fairfax Street, Alexandria, Virginia 22314. Quarterly.

University Research News. Capitol Publications, Inc., 2430 Pennsylvania Avenue, N.W., Washington, D.C. 20037. Biweekly.

Voluntary Action Leadership. Volunteer: The National Center for Citizen Involvement, Box 4179, Boulder, Colorado 80306. Quarterly. Advertising. Book reviews. Circulation: 7,000.

The Volunteer Gazette. Volunteers of America, 3813 North Causeway Boulevard, Metairie, Louisiana 70002. Monthly.

Volunteer Services Administration. American Society of Directors of Volunteer Services, American Hospital Association, 840 North Lakeshore Drive, Chicago, Illinois 60611. Quarterly.

Volunteering. Volunteer: The National Center for Citizen Involvement, Box 4179, Boulder, Colorado 80306. Monthly.

Washington Foundation Journal. Capitol Publications, Inc., 2430 Pennsylvania Avenue, N.W., Washington, D.C. 20037. Monthly.

Washington International Arts Letter. Box 9005, Washington, D.C. 20003. 10 times per year. Book reviews. Charts. Illustrations. Circulation: 16,359.

Women and Foundations/Corporate Philanthropy Newsletter. Women and Foundations/Corporate Philanthropy, 70 West 40th Street, New York, New York 10018. Quarterly.

Section II:
Subject
Information
Sources

The second section of this bibliography is arranged by subject. Some of the subject areas included are Foundations and Foundation Grants; Fund-raising; Grantsmanship and Proposal Writing; Not-for-Profit Organizations and Agencies; and Volunteerism.

Other subjects covered in this section, such as Computers or Taxation, might be considered tangential, but are included as necessary to an understanding of the successful and efficient operation of a fund-raising "business." The entries under the subheading Corporate Social Responsibility and Philanthropy provide useful and interesting sources of background information.

ACCOUNTING, BUSINESS METHODS, AND MANAGEMENT

In a "charity business" grossing over $60 billion yearly, trained accounting and management methods are clearly in order. Not-for-profit courses are appearing more and more frequently in business school curricula. There are workshops, seminars, and extension courses with particular application to the not-for-profit sector.

The literature on the subject expands apace. Of the titles listed below, various books are helpful to the nonaccountant. The expanded third edition of Gross and Warshauer, *Financial and Accounting Guide for Nonprofit Organizations,* Wiley, 1983, is especially recommended.

Accounting and Financial Reporting: A Guide for United Ways and Not-for-Profit Human Service Organizations. United Way of America, 801 North Fairfax Street, Alexandria, Virginia 22314. 1974. 95p.

Accounting and Reporting Practices of Private Foundations: A Critical Evaluation. Jack Traub. Praeger Publishers, 521 Fifth Avenue, New York, New York 10175. 1977. 240p.

Accounting for Librarians and Other Not-for-Profit Managers. G. Stevenson Smith. American Library Association, 50 East Huron Street, Chicago, Illinois 60611. 1983. 470p.

Accounting for Non-Accountants. John N. Myer. Revised second edition. Hawthorn Books, Inc., 260 Madison Avenue, New York, New York 10016. 1980. 249p.

Accounting for Non-Profit Organizations. Third edition. Emerson O. Henke. Wadsworth Publishing Company, 10 Davis Drive, Belmont, California 94002. 1983. 288p.

Accounting Fundamentals for Non-Accountants. Stephen A. Mosgrove. Reston Publishing Company, 11480 Sunset Hills Road, Reston, Virginia 22090. 1981. 301p.

Accounting Handbook for Non-Accountants. Second edition. Clarence B. Nickerson. CBI Publishing Company, Inc., 51 Sleeper Street, Boston, Massachusetts 02210. 1979. 701p.

An Accounting Manual for Voluntary Social Welfare Organizations. Child Welfare League of America. Family Service Association of America, 44 East 23rd Street, New York, New York 10010. 1971. 67p.

Artsfax '81: A Report on the Finances, Personnel and Programs of Bay Area Arts Organizations. Virginia H. Baer. The San Francisco Foundation, 425 California Street, Suite 1600, San Francisco, California 94104. 1981. 161p.

Bookkeeping for Nonprofits. Public Management Institute, 358 Brannan Street, San Francisco, California 94107. 1979. 221p.

Breaking Even: Financial Management in Human Service Organizations. Roger A. Lohman. Temple University Press, Philadelphia, Pennsylvania 19122. 1980. 336p.

Budgeting: A Guide for United Ways and Other Not-for-Profit Human Services Organizations. United Way of America, 801 North Fairfax Street, Alexandria, Virginia 22314. 1975. 55p.

Budgeting for Nonprofits. Second edition. V. Srikanth and Lyn Levy. Public Management Institute, 358 Brannan Street, San Francisco, California 94107. 1980. 321p.

Budgeting Procedures for Hospitals. Second edition. Truman H. Esmond, Jr. American Hospital Association, 840 North Lakeshore Drive, Chicago, Illinois 60611. 1982. 92p.

The California Nonprofit Corporation Handbook. Third edition. Ralph Warren, editor. Nolo Press, Box 544, Occidental, California 95465. 1983. 288p.

Capital Financing for Hospitals. American Hospital Association. 840 North Lakeshore Drive, Chicago, Illinois 60611. 1974. 60p.

College and University Endowment: Status and Management. D. Kent Halstead. U.S. Office of Education. Available from U.S. Government Printing Office, Washington, D.C. 20402. 1977. 81p.

A Communications Manual for Nonprofit Organizations. Lucille A. Maddalena. American Management Association, Inc., 135 West 50th Street, New York, New York 10020. 1981. 222p.

Corporate Planning for Nonprofit Organizations. James M. Hardy. Association Press, 291 Broadway, New York, New York 10007. 1973. 119p.

Cost Principles Applicable to Grants and Contracts with State and Local Governments. U.S. General Services Administration, Office of Federal Management Policy, Washington, D.C. 20405. 1974. 25p.

Culture and Management: Text and Readings in Comparative Management. Ross A. Webber, compiler. Richard D. Irwin, Inc., 1818 Ridge Road, Homewood, Illinois 60430. 1969. 598p.

Decision Making for Library Management. Michael R. W. Bommer and Ronald W. Chorba. Knowledge Industry Publications, Inc., 701 Westchester Avenue, White Plains, New York 10604. 1982. 178p.

Development Today: A Guide for Non-Profit Organizations. Jeffrey L. Lant. Robert D. Anderson Publishing Company, 7000 Franklin Boulevard, Suite 820, Box 22324, Sacramento, California 95882. 1980. 200p.

Do or Die: Survival for Nonprofits. James C. Lee. Taft Group, 5125 MacArthur Boulevard, N.W., Suite 300, Washington, D.C. 20016. 1974. 110p.

Economic Factors in the Growth of Corporation Giving. Ralph L. Nelson. Russell Sage Foundation, 112 East 64th Street, New York, New York 10021. 1970. 116p.

The Effect of Tax Deductibility on the Level of Charitable Contributions and Variations on the Theme. The Lock-In Problem for Capital Gains: An Analysis of the 1970-71 Experience. Buildings and the Income Tax. Gerard M. Brannon. Fund for Public Policy Research, 1156 15th Street, N.W., Washington, D.C. 20005. 1974. 59p.

Effective Nonprofit Executive Handbook. Stephen Hitchcock, editor. Public Management Institute, 358 Brannan Street, San Francisco, California 94107. 1983. 600p.

Evaluation: A Systematic Approach. Peter H. Rossi and Howard E. Freeman. Sage Publications, Inc., P.O. Box 5024, Beverly Hills, California 90210. 1982. 384p.

Evaluation Handbook. Public Management Institute, 358 Brannan Street, San Francisco, California 94107. 1980. 400p.

Financial and Accounting Guide for Nonprofit Organizations. Expanded third edition. Malvern J. Gross and William Warshauer, Jr. John Wiley and Sons, Inc., 605 Third Avenue, New York, New York 10158. 1983. 564p.

Financial Aspects of Administration of Grants-In-Aid, Loans and Contracts with Program Participants. U.S. Department of Housing and Urban Development, Office of Administration, 451 7th Street, N.W., Washington, D.C. 20410. Updated by continuing supplements and cumulated irregularly.

Financial Management for Arts Organizations. Mary M. Wehle. Arts Administration Research Institute, 75 Sparks Street, Cambridge, Massachusetts 02138. 1975. 163p.

Financial Management for the Arts. Revised edition. Frederick J. Turk. American Council for the Arts, 570 Seventh Avenue, New York, New York 10018. 1982. 102p.

Financial Management of Federal Aid. U.S. Executive Office of the President, Office of Management and Budget. Available from U.S. Government Printing Office, Washington, D.C. 20402. 1981. 24p.

Financing the Nonprofit Organization for Recreation and Leisure Services. Harry E. Moore, Jr. Groupwork, Inc., Box 258, South Plainfield, New Jersey 07080. 1981. 24p.

The Foundation Administrator: A Study of Those Who Manage America's Foundations. Arnold J. Zurcher and Jane Dustan. Russell Sage Foundation, 112 East 64th Street, New York, New York 10021. 1972. 171p.

Fund Accounting: Theory and Practice. Second edition. Edward S. Lynn and Robert J. Freeman. Prentice-Hall, Inc., Englewood Cliffs, New Jersey 07632. 1983. 896p.

Getting a Grant in the Nineteen Eighties: Readings in Cost and Managerial Accounting. Third edition. Alfred Rappaport, editor. Prentice-Hall, Inc., Englewood Cliffs, New Jersey 07632. 1982. 176p.

Glossary of Tools and Concepts for Nonprofit Managers. Barbara Schilling. The Management Center, 150 Post Street, Suite 640, San Francisco, California 94108. 1980. 22p.

Grant Budgeting and Finance: Getting the Most out of Your Grant Dollar. Frea E. Sladek and Eugene L. Stein. Plenum Publishing Corporation, 233 Spring Street, New York, New York 10013. 1981. 375p.

Grant Proposals: A Practical Guide to Planning, Funding and Managing. Lawrence Blaine. Psyon Publications, 220 Redwood Highway, Number 102, Mill Valley, California 94941. 1981. 105p.

Growth in the Eighties: A Manager's Guide to Financial Productivity for Non-Profit Organizations. The Not for Profit Group, Chemical Bank, 1212 Sixth Avenue, New York, New York 10036. n.d. n.p.

A Guide for Preparing a Statement of Accountability. National Catholic Development Conference, 119 North Park Avenue, Suite 409, Rockville Centre, New York 11570. 1982. 21p.

A Guide for State and Local Government Agencies: Cost Principles and Procedures for Establishing Cost Allocation Plans and Indirect Cost Rates for Grants and Contracts with the Federal Government. U.S. Department of Health, Education and Welfare, Division of Financial Management Standards and Procedures. Available from U.S. Government Printing Office, Washington, D.C. 20402. 1976. 88p.

Guide to the Administration of Charitable Remainder Trusts. Fourth edition. Winton Smith. Council for Advancement and Support of Education, 11 Dupont Circle, N.W., Suite 400, Washington, D.C. 20036. 1984. 350p.

How to Be an Effective Board Member. Public Management Institute, 358 Brannan Street, San Francisco, California 94107. 1980. 400p.

How to Manage a Non-Profit Organization. John Fisher. Management and Fund Raising Center. Available from Public Service Materials Center, 111 North Central Avenue, Hartsdale, New York 10530. 1978. 214p.

How to Secure and Manage Foundation and Federal Funds in the 1980's. Theodore M. Lawe. MRDC Educational Institute, Box 15127, Dallas, Texas 75201. 1980. 185p.

Improving the Financial Management and Auditing of Federal Assistance Programs: The "Single Audit" Concept. U.S. Congress, House, Committee on Government Operations, Intergovernmental Relations and Human Resources Subcommittee. Available from House Documents Room, Washington, D.C. 20402. 1982. 38p.

Introduction to Fund Accounting. Edward S. Lynn and Joan W. Thompson. Reston Publishing Company, 11480 Sunset Hills Road, Reston, Virginia 22090. 1974. 134p.

Linkages: Improving Financial Management in Local Government. Frederick Hayes. Urban Institute Press, 2100 M Street, N.W., Washington, D.C. 20037. 1982. 184p.

Management Assistance for the Arts: A Survey of Programs. Ellen Thurston, compiler; Stephen Benedict, editor. Center for Arts Information, 625 Broadway, New York, New York 10012. 1980. 51p.

Management Control in Nonprofit Organizations. Revised edition. Robert N. Anthony and Regina E. Herzlinger. Richard D. Irwin, Inc., 1818 Ridge Road, Homewood, Illinois 60430. 1980. 600p.

Management Control in Nonprofit Organizations: Text and Cases. Kavasseri V. Ramanathan. John Wiley and Sons, Inc., 605 Third Avenue, New York, New York 10158. 1982. 612p.

The Management of American Foundations: Administration, Policies, and Social Role. Arnold J. Zurcher. New York University Press. Distributed by Columbia University Press, 562 West 113th Street, New York, New York 10025. 1972. 184p.

The Management of Small History Museums. Second edition. Carl E. Guthe. American Association for State and Local History, 708 Berry Road, Nashville, Tennessee 37204. 1964. 80p.

Management Principles for Non-Profit Agencies and Organizations. Gerald Zaltman. American Management Association, Inc., 135 West 50th Street, New York, New York 10020. 1979. 584p.

Management Reporting Standards for Educational Institutions: Fund Raising and Related Activities. Cosponsored by CASE and the National Association of College and University Business Officers. Council for Advancement and Support of Education, 11 Dupont Circle, Suite 400, Washington, D.C. 20036. 1983. 18p.

Managing Corporate Contributions. Kathryn Troy. The Conference Board, Inc., 845 Third Avenue, New York, New York 10022. 1980. 95p.

Managing Educational Endowments: Report to the Ford Foundation. Advisory Committee on Endowment Management. Ford Foundation, 320 East 43rd Street, New York, New York 10017. 1969. 65p.

Managing Federal Assistance in the 1980's: A Report to the Congress of the United States Pursuant to the Federal Grant and Cooperative Agreement Act of 1977. U.S. Executive Office of the President, Office of Management and Budget, Washington, D.C. 20503. 1980. 69p.

Managing Federal Assistance in the 1980's: A Report to the Congress of the United States Pursuant to the Federal Grant and Cooperative Agreement Act of 1977: Working Papers. U.S. Executive Office of the President, Office of Management and Budget. Available from U.S. Government Printing Office, Washington, D.C. 20402. 1980. Two volumes.

Managing Federal Assistance in the 1980's: A Study of Federal Assistance Management Pursuant to the Federal Grant and Cooperative Agreement Act of 1977. U.S. Executive Office of the President, Office of Management and Budget, Washington, D.C. 20503. 1979. Nine volumes.

Managing Nonprofit Agencies for Results: A Systems Approach to Long-Range Planning. Paul Hennessey. Public Management Institute, 358 Brannan Street, San Francisco, California 94107. 1979. 250p.

Managing Nonprofit Organizations. Diane Borst and Patrick J. Montana. American Management Association, Inc., 135 West 50th Street, New York, New York 10020. 1977. 328p.

Managing Staff for Results. Joanne Pugh. Public Management Institute. Available from Gale Research Company, Book Tower, Detroit, Michigan 48226. 1980. 411p.

Managing Volunteers for Results. Audrey Richards. Public Management Institute, 358 Brannan Street, San Francisco, California 94107. 1979. 354p.

Managing Your Public Relations: Guidelines for Nonprofit Organizations. National Communication Council for Human Services and Public Relations Society of America. Public Relations Society of America, 845 Third Avenue, New York, New York 10022. 1977. Set of six guides: *Making the Most of Special Events* (Harold N. Weiner, 20p.); *Measuring*

Potential and Evaluating Results (Alice Norton, 20p.); *Planning and Setting Objectives* (Frances E. Koestler, 22p.); *Using Publicity to Best Advantage* (Frances Schmidt, 20p.); *Using Standards to Strengthen Public Relations* (Anne L. New and Don Bates, 18p.); and *Working with Volunteers* (Dorothy Ducas, 16p.).

Market the Arts. Joseph V. Melillo, editor. Foundation for the Extension and Development of American Professional Theater, 1500 Broadway, New York, New York 10036. 1983. 287p.

Marketing for Nonprofit Organizations. Second edition. Philip Kotler. Prentice-Hall, Inc., Englewood Cliffs, New Jersey 07632. 1982. 592p.

Marketing for Public and Nonprofit Managers. Christopher H. Lovelock and Charles B. Weinberg. John Wiley and Sons, Inc., 605 Third Avenue, New York, New York 10158. 1984. 624p.

Marketing Higher Education: A Practical Guide. Robert S. Topor. Council for Advancement and Support of Education, 11 Dupont Circle, Suite 400, Washington, D.C. 20036. 1983. 90p.

Marketing in Nonprofit Organizations. Patrick J. Montana, editor. American Management Association, Inc., 135 West 50th Street, New York, New York 10020. 1978. 302p.

Marketing in Nonprofit Organizations. Benson P. Shapiro. Marketing Science Institute, 14 Story Street, Cambridge, Massachusetts 02138. 1972. 47p.

Marketing the Arts. Michael P. Mokwa, William M. Dawson, and E. Arthur Prieve, editors. Praeger Publishers, 521 Fifth Avenue, New York, New York 10175. 1980. 304p.

Marketing the Arts in a Rural Environment: The Monadnock Arts Study. George Miaolis and David Lloyd. Wright State University, 7751 Colonel Glenn Highway, Dayton, Ohio 45431. 1979. 66p.

Marketing the Library. Benedict A. Leerburger. Knowledge Industry Publications, Inc., 701 Westchester Avenue, White Plains, New York 10604. 1982. 124p.

Marketing Your Hospital: A Strategy for Survival. Norman H. McMillan. American Hospital Association, 840 North Lakeshore Drive, Chicago, Illinois 60611. 1981. 128p.

MBO for Nonprofit Organizations. Dale D. McConkey. American Management Association, Inc., 135 West 50th Street, New York, New York 10020. 1975. 223p.

The Money Game: Financing Collegiate Athletics. Robert H. Atwell, et al. American Council on Education, One Dupont Circle, Washington, D.C. 20036. 1980. 72p.

Needs Assessment Handbook. Public Management Institute, 358 Brannan Street, San Francisco, California 94107. 1980. 400p.

Nonprofit CEOs Speak Out on Importance of Communication. International Association of Business Communicators, 870 Market Street, Suite 940, San Francisco, California 94102. 1982. 212p.

Nonprofit Corporations, Organizations and Associations. Fourth edition. Howard L. Oleck. Prentice-Hall, Inc., Englewood Cliffs, New Jersey 07632. 1980. 1,221p.

Nonprofit Financial Management. Christian P. Frederiksen. Public Management Institute, 358 Brannan Street, San Francisco, California 94107. 1979. 232p.

Nonprofit Management Skills for Women Managers. Public Management Institute. Available from Gale Research Company, Book Tower, Detroit, Michigan 48226. 1980. 280p.

Nonprofit Organization Handbook. Tracy D. Connors, editor. McGraw-Hill Book Company, 1221 Avenue of the Americas, New York, New York 10020. 1979. 740p.

The Nonprofit Secretary Handbook. Susan Fox and Stephen Hitchcock. Public Management Institute, 358 Brannan Street, San Francisco, California 94107. 1983.

Organizational Survival in the Performing Arts: The Making of the Seattle Opera. Mahmoud Salem. Praeger Publishers, 521 Fifth Avenue, New York, New York 10175. 1976. 210p.

Organizing the Library's Support: Donors, Volunteers, Friends. Donald W. Krummel, editor. Graduate School of Library Science, University of Illinois, Publications Office, 249 Armory Building, 505 East Armory Street, Champaign, Illinois 61820. 1980. 119p.

Philanthropy and Marketing: New Strategies for Fund Raising. James Gregory Lord. The Third Sector Press, 2000 Euclid Avenue, Box 18044, Cleveland, Ohio 44118. 1981. Looseleaf.

Principles of Accounting and Financial Reporting for Nonprofit Organizations. Malvern J. Gross and Stephen F. Jablonsky. John Wiley and Sons, Inc., 605 Third Avenue, New York, New York 10158. 1979. 415p.

Proposal Preparation and Managment Handbook. Roy J. Loring and Harold Kerzner. Van Nostrand Reinhold, 135 West 50th Street, New York, New York 10020. 1982. 416p.

Readings in Public and Nonprofit Marketing. Christopher H. Lovelock and Charles B. Weinberg. Scientific Press, The Stanford Barn, Palo Alto, California 94304. 1978. 304p.

Resource Directory for the Funding and Managing of Non-Profit Organizations. Ingrid Lemaire. The Edna McConnel Clark Foundation, 250 Park Avenue, Room 900, New York, New York 10017. 1977. 127p.

Setting National Priorities. The Brookings Institution, 1755 Massachusetts Avenue, N.W., Washington, D.C. 20036. Annual.

Simplified Accounting for Non-Accountants. R. S. Hayes and C. R. Baker. John Wiley and Sons, Inc., 605 Third Avenue, New York, New York 10158. 1980. 291p.

The Small College Advancement Program: Managing for Results. Wesley K. Willmer. Council for Advancement and Support of Education, 11 Dupont Circle, Suite 400, Washington, D.C. 20036. 1981. 145p.

The Small Theatre Handbook: A Guide to Management and Production. Joann Green. Harvard Common Press, 535 Albany Street, Boston, Massachusetts 02172. 1982. 163p.

Successful Meetings. Public Management Institute. Available from Gale Research Company, Book Tower, Detroit, Michigan 48226. 1980. 360p.

Successful Seminars, Conferences and Workshops. Public Management Institute, 358 Brannan Street, San Francisco, California 94107. 1980. 410p.

Theatre Profiles/2: An Informational Handbook of Nonprofit Professional Theatres in the United States. Lindy Zesch, editor; Marsue Cumming, associate editor. Theatre Communications Group, Inc., 355 Lexington Avenue, New York, New York 10017. 1975. 219p.

Trusteeship and the Managment of Foundations. Donald R. Young and Wilbert E. Moore. Russell Sage Foundation, 112 East 64th Street, New York, New York 10020. 1969. 158p.

Up Your Accountability: How to Up Your Serviceability and Funding Credibility by Upping Your Accounting Ability. Paul Bennett. Taft Group, 5125 MacArthur Boulevard, N.W., Suite 300, Washington, D.C. 20016. 1973. 66p.

COMPUTERS AND THE AUTOMATED OFFICE

As was already noted in the discussion of **Online Databases**, the computer is a major subject of current nonfiction publication. The automated office is now the *sine qua non* of the business world. It is hard to realize that the once-prized Selectric II correcting typewriter will soon be, if it is not already, an office dinosaur. The subject of computers and the automated office is so extensive and diverse, that for the sake of convenience we have subdivided it into eight sections:

Computers: General Works

Computers: Reference Sources

Computers: Directories

Computers: Buying a Computer

Computers: Journals and Looseleaf Services

The Automated Office: General Works

The Automated Office: Guides and Handbooks

The Automated Office: Journals and Looseleaf Services

Note: While it is not our policy to include journal articles in this bibliography, we have to make an exception for the excellent article in the July/August 1983 *Grantsmanship Center News*, "Computer Basics for Nonprofit Organizations," pages 15-29, by Ralph J. Megna. It is highly recommended.

Computers: General Works

Computer Graphics: A Programming Approach. Steven Harrington. James A. Vastyan, editor. McGraw-Hill Book Company, 1221 Avenue of the Americas, New York, New York 10020. 1983. 480p.

Computer Publishers and Publications 1984. Gale Research Company, Book Tower, Detroit, Michigan 48226. 1983. 400p. Supplements to update.

Computers and Information Processing in Business. James A. O'Brien. Richard D. Irwin, Inc., 1818 Ridge Road, Homewood, Illinois 60430. 1983. 533p.

Computers and Management in a Changing Society. Second edition. Donald H. Sanders and Stanley J. Birkin. McGraw-Hill Book Company, 1221 Avenue of the Americas, New York, New York 10020. 1980. 490p.

Computers for Nonprofits. Second edition. Kenneth Gilman. Public Management Institute, 358 Brannan Street, San Francisco, California 94107. 1982. 600p.

Fund Raising by Computer. Fund Raising Institute, Box 365, Ambler, Pennsylvania 19002. 1977. 135p.

GSM Library Guides. Management Series Number 6: *Computers and Management.* Compiled by Karen Sternheim. Graduate School of Management Library, University of California, Los Angeles, California 90024. 1983. 2p. ($1).

Note: Useful information may be obtained by writing directly to major microcomputer companies:

Apple Computer. 10260 Bandley Drive, Cupertino, California 95104.

Commodore Computer Systems, 681 Moore Road, King of Prussia, Pennsylvania 19406.

IBM. General Systems Division, 4111 Northside Parkway, Atlanta, Georgia 30301.

Radio Shack. One Tandy Center, Fort Worth, Texas 76102.

Wang. 1 Industrial Avenue, Lowell, Massachusetts 01851.

Computers: Reference Sources

Beginner's Guide to Buying a Personal Computer. Richard Mansfield and Myron D. Miller. Compute! Publications, Inc., Box 5406, Greensboro, North Carolina 27403. 1982. 78p.

Bowker/Bantam 1984 Complete Sourcebook of Personal Computing. R. R. Bowker Company, 1180 Avenue of the Americas, New York, New York 10036. 1983. 704p.

Compu-Guide. Martha Eischen. Dilithium Press, 8285 S.W. Nimbus Street, Suite 151, Beaverton, Oregon 97005. 1982. 157p.

Computer Resource Guide for Nonprofits. Second edition. Kenneth Gilman. Public Management Institute, 358 Brannan Street, San Francisco, California 94107. 1982. 600p.

Dictionary of Computers, Data Processing, and Telecommunications. Jerry M. Rosenberg. John Wiley and Sons, Inc., 605 Third Avenue, New York, New York 10158. 1983. 528p.

Encyclopedia of Computer Science and Technology. Jack Belzer, Albert G. Holzman, and Allen Kent, editors. Marcel Dekker, Inc., 270 Madison Avenue, New York, New York 10016. 1975-1981. 16 volumes.

The Microcomputer User's Handbook, 1983-84. Dennis Longley and Michael Shain. John Wiley and Sons, Inc., 605 Third Avenue, New York, New York 10158. 1983. 400p.

Practical Guide to Small Computers for Business and Professional Use. Revised edition. Robert M. Rinder. Monarch Press, 1230 Avenue of the Americas, New York, New York 10020. 1981. 288p.

Computers: Directories

Datapro Reports on Minicomputers. Datapro Research Corporation, 1805 Underwood Boulevard, Delran, New Jersey 08075. Three looseleaf volumes with monthly updates.

Directory of Information Management Software for Libraries, Information Centers and Record Centers. Cibbarelli and Associates, Inc., 11684 Ventura Boulevard, Suite 295, Studio City, California 91604. 1983. 133p.

Information Sources. Information Industry Association, 316 Pennsylvania Avenue, S.E., Suite 400, Washington, D.C. 20003. Annual.

Microcomputer Market Place 1983. Robert Driscoll, editor. Available from Gale Research Company, Book Tower, Detroit, Michigan 48226. 1982. 207p.

Terminal/Microcomputer Guide and Directory. Third edition. Online, Inc., 11 Tannery Lane, Weston, Connecticut 06883. 1981. 290p. Supplements November 1982, November 1983.

Computers: Buying a Computer

How to Buy a Home Computer: A Guide for Consumers. Electronics Industries Association, Consumer Electronics Group, Box 19100, Washington, D.C. 20036. 1983. Single complimentary copy sent in return for self-addressed, 6" x 9", $.54 stamped envelope.

How to Buy an Office Computer or Word Processor. Brian C. Donohue. Prentice-Hall, Inc., Englewood Cliffs, New Jersey 07632. 1983. 232p.

Simplified Guide to Small Computers for Business. Daniel R. McGlynn. John Wiley and Sons, Inc., 605 Third Avenue, New York, New York 10158. 1983. 241p.

Understanding and Buying a Small Business Computer. Susan Blumenthal. Howard W. Sams and Company, Inc., 4300 West 62nd Street, Indianapolis, Indiana 46206. 1983. 157p.

Understanding Computers: What Managers and Users Need to Know. Myles E. Walsh. John Wiley and Sons, Inc., 605 Third Avenue, New York, New York 10158. 1982. 266p.

Your First Business Computer. Donald R. Shaw. Van Nostrand Reinhold, 135 West 50th Street, New York, New York 10020. 1981. 256p.

Computers: Journals and Looseleaf Services

Byte. McGraw-Hill Publications Company, 70 Main Street, Peterborough, New Hampshire 03458. Monthly.

Compute! Small Systems Services, Inc., Box 5406, Greensboro, North Carolina 27403. Monthly.

Computerworld. C. W. Communications, Inc., 375 Cochituate Road, Box 880, Farmingham, Massachusetts 01701. Weekly. Advertising. Book reviews. Bibliographies. Charts. Illustrations. Patents. Statistics. Circulation: 117,000.

Creative Computing. Ziff-Davis Publishing Company, Consumer Division, One Park Avenue, New York, New York 10016. Monthly. Advertising. Book reviews. Charts. Illustrations. Statistics. Circulation: 8,000.

Datapro Directory of Small Computers. Datapro Research Corporation, 1805 Underwood Boulevard, Delran, New Jersey, 08075. Two looseleaf volumes with monthly updates.

Datapro Directory of Software. Datapro Research Corporation, 1805 Underwood Boulevard, Delran, New Jersey 08075. Two looseleaf volumes with monthly updates.

Interface Age. McPheters, Wolfe & Jones, 16704 Marquard Avenue, Box 1234, Cerritos, California 90701. Monthly. Advertising. Book reviews. Circulation: 70,000.

Microcomputing. 1001001, Inc., 80 Pine Street, Peterborough, New Hampshire 03458. Monthly.

Personal Computing. Benwill Publishing Corporation, 1050 Commonwealth Avenue, Boston, Massachusetts 02215. Monthly.

Note: Recommended publishers of looseleaf directories and reports on data communications, minicomputers, office systems, software, suppliers, et al. Expensive.

Auerbach Publications. 6560 North Park Drive, Pennsauken, New Jersey 08109.

Datapro Research Corporation (A McGraw-Hill Company). 1805 Underwood Boulevard, Delran, New Jersey 08075.

The Automated Office: General Works

Administrative Procedures for the Electronic Office. Arnold Rosen, Eileen Feretic Tunison, and Margaret Hilton Bahniuk. John Wiley and Sons, Inc., 605 Third Avenue, New York, New York 10158. 1982. 520p.

Affordable Word Processing. Richard A. McGrath. Prentice-Hall, Inc., Englewood Cliffs, New Jersey 07632. 1983. 160p.

Electronic Mail: A Revolution in Business Communications. Stephen Connell and Ian A. Galbraith. Knowledge Industry Publications, Inc., 701 Westchester Avenue, White Plains, New York 10604. 1982. 141p.

Managing Paperwork: The Key to Productivity. Frank M. Knox. Thomond Press. Distributed by Van Nostrand Reinhold, 135 West 50th Street, New York, New York 10020. 1980. 249p.

Office Automation. Andrew Doswell. John Wiley and Sons, Inc., 605 Third Avenue, New York, New York 10158. 1983. 283p.

Office Automation: The Productivity Challenge. Dimitris N. Chorafas. Prentice-Hall, Inc., Englewood Cliffs, New Jersey 07632. 1982. 304p.

Office Automation and Word Processing Fundamentals. Second edition. Shirley A. Waterhouse. Harper and Row, 10 East 53rd Street, New York, New York 10022. 1983. 336p.

Office Management and Control: The Administrative Managing of Information. Eighth edition. George R. Terry and John J. Stallard. Dow Jones-Irwin, 1818 Ridge Road, Homewood, Illinois 60430. 1980. 571p.

Records Management: Controlling Business Information. Irene Place and David Hyslop. Reston Publishing Company, 11480 Sunset Hills Road, Reston, Virginia 22090. 1982. 371p.

Teleconferencing: New Media for Business Meetings. Martin C. J. Elton. American Management Association, Inc., 135 West 50th Street, New York, New York 10020. 1982. 57p.

The Automated Office: Guides and Handbooks

GSM Library Guides. Management Series Number 11: *The Automated Office/ Office of the Future.* Compiled by Eloisa G. Yeargain. Graduate School of Management Library, University of California, Los Angeles, California 90024. 1983. 2p. ($1).

A Guide to the Electronic Office. Malcom Peltu. John Wiley and Sons, Inc., 605 Third Avenue, New York, New York 10158. 1981. 200p.

The Library Manager's Guide to Automation. Second edition. Richard W. Boss. Knowledge Industry Publications, Inc., 701 Westchester Avenue, White Plains, New York 10604. 1983. 165p.

Office Automation: A Manager's Guide. Harry Katzan. American Management Association, Inc., 135 West 50th Street, New York, New York 10020. 1982. 224p.

Office Automation and Word Processing Buyer's Guide. Tony Webster, Richard Dougan, Jenny Green with assistance from Datapro Research Corporation. Computer Reference Guide, Coopers & Lybrand International, Australia. McGraw-Hill Book Company, 1221 Avenue of the Americas, New York, New York 10020. 1984. 320p.

The Professional Secretary's Handbook: A Guide to the Electronic and Conventional Office. Houghton Mifflin Company, Two Park Street, Boston, Massachusetts 02108. 1984. 394p.

The Word Processing Handbook: A Step-by-Step Guide to Automating Your Office. Katherine Aschner. Knowledge Industry Publications, Inc., 701 Westchester Avenue, White Plains, New York 10604. 1982. 193p.

The Automated Office: Journals and Looseleaf Services

Datapro Automated Office Solutions. Datapro Research Corporation, 1805 Underwood Boulevard, Delran, New Jersey 08075. Two looseleaf volumes with monthly updates.

Datapro Reports on Office Systems. Datapro Research Corporation, 1805 Underwood Boulevard, Delran, New Jersey 08075. Three looseleaf volumes with monthly updates.

Office. Office Publications, Inc., 1200 Summer Street, Stamford, Connecticut 06904. Monthly. Advertising. Book reviews. Illustrations. Index. Circulation: 132,000.

Office Administration and Automation. Box 1129, Dover, New Jersey 07801. Monthly.

CORPORATE SOCIAL RESPONSIBILITY AND PHILANTHROPY

In 1982, corporations gave over $3 billion in grants and charitable contributions. Like the Italian Renaissance popes and princes, the modern corporate nobility have recognized their responsibility to the human welfare and cultural advancement of the society from which they profit.

Unquestionably, the best book on the subject, which also includes a definitive bibliography, is George Steiner and John Steiner, *Business, Government, and Society: A Managerial Perspective*, fourth edition to be published in 1985 by Random House.

American Business History. Herman E. Kroos and Charles Gilbert. Prentice-Hall, Inc., Englewood Cliffs, New Jersey 07632. 1972. 352p.

American Business Values in Transition. Gerald F. Cavanagh. Prentice-Hall, Inc., Englewood Cliffs, New Jersey 07632. 1976. 216p.

America's Wealthiest People: Their Philanthropic and Nonprofit Affiliations. Taft Group, 5125 MacArthur Boulevard, N.W., Suite 300, Washington, D.C. 20016. 1983. 482p.

Annual Survey of Corporate Contributions. The Conference Board, Inc., 845 Third Avenue, New York, New York 10022. Annual.

The Art of Winning Corporate Grants. Howard Hillman. The Vanguard Press, Inc., 424 Madison Avenue, New York, New York 10017. 1980. 180p.

Asking and Giving: A Report on Hospital Philanthropy. Robert Maris Cunningham. American Hospital Association, 840 North Lakeshore Drive, Chicago, Illinois 60611. 1980. 148p.

Better Giving: The New Needs of American Philanthropy. George C. Kirstein. Houghton Mifflin Company, Two Park Street, Boston, Massachusetts 02107. 1975. 196p.

Bibliography of Fund Raising and Philanthropy. Second edition. George T. Holloway, executive director; Rosy B. Gonzales, editor and director of research. National Catholic Development Conference, 119 North Park Avenue, Suite 409, Rockville Centre, New York 11570. 1982. 76p.

Business and Society: A Managerial Approach. Frederick D. Sturdivant. Richard D. Irwin, Inc., 1818 Ridge Road, Homewood, Illinois 60430. 1977. 502p.

Business and Society: Concepts and Policy Issues. Fourth edition. Keith Davis, William C. Frederick and Robert L. Blostrom. McGraw-Hill Book Company, 1221 Avenue of the Americas, New York, New York 10020. 1980. 672p.

Business and Society: Environment and Responsibility. Third edition. Keith Davis and Robert L. Blostrom. McGraw-Hill Book Company, 1221 Avenue of the Americas, New York, New York 10020. 1975. 597p.

Business and Society: Managing Corporate Social Impact. George C. Sawyer. Houghton Mifflin Company, Two Park Street, Boston, Massachusetts 02107. 1979. 425p.

Business and Society: Managing Corporate Social Performance. Archie B. Carroll. Little, Brown and Company, 34 Beacon Street, Boston, Massachusetts 02106. 1981. 453p.

Business and Society: 1976-2000. John L. Paluszek. American Management Association, Inc., 135 West 50th Street, New York, New York 10020. 1976. 46p.

Business and Society: Strategies for the 1980's. Report of the Task Force on Corporate Social Performance. U.S. Department of Commerce, Washington, D.C. 20230. 1980. 193p. Includes John F. Filer Report, "The Social Goals of the Corporation."

Business Ethics: Concepts and Cases. Manuel G. Velasquez. Prentice-Hall, Inc., Englewood Cliffs, New Jersey 07632. 1982. 416p.

Business Ethics in America. George C. Benson. D. C. Heath Company, 125 Spring Street, Lexington, Massachusetts 02173. 1982. 320p.

Business, Government and Society: A Managerial Perspective. Fourth edition. George A. Steiner and John F. Steiner. Random House, Inc., 201 East 50th Street, New York, New York 10022. (To be published 1985, ca. 650p.)

Business in the Humane Society. John J. Corson. McGraw-Hill Book Company, 1221 Avenue of the Americas, New York, New York 10020. 1971. 314p.

Casebook in Business, Government and Society. Second edition. George A. Steiner and John F. Steiner. Random House, Inc., 201 East 50th Street, New York, New York 10022. 1980. 241p.

The Changing Position of Philanthropy in the American Economy. Frank G. Dickinson. National Bureau of Economic Research. Distributed by Columbia University Press, 562 West 113th Street, New York, New York 10025. 1970. 222p.

Charitable Giving and Solicitation. Sue S. Stern, Jon L. Schumacher, and Patrick D. Martin. Prentice-Hall, Inc., Information Services Division, Englewood Cliffs, New Jersey 07632. Looseleaf service basis.

Community and the Bank: Bank of America Corporate Responsibility Report. Bank of America, Editorial Services Department 3124, Box 37000, San Francisco, California 94137. Annual.

The Complete Guide to Corporate Fund Raising. Joseph Dermer and Stephen Wertheimer. Public Service Materials Center, 111 North Central Avenue, Hartsdale, New York 10530. 1982. 112p.

Contemporary Challenges in the Business-Society Relationship. George A. Steiner, editor. Graduate School of Management, University of California, Los Angeles, California 90024. 1972.

Corporate Community Involvement. Partnerships Dataline USA. Citizens Forum/NML, New York, New York 10036. 1983. n.p.

Corporate 500: The Directory of Corporate Philanthropy. Public Management Institute, 358 Brannan Street, San Francisco, California 94107. Annual.

Corporate Giving Yellow Pages. Benjamin Lord, editor. Taft Group. 5125 MacArthur Boulevard, N.W., Suite 300, Washington, D.C. 20016. 1983. 88p.

Corporate Performance: The Key to Public Trust. Francis W. Steckmest, editor. McGraw-Hill Book Company, 1221 Avenue of the Americas, New York, New York 10020. 1982. 295p.

Corporate Philanthropic Public Service Activities. James F. Harris and Anne Klepper. The Conference Board, Inc., 845 Third Avenue, New York, New York 10022. 1976. 61p.

Corporate Philanthropy. Kenneth A. Bertsch. Investor Responsibility Research Center, 1319 F Street, N.W., Washington, D.C. 20004. 1982. 84p.

Corporate Philanthropy in the Eighties: Expert Advice for Those Who Give or Seek Funds. National Chamber Foundation, 1615 H Street, N.W., Washington, D.C. 20062. 1980. 31p.

Corporate Power and Social Responsibility. Neil H. Jacoby. Macmillan Publishing Company, 866 Third Avenue, New York, New York 10022. 1980. 274p.

Corporate Responsibility for Social Problems: A Bibliography. Bank of America, Editorial Services Department 3124, Box 37000, San Francisco, California 94137. 1975. 78p.

The Corporate Social Audit. Raymond A. Bauer and Dan H. Fenn, Jr. Russell Sage Foundation, 112 East 64th Street, New York, New York 10021. 1972. 109p.

Corporate Social Responsibility. Richard N. Farmer and W. Dickerson Hogue. Science Research Associates, Inc., 155 North Wacker Drive, Chicago, Illinois 60606. 1973. 223p.

Corporate Social Responsibility: Policies, Programs and Publications. Council for Financial Aid to Education, 680 Fifth Avenue, New York, New York 10019. 1982. 28p.

Corporate Strategies for Social Performance. Melvin Anshen. Macmillan Publishing Company, 866 Third Avenue, New York, New York 10022. 1980. 274p.

Corporate Support. Council for Advancement and Support of Education, 11 Dupont Circle, Suite 400, Washington, D.C. 20036. 1981. 56p.

Corporate Support of Higher Education, 1979. Council for Financial Aid to Education, 680 Fifth Avenue, New York, New York 10019. 1980. 20p.

The Corporation and the Campus. Robert H. Connery, editor. Praeger Publishers, 521 Fifth Avenue, New York, New York 10175. 1970. 187p.

Corporations and Their Critics: Issues and Answers to the Problems of Corporate Social Responsibility. Thornton Bradshaw and David Fogel, editors. McGraw-Hill Book Company, 1221 Avenue of the Americas, New York, New York 10020. 1981. 288p.

The Cox Report on the American Corporation. Allan Cox. Delacorte Press, One Dag Hammarskjold Plaza, 245 East 47th Street, New York, New York 10017. 1982. 448p.

Creative Philanthropy: Carnegie Corporation in Africa, 1953-1974. E. Jefferson Murphy. Teachers College Press, Columbia University, 1234 Amsterdam Avenue, New York, New York 10027. 1976. 286p.

Economic Factors in the Growth of Corporation Giving. Ralph L. Nelson. Russell Sage Foundation, 112 East 64th Street, New York, New York 10021. 1970. 116p.

Effective Corporate Fundraising. W. Grant Brownrigg. American Council for the Arts, 570 Seventh Avenue, New York, New York 10018. 1982. 162p.

The Endangered Sector. Waldemar A. Nielson. Columbia University Press, 562 West 113th Street, New York, New York 10025. 1979. 279p.

The Ethics of Corporate Conduct. Clarence Walton, editor. Prentice-Hall, Inc., Englewood Cliffs, New Jersey 07632. 1977. 216p.

Filer Report. See *Business and Society: Strategies for the 1980's,* above.

5,123 Examples of How BCA Companies Supported the Arts. Business Committee for the Arts, 1775 Broadway, New York, New York 10019. 1983.

Fund Raising for Philanthropy. Gerald Soroker. Pittsburgh Jewish Publishing and Education Foundation, 315 South Bellefield Avenue, Pittsburgh, Pennsylvania 15213. 1974. 190p.

The Future Role of Business in Society. Lillian W. Kay, editor. The Conference Board, Inc., 845 Third Avenue, New York, New York 10022. 1977. 57p.

Give! Who Gets Your Charity Dollar? Harvey Katz. Doubleday and Company, Inc., 501 Franklin Avenue, New York, New York 11530. 1974. 252p.

Giving and Getting: A Chemical Bank Study of Charitable Contributions 1983 through 1988. The Not for Profit Group, Chemical Bank, 1212 Sixth Avenue, New York, New York 10036. 1983. 12p.

Giving USA: Annual Report. American Association of Fund Raising Counsel, Inc., 25 West 43rd Street, New York, New York 10036. Annual.

Guide to Corporate Giving in the Arts. Robert Porter. American Council for the Arts, 570 Seventh Avenue, New York, New York 10018. Biennial.

Guide to Creative Giving. Bernard P. Taylor. Groupwork, Inc., Box 258, South Plainfield, New Jersey 07080. 1980. 89p.

The Handbook of Corporate Social Responsibility: Profiles of Involvement. Second edition. Human Resources Network. Chilton Book Company, Chilton Way, Radnor, Pennsylvania 19089. 1975. 629p.

How to Be a Good Corporate Citizen: A Manager's Guide to Making Social Responsibility Work—and Pay. David Clutterbuck. McGraw-Hill Book Company, 1221 Avenue of the Americas, New York, New York 10020. 1982. 254p.

How to Create New Ideas for Corporate Profit and Personal Success. Eugene Raudsepp. Prentice-Hall, Inc., Englewood Cliffs, New Jersey 07632. 1982. 176p.

How to Get Corporate Grants. Daniel Lynn Conrad. Public Management Institute, 358 Brannan Street, San Francisco, California 94107. 1981. 351p.

How to Write Successful Corporate Appeals/With Full Examples. James P. Sinclair. Public Service Materials Center, 111 North Central Avenue, Hartsdale, New York 10530. 1982. 110p.

International Business Philanthropy: Papers from a Symposium Cosponsored by the National Council on Philanthropy and Seven Springs Center, an

Affiliate of Yale University. Richard Eells, editor. The Free Press, 866 Third Avenue, New York, New York 10022. 1979. 169p.

International Philanthropy: A Compilation of Grants by U.S. Foundations. Martha R. Keens. Foundation Center, 888 Seventh Avenue, New York, New York 10106. 1981. 240p.

Issues in Business and Society. Second edition. George A. Steiner and John F. Steiner, compilers. Random House, 201 East 50th Street, New York, New York 10022. 1977. 560p.

The Limits of Corporate Responsibility. Neil W. Chamberlain. Basic Books, 10 East 53rd Street, New York, New York 10022. 1973. 236p.

Management: Toward Accountability for Performance. Robert Albanese. Richard D. Irwin, Inc., 1818 Ridge Road, Homewood, Illinois 60430. 1975. 569p.

Managing a Business Contributions Program. Mike White and Jerry Cronin. Independent Community Consultants, Inc., Box 141, Hampton, Arkansas 71744. 1983. 48p.

Managing Corporate Contributions. Kathryn Troy. The Conference Board, Inc., 845 Third Avenue, New York, New York 10022. 1980. 95p.

Managing Smaller Corporate Giving Programs. Council on Foundations, 1828 L Street, N.W., Washington, D.C. 20036. 1983. 35p.

Measuring Business's Social Performance: The Corporate Social Audit. John J. Corson and George A. Steiner. Committee for Economic Development, 477 Madison Avenue, New York, New York 10022. 1974. 75p.

Meeting Human Needs: Toward a New Public Philosophy. Jack A. Meyer. American Enterprise Institute for Public Policy Research, 1150 17th Street, N.W., Washington, D.C. 20036. 1982. 469p.

Memorandum on Corporate Giving. Council on Foundations, 1828 L Street, N.W., Washington, D.C. 20036. 1981. 32p.

The Money Givers. Joseph C. Goulden. Random House, Inc., 201 East 50th Street, New York, New York 10022. 1971. 341p.

Motivations for Charitable Giving: A Reference Guide. Astrida Butners and Norman Buntaine. The 501 (c) (3) Group, Suite 600, One Dupont Circle, Washington, D.C. 20036. 1973. 69p.

National Corporations: Analysis of Corporate and Employee Giving in 1981 United Way Campaigns. United Way of America, Research Division, 801 North Fairfax Street, Alexandria, Virginia 22314. 1982. 65p.

National Directory of Arts and Education Support by Business Corporations. Second edition. Daniel Millsaps, editor. Washington International Arts Letter, Box 9005, Washington, D.C. 20003. 1982. 234p.

National Directory of Corporate Charity (California Edition). Compiled by Sam Sternberg. Regional Young Adult Project, 944 Market Street, #705, San Francisco, California 94102. 1981. 512p.

The New Corporate Philanthropy: How Society and Business Can Profit. Frank Koch. Plenum Publishing Corporation, 233 Spring Street, New York, New York 10013. 1979. 315p.

New Models for Creative Giving. Raymond B. Knudsen. New Century Publications, Inc., 220 Old New Brunswick Road, Piscataway, New Jersey 08854. 1976. 143p.

The New Philanthropy. Craig W. Smith. Harper and Row Publishers, Inc., 10 East 53rd Street, New York, New York 10022. (in press).

The Next 200 Years. Herman Kahn, William Brown, and Leon Martel. William Morrow and Company, 105 Madison Avenue, New York, New York 10016. 1976. 241p.

Opportunities for Philanthropy—1976: Report of an International Conference. Sponsored by the Ciba Foundation, Council on Foundations and the Josiah Macy, Jr. Foundation. Edited by John Z. Bowers and Elizabeth F. Purcell. Josiah Macy, Jr. Foundation, One Rockefeller Plaza, New York, New York 10020. 1977. 223p.

Partners: A Practical Guide to Corporate Support of the Arts. Cultural Assistance Center. Available from American Council for the Arts, 570 Seventh Avenue, New York, New York 10018. 1982. 112p.

The Philanthropoids: Foundations and Society, Unsubsidized Anatomy of the Burden of Benevolence. Benjamin Charles George Whitaker. William Morrow and Company, Inc., 105 Madison Avenue, New York, New York 10016. 1974. 256p.

Philanthropy and Marketing: New Strategies for Fund Raising. James Gregory Lord. The Third Sector Press, 2000 Euclid Avenue, Box 18044, Cleveland, Ohio 44118. 1981. Looseleaf.

Philanthropy and the Business Corporation. Marion R. Fremont-Smith. Russell Sage Foundation, 112 East 64th Street, New York, New York 10021. 1972. 110p.

Philanthropy in the 70's: An Anglo-American Discussion. A report on the Anglo-American Conference on the Role of Philanthropy in the 1970s, Ditchley Park, England, April 28 to May 1, 1972. Edited by John J. Corson and Harry V. Hodson. Council on Foundations, 1828 L Street, N.W., Washington, D.C. 20036. 1973. 116p.

Philanthropy in the United States. Frank Emerson Andrews. Foundation Center, 888 Seventh Avenue, New York, New York 10106. 1974. 48p.

The Planned Giving Idea Book. Robert F. Sharpe. Public Service Materials Center, 111 North Central Avenue, Hartsdale, New York 10530. 1981. 285p.

Planned Giving Ideas. Edited by Virginia Carter Smith and Catherine E. Garigan. Council for Advancement and Support of Education, 11 Dupont Circle, Suite 400, Washington, D.C. 20036. 1979. 30p.

Private Enterprise and Public Purpose. S. Prakash Sethi and Carl L. Swanson, editors. John Wiley and Sons, Inc., 605 Third Avenue, New York, New York 10158. 1981. 461p.

Private Management and Public Policy: The Principle of Public Responsibility. Lee E. Preston and James E. Post. Prentice-Hall, Inc., Englewood Cliffs, New Jersey 07632. 1975. 192p.

Private Philanthropy and Public Welfare: The Joseph Rowntree Memorial Trust, 1954-1979. Lewis E. Waddilove. Allen and Unwin, Inc., 9 Winchester Terrace, Winchester, Massachusetts 01890. 1983. 272p.

A Profile of Corporate Contributions. Hayden W. Smith. Council for Financial Aid to Education, 680 Fifth Avenue, New York, New York 10019. 1983. 46p.

Prospecting: Searching Out the Philanthropic Dollar. Elizabeth Koochoo. Taft Group, 5125 MacArthur Boulevard, N.W., Suite 300, Washington, D.C. 20016. 1979. 69p.

The Public Image of Big Business in America, 1880-1940: A Quantitative Study in Social Change. Louis B. Galambos and Barbara Barrow Spence. Johns Hopkins University Press, Baltimore, Maryland 21218. 1975. 336p.

Public-Private Partnership: An Opportunity for Urban Communities. Research and Policy Committee, Committee for Economic Development, 477 Madison Avenue, New York, New York 10022. 1982. 106p.

Public-Private Partnership in American Cities: Seven Case Studies. R. Scott Fosler and Renee A. Berger, editors. Committee for Economic Development, 477 Madison Avenue, New York, New York 10022. 1982. 336p.

Research in Corporate Social Performance and Policy. JAI Press, Inc., 36 Sherwood Place, Greenwich, Connecticut 06836. Annual.

The Rich: A Study of the Species. William Davis. Franklin Watts, Inc., 730 Fifth Avenue, New York, New York, 10019. 1983. 267p.

Scholars, Dollars, and Public Policy: New Frontiers in Corporate Giving. Ernest W. Lefever, Raymond English, and Robert L. Schuettinger. Ethics and Public Policy Center, Inc., 1211 Connecticut Avenue, N.W., Washington, D.C. 20036. 1983. 63p.

Self-Portrait with Donors: Confessions of an Art Collector. John Walker. Little, Brown, and Company, 34 Beacon Street, Boston, Massachusetts 02106. 1974. 320p.

The Social Audit for Management. Clark C. Abt. American Management Association, Inc., 135 West 50th Street, New York, New York 10020. 1977. 278p.

The Social Challenge to Business. Robert W. Ackerman. Harvard University Press, 79 Garden Street, Cambridge, Massachusetts 02138. 1975. 345p.

Social Costs and Benefits of Business. Thomas A. Klein. Prentice-Hall, Inc., Englewood Cliffs, New Jersey 07632. 1977. 199p.

Social Strategy and Corporate Structure. Neil W. Chamberlain. Macmillan Publishing Company, 866 Third Avenue, New York, New York 10022. 1982. 192p.

Strategic Planning: What Every Manager Must Know. George A. Steiner. The Free Press, 866 Third Avenue, New York, New York 10022. 1979. 383p.

Taft Corporate Directory: Profiles and Analyses of America's Corporate Foundations and Giving Committees. Taft Group, 5125 MacArthur Boulevard, N.W., Suite 300, Washington, D.C. 20016. Annual. Includes *Corporate Updates*, monthly, and *Corporate Giving Watch*, monthly.

Taft Trustees of Wealth: A Biographical Directory of Private Foundations and Corporate Foundation Officers. Fifth edition. Taft Group, 5125 MacArthur Boulevard, N.W., Suite 300, Washington, D.C. 20016. 1979. 565p.

Tips on Charitable Giving. Philanthropic Advisory Service, Council on Better Business Bureaus, 1515 Wilson Boulevard, Arlington, Virginia 22209. 1982. n.p.

Voluntary Support for Public Higher Education, 1977-78. Brakely, John Price Jones, Inc., 6 East 43rd Street, New York, New York 10017. 1980. 24p.

Voluntary Support of Education. Council for Financial Aid to Education, 680 Fifth Avenue, New York, New York 10019. Annual.

FOUNDATIONS AND FOUNDATION GRANTS

The ninth edition of *The Foundation Directory*, the bible of the field, lists over 4,000 corporate, community, and independent foundations. These organizations report assets of over $47 billion and make grants of $3.5 billion annually. More than 700 have assets of over a million or make annual grants totaling more than $100,000.

The Foundation Center, the premier source of information on the subject, publishes a wide array of useful and interesting materials. A postcard to their address, 888 Seventh Avenue, New York, New York 10106, asking to be put on their mailing list, will be the best 13 cent investment you could make. For additional information, see Section III: **A Basic Fund-raising Library.**

About Foundations: How to Find the Facts You Need to Get a Grant. Judith B. Margolin. The Foundation Center, 888 Seventh Avenue, New York, New York 10101. 1975. 38p.

Accounting and Reporting Practices of Private Foundations: A Critical Evaluation. Jack Traub. Praeger Publishers, 521 Fifth Avenue, New York, New York 10175. 1977. 240p.

The Art of Winning Foundation Grants. Howard Hillman and Karin Abarbanel. Vanguard Press, Inc., 424 Madison Avenue, New York, New York 10017. 1975. 192p.

The Big Foundations. Waldemar A. Nielsen. Columbia University Press, 562 West 113th Street, New York, New York 10025. 1972. 475p.

Charities and Charitable Foundations. Edith L. Fisch, Doris Jonas Freed, and Esther R. Schachter. Prentice-Hall, Inc., Englewood Cliffs, New Jersey 07632. 1974. 869p.

The Charity Racket. Robert A. Liston. Thomas Nelson Publishers, P.O. Box 14100, Nelson Place at Elmhill Pike, Nashville, Tennessee 37214. 1976. 160p.

The Community College Foundation. Edited by W. Harvey Sharron, Jr. Council for Advancement and Support of Education, 11 Dupont Circle, Suite 400, Washington, D.C. 20036. 1982. 321p.

Corporate Foundation Profiles. Third edition. The Foundation Center, 888 Seventh Avenue, New York, New York 10106. 1983. 550p.

The First Five Years: Fiscal 1966 through Fiscal 1970. National Council on the Arts, National Endowment for the Arts, Washington, D.C. 20506. 1970. various pagings.

Ford Foundation: Report. Ford Foundation, 320 East 43rd Street, New York, New York 10017. Annual.

The Ford Foundation at Work: Philanthropic Choices, Methods and Styles. Richard Magat. Plenum Publishing Corporation, 233 Spring Street, New York, New York 10013. 1979. 208p.

The Foundation Administrator: A Study of Those Who Manage America's Foundations. Arnold J. Zurcher and Jane Dustan. Russell Sage Foundation, 112 East 64th Street, New York, New York 10021. 1972. 171p.

Foundation 500. Douglas M. Lawson Associates, 39 East 51st Street, New York, New York 10022. Annual.

Foundation Fundamentals: A Guide for Grant Seekers. Revised edition. Carol M. Kurzig. Foundation Center, 888 Seventh Avenue, New York, New York 10106. 1980. 148p.

Foundation Gamesmanship. June Wayne. Tamarind Lithography Workshop, 1112 Tamarind, Los Angeles, California 90038. 1966. 13p.

Foundation Guide for Religious Grant Seekers. Peter S. Robinson, editor. Scholars Press, 101 Salem Street, Box 2268, Chico, California 95927. 1979. 98p.

Foundation Primer. M. Jane Williams. Fund Raising Institute, Box 365, Ambler, Pennyslvania 19002. 1981. 150p.

Foundation Watcher. Frank Emerson Andrews. Franklin and Marshall College, Box 3003, Lancaster, Pennsylvania 17604. 1973. 321p.

The Foundations: Their Use and Abuse. William H. Rudy. Public Affairs Press, 419 New Jersey Avenue, Washington, D.C. 20003. 1970. 75p.

Foundations: Twenty Viewpoints. Frank Emerson Andrews, editor. Russell Sage Foundation, 112 East 64th Street, New York, New York 10021. 1965. 108p.

Foundations and Fund Raising: A Bibliography of Books to 1980. John J. Miletich. Vance Bibliographies, Box 229, Monticello, Illinois 61856. 1981. 10p.

Foundations and Government: State and Federal Law and Supervision. Marion R. Fremont-Smith. Russell Sage Foundation, 112 East 64th Street, New York, New York 10021. 1965. 564p.

Foundations, Private Giving, and Public Policy: Report and Recommendations. Commission on Foundations and Private Philanthropy. University of Chicago Press, 5801 Ellis Avenue, Chicago, Illinois 60637. 1970. 287p.

The Future of Philanthropic Foundations. Ciba Foundation. Elsevier Science Publishing Company, 52 Vanderbilt Avenue, New York, New York 10017. 1975. 300p.

Giving and Taking: Across the Foundation Desk. John M. Russell. Teachers College Press, Columbia University, 1234 Amsterdam Avenue, New York, New York 10027. 1977. 90p.

The Guggenheims. John H. Davis. William Morrow and Company, Inc., 105 Madison Avenue, New York, New York 10016. 1978. 608p.

The Handbook on Private Foundations. David F. Freeman. Published for the Council on Foundations by Seven Locks Press, Box 72, 6600 81st Street, Cabin John, Maryland 20731. 1981. 452p.

How to Get Your Fair Share of Foundation Grants. Manning Patillo, Jr., Robert F. Semple, Martha R. Wallace, et al. Public Service Materials Center, 111 North Central Avenue, Hartsdale, New York 10530. 1983. 143p.

How to Secure and Manage Foundation and Federal Funds in the 1980's. Theodore M. Lawe. MRDC Educational Institute, Box 15127, Dallas, Texas 75201. 1980. 185p.

How to Write Successful Foundation Presentations. Joseph Dermer. Public Service Materials Center, 111 North Central Avenue, Hartsdale, New York 10530. 1980. 80p.

The Instant Foundation Telephone Index. Burton J. Eckstein and Richard M. Eckstein. Research Grant Guides, Box 357, Oceanside, New York 11572. 1980. 32p.

International Philanthropy: A Compilation of Grants by U.S. Foundations. Martha R. Keens. Foundation Center, 888 Seventh Avenue, New York, New York 10106. 1981. 240p.

The Investment Policies of Foundations. Ralph L. Nelson. Russell Sage Foundation, 112 East 64th Street, New York, New York 10021. 1967. 203p.

Management of American Foundations: Administration, Policies and Social Role. Arnold J. Zurcher. New York University Press. Distributed by Columbia University Press, 562 West 113th Street, New York, New York 10025. 1972. 184p.

The Mellons. David E. Koskoff. Thomas Y. Crowell Company, 10 East 53rd Street, New York, New York 10022. 1978. 602p.

Models for Money: Obtaining Government and Foundation Grants and Assistance. Second edition. Louis Urgo. Suffolk University Management Center, 41 Temple Street, Boston, Massachusetts 02114. 1978. 187p.

National Development Foundations: A Private Sector Response to the Development Needs and Opportunities within Latin America. First Seminar on National Development Foundations, Washington, 1968. Pan American Development Foundation, 1889 F Street, N.W., Washington, D.C. 20006. 1969. various pagings.

The New How to Raise Funds from Foundations. Third edition. Joseph Dermer. Public Service Materials Center, 111 North Central Avenue, Hartsdale, New York 10530. 1979. 96p.

New Ways to Succeed with Foundations—A Guide for the Reagan Years. Joseph Dermer. Public Service Materials Center, 111 North Central Avenue, Hartsdale, New York 10530. 1982. 96p.

Patterns of Concentration in Large Foundations' Grants to U.S. Colleges and Universities. Richard Colvard and A. M. Bennett. Research and Development Division, American College Testing Program, 2201 North Dodge Street, Box 168, Iowa City, Iowa 52243. 1974. 30p.

Persuade and Provide: The Story of the Arts and Education Council in St. Louis. Michael Newton and Scott Hadley. American Council for the Arts, 570 Seventh Avenue, New York, New York 10018. 1970. 249p.

104 / II–Subject Information Sources

The Philanthropoids: Foundations and Society, Unsubsidized Anatomy of the Burden of Benevolence. Benjamin Charles George Whitaker. William Morrow and Company, 105 Madison Avenue, New York, New York 10016. 1974. 256p.

Private Money and Public Service: The Role of Foundations in American Society. Merrimon Cuninggim. McGraw-Hill Book Company, 1221 Avenue of the Americas, New York, New York 10020. 1972. 267p.

Public Accountability of Foundations and Charitable Trusts. Eleanor Kendrick Taylor. Russell Sage Foundation, 112 East 64th Street, New York, New York 10021. 1973. 231p.

Public Information Handbook for Foundations. Saul Richman. Foreword by Robert F. Goheen. Council on Foundations, Inc., 1828 L Street, N.W., Washington, D.C. 20036. 1973. 95p.

Statistics of Income 1974-1978: Private Foundations. U.S. Internal Revenue Service. Available from U.S. Government Printing Office, Washington, D.C. 20402. 1981. 113p.

The Tax-Exempt Scandal: America's Leftist Foundations. William H. McIlhany. Crown Publications, Inc., One Park Avenue, New York, New York 10016. 1980. 367p.

Trustees and the Future of Foundations. John W. Nason. Council on Foundations, Inc., 1828 L Street, N. W., Washington, D.C. 20036. 1977. 112p.

Understanding and Increasing Foundation Support. Edited by J. Davis Ross. Council for Advancement and Support of Education, 11 Dupont Circle, Suite 400, Washington, D.C. 20036. 1981. 94p.

Why Establish a Private Foundation. Southeastern Council of Foundations, 134 Peachtree Street, N.E., Atlanta, Georgia 30303. 1980. 26p.

FUND-RAISING

Fund-raising, of course, is what this bibliography is all about. The literature on this vast subject, with all of its peripheral interests is, while wide and varied, also limited and specific.

Giving USA, the annual publication of the American Association of Fund Raising Counsel, is the authoritative statistical compendium in the field, quoted extensively throughout these remarks. As its subtitle denotes, it is "A Compilation of Facts and Trends on American Philanthropy."

It is included in the **Basic Fund-raising Library** in Section III, as are the Hoke Communications bimonthly *Fund Raising Management*, and the publications of the Public Services Materials Center, the Taft Corporation, and the Third Sector Press.

The A-V Connecton: The Guide to Federal Funds for Audio-Visual Programs. American Library Association, 50 East Huron Street, Chicago, Illinois 60611. 1981. 248p.

America's Most Successful Fund Raising Letters. Joseph Dermer. Public Service Materials Center, 111 North Central Avenue, Hartsdale, New York 10530. 1976. 141p.

The Anatomy of an Art Auction; a Vital Guide for Organization Fund Raisers. Arnold Harvey Associates, P.O. Box 89, Commack, New York 11725. 1972. 77p.

The Annual Fund. Council for Advancement and Support of Education, 11 Dupont Circle, Suite 400, Washington, D.C. 20036. 1982. 64p.

Annual Fund Ideas. Virginia L. Carter. Council for Advancement and Support of Education, 11 Dupont Circle, Suite 400, Washington, D.C. 20036. 1979. 48p.

The Art of Asking: A Handbook for Successful Fund Raising. Paul H. Schneiter. Walker and Company, 720 Fifth Avenue, New York, New York 10019. 1978. 198p.

The Art of Fund Raising. Irving R. Warner. Harper and Row Publishers, Inc., 10 East 53rd Street, New York, New York 10022. 1975. 176p.

Arts Money: Raising It, Saving It, and Earning It. Joan Jeffri. Neal-Schuman Publishers, Inc., 23 Cornelia Street, New York, New York 10014. 1983. 240p.

Ayer Fund-raising Dinner Guide. Ayer Press, One Bala Avenue, Bala Cynwyd, Pennsylvania 19004. 1974. 120p.

Basic Funding Development. Clark C. Nichols. Grantsman, Inc., Pine City, Minnesota 55063. 1974. 198p.

Before You Give Another Dime. Robert F. Sharpe. Thomas Nelson Publishers, Box 141000, Nelson Place at Elm Hill Pike, Nashville, Tennessee 37214. 1979. 189p.

Bibliography of Fund Raising and Philanthropy. Second edition. George T. Holloway, executive editor; Rosy B. Gonzales, editor and director of research. National Catholic Development Conference, 119 North Park Avenue, Suite 409, Rockville Centre, New York 11570. 1982. 76p.

A Bibliography on Fundraising. Alfreda C. Doyle, editor. Bibliotheca Press, Box 98378, Atlanta, Georgia 30359. 1982. 50p.

The Big Gift. Council for Advancement and Support of Education, 11 Dupont Circle, Suite 400, Washington, D.C. 20036. 1982. 56p.

The Bread Game: The Realities of Foundation Fund Raising. Fourth revised edition. Herb Allen, editor. Regional Young Adult Project, 944 Market Street, #705, San Francisco, California 94102. 1981. 150p.

The Capital Campaign. Council for Advancement and Support of Education, 11 Dupont Circle, Suite 400, Washington, D.C. 20036. 1979. 64p.

Capital Financing for Hospitals. American Hospital Association, 840 North Lakeshore Drive, Chicago, Illinois 60611. 1974. 60p.

Capital Ideas: Step-by-Step—How to Solicit Major Gifts from Private Sources. Second edition. M. Jane Williams. Fund Raising Institute, Box 365, Ambler, Pennsylvania 19002. 1979. 320p.

Charitable Giving and Solicitation. Sue S. Stern, Jon L. Schumacher, and Patrick D. Martin. Prentice-Hall, Inc., Information Services Division, Englewood Cliffs, New Jersey 07632. Looseleaf service basis.

The Charity Racket. Robert A. Liston. Thomas Nelson Publishers, Box 141000, Nelson Place at Elm Hill Pike, Nashville, Tennessee 37214. 1977. 160p.

Charity under Siege: Government Regulation of Fund-raising. Bruce R. Hopkins. John Wiley and Sons, Inc., 605 Third Avenue, New York, New York 10158. 1980. 274p.

Charity U.S.A.: An Investigation into the Hidden World of the Multibillion Dollar Charity Industry. Carl Bakal. Times Books, Three Park Avenue, New York, New York 10016. 1979. 498p.

Communicating and Moneymaking: A Guide for Using Public Relations to Improve Fundraising Success. Don Bates. Heladon Press, Box 2827, Grand Central Station, New York, New York 10017. 1980. 20p.

The Complete Fund Raising Guide. Howard R. Mirkin. Public Service Materials Center, 111 North Central Avenue, Hartsdale, New York 10530. 1978. 159p.

The Complete Guide to Corporate Fund Raising. Joseph Dermer and Stephen Wertheimer. Public Services Materials Center, 111 North Central Avenue, Hartsdale, New York 10530. 1982. 112p.

The Complete Guide to Successful Fund-raising. Andrew Yiannakis with Susan Braunstein. American Sports Education Institute, 200 Castlewood Drive, North Palm Beach, Florida 33408. 1983. 298p.

The Constant Quest: Raising Billions through Capital Campaigns. Sharon L. Coldren. American Council on Education, One Dupont Circle, Washington, D.C. 20036. 1982. 118p.

Coping with Reduced Resources. Richard L. Alfred. Jossey-Bass, 433 California Street, San Francisco, California 94104. 1978. 102p.

Corporate Fund Raising: A Practical Plan of Action. W. Grant Brownrigg. American Council for the Arts, 570 Seventh Avenue, New York, New York 10018. 1978. 73p.

Corporate Fund Raising Directory. Public Service Materials Center, 111 North Central Avenue, Hartsdale, New York 10530. Annual.

The Corporation and the Campus. Robert H. Connery, editor. Published for the Academy of Political Science by Praeger Publishers, 521 Fifth Avenue, New York, New York 10175. 1970. 187p.

Cost Effective Analysis in Fund Raising for Colleges and Universities. Warren Heeman. Jossey-Bass, 433 California Street, San Francisco, California 94104. 1979. 342p.

The Costs and Benefits of Deferred Giving. Norman S. Fink and Howard C. Metzler. Public Service Materials Center, 111 North Central Avenue, Hartsdale, New York 10530. 1982. 224p.

Cultural Directory II: Federal Funds and Services for the Arts and Humanities. Linda C. Coe, Rebecca Denny, and Anne Rogers. Prepared for the Federal Council on the Arts and Humanities. Smithsonian Institution Press, Room 2280, Arts and Industries Building, Washington, D.C. 20560. 1980. 270p.

Deferred Gifts: How to Get Them. George V. King. Fund Raising Institute, Box 365, Ambler, Pennsylvania 19002. 1980. 198p.

Designs for Fund Raising: Principles, Patterns, Techniques. Harold J. Seymour. Fund Raising Institute, Box 365, Ambler, Pennsylvania 19002. 1966. 210p.

Direct Mail Fund Raising. Public Management Institute, 358 Brannan Street, San Francisco, California 94107. 1980. 467p.

Dollars and Sense: A Community Fundraising Manual for Women's Shelters and Other Non-Profit Organizations. Western States Shelter Network, 870 Market Street, Suite 1058, San Francisco, California 94102. 1982. 135p.

Encyclopedia of Fund Raising. Gerald M. Plessner. Fund Raisers, Inc., 59 West La Sierra Drive, Arcadia, California 91006. Looseleaf. 1979-80. Volume 1: Charity Auction Management Manual. Volume 2: Golf Tournament Management Manual. Volume 3: Testimonial Dinner and Industry Luncheon Management Manual.

Escape from the Money Trap. Henry B. Clark. Judson Press, Valley Forge, Pennsylvania 19481. 1973. 128p.

Evaluating Development Performance. Richard J. Taft. Taft Group, 5125 MacArthur Boulevard, N.W., Suite 300, Washington, D.C. 20016. 1983. n.p.

External Fund Raising. Systems and Procedures Exchange Center. Association of Research Libraries, Office of University Library Management Studies, 1527 New Hampshire Avenue, N.W., Washington, D.C. 20036. 1978. 106p.

Federal Funding Forum. Four-One-One, 7304 Beverly Street, Annandale, Virginia 22003. Annual.

Federal Funding Guide. Government Information Services, 752 National Press Building, N.W., Washington, D.C. 20045. Annual.

Five Hundred Ways for Small Charities to Raise Money. Phillip T. Drotning. Public Service Materials Center, 111 North Central Avenue, Hartsdale, New York 10530. 1981. 177p.

Foundations and Fund Raising: A Bibliography of Books to 1980. John J. Miletich. Vance Bibliographies, Box 229, Monticello, Illinois 61856. 1981. 10p.

Fund-raising: A Comprehensive Handbook. Hilary Blume. Routledge & Kegan Paul, Ltd., Nine Park Street, Boston, Massachusetts 02108. 1977. 188p.

Fund Raising: A Guide for Non-Profit Corporations. Othniel Alsop Pendleton. Prentice-Hall, Inc., Englewood Cliffs, New Jersey 07632. 1981. 207p.

Fund Raising: A Guide for Research on Individuals. Gary W. Phillips & Associates, 1100 Glendon Avenue, Suite 1754, Los Angeles, California 90024. 1978.

Fund Raising: A Professional Guide. William R. Cumerford. Ferguson E. Peters Company, Box 21587, Fort Lauderdale, Florida 33335. 1978. 347p.

Fund Raising: The Guide to Raising Money from Private Sources. Thomas E. Broce. University of Oklahoma Press, 1005 Asp Avenue, Norman, Oklahoma 73019. 1979. 254p.

Fund-raising and Grant-aid: A Practical and Legal Guide to Charities and Voluntary Organizations. Ann Darnbrough and Derek Kinrade. State Mutual Book and Periodical Service, Ltd., 521 Fifth Avenue, New York, New York 10017. 1980. 160p.

Fund Raising by Computer. Fund Raising Institute, Box 365, Ambler, Pennsylvania 19002. 1977. 135p.

Fund Raising Consultancy and Public Relations. Andrew DeMille. State Mutual Book and Periodicals Service, Ltd., 521 Fifth Avenue, New York, New York 10017. 1981. 292p.

Fund Raising for Non-Profit Groups. Second edition. Joyce Young. Self Counsel Press, Inc., 1303 North Northgate Way, Seattle, Washington 98133. 1981. 102p.

Fund Raising for Philanthropy. Gerald Soroker. Pittsburgh Jewish Publishing and Education Foundation, 315 South Bellefield Avenue, Pittsburgh, Pennsylvania 15213. 1974. 190p.

Fund Raising for Small Charities and Organizations. H. R. Humphries. David and Charles, Inc., Box 57, North Pomfret, Vermont 05053. 1972. 124p.

Fund Raising in ARL Libraries. Systems and Procedures Exchange Center. Association of Research Libraries, Office of Management Studies, 1527 New Hampshire Avenue, N.W., Washington, D.C. 20036. 1983. 103p.

Fund Raising in the Black Community: History, Feasibility, and Conflict. King E. Davis. Scarecrow Press, Inc., 52 Liberty Street, Box 656, Metuchen, New Jersey 08840. 1975. 169p.

Fund-raising Letter Collection. William E. Sheppard, compiler. Fund Raising Institute, Box 365, Ambler, Pennsylvania 19002. 1978. 150p.

Fund Raising Letters: A Comprehensive Study Guide to Raising Money by Direct Response Marketing. Jerry Huntsinger. Emerson Publishers, Box 15274, Richmond, Virginia 23227. 1982. 391p.

The Fund Raising Manual: Strategies for Non-Profit Organizations. Thomas W. Tenbrunsel. Prentice-Hall, Inc., Englewood Cliffs, New Jersey 07632. 1982. 192p.

Fund Raising—Marketing for Human Needs. Francis S. Andrews. Direct Mail Marketing Association, 28 West 44th Street, Suite 1215, New York, New York 10036. 1976. 19p.

Fund Raising Practices of United Way Agencies in New York City. Greater New York Fund/United Way, 99 Park Avenue, New York, New York 10016. 1980. 114p.

The Fund Raising Resource Manual. Thomas W. Tenbrunsel. Prentice-Hall, Inc., Englewood Cliffs, New Jersey 07632. 1982. 182p.

Fund Raising Techniques. Edgar H. Phillips. Business Books, Ltd., Mercury House, Waterloo Road, London SE 1, England. 1969. 189p.

Funding in Aging: Public, Private and Voluntary. Second edition, revised and enlarged. Lily Cohen, Marie Oppedisano-Reich, and Kathleen Hamilton Gerardi. Adelphi University Press, Garden City, New York 11530. 1979. 308p.

Funding Sources and Technical Assistance for Museums and Historical Agencies: A Guide to Public Programs. Hedy A. Hartman. American Association for State and Local History, 708 Berry Road, Nashville, Tennessee 37204. 1979. 144p.

The Funding Workbook. Barry Nickelsberg. Funding Center, 1712 I Street, Suite 1005, Washington, D.C. 20006. 1981. 318p.

Getting Your Share: An Introduction to Fundraising. Women's Action Alliance, Inc., 370 Lexington Avenue, New York, New York 10017. 1976. 36p.

Getting Yours: The Complete Guide to Government Money. Mathew Lesko. Penguin Books, Inc., 625 Madison Avenue, New York, New York. 10022. 1982. 346p.

Give! Who Gets Your Charity Dollar? Harvey Katz. Doubleday and Company, Inc., 501 Franklin Avenue, Garden City, New York 11530. 1974. 252p.

Giving USA: Annual Report. American Association of Fund Raising Counsel, Inc., 25 West 43rd Street, New York, New York 10036. Annual.

The Grass Roots Fundraising Book: How to Raise Money in Your Community. Second edition. Joan Flanagan. Youth Project, 1555 Connecticut Avenue, N.W., Washington, D.C. 20036. 1982. 344p.

Guide for Fundraisers. Alfreda Doyle. Bibliotheca Press, Box 98378, Atlanta, Georgia 30359. 1981. 52p.

A Guide to Successful Fund Raising. Albert A. Hutler. Business Reports, Inc., One West Avenue, New York, New York 10538. 1977. 172p.

Guide to Successful Fund Raising: For Authentic Charitable Purposes. Bernard P. Taylor. Revised edition. Groupwork Today, Inc., Box 258, South Plainfield, New Jersey 07080. 1981. 131p.

A Guide to Successful Phonathons. Nelson Cover. Council for Advancement and Support of Education, 11 Dupont Circle, Suite 400, Washington, D.C. 20036. 1980. 89p.

The Handbook for Direct Mail Fundraising. Direct Mail Fundraisers Association, 151 Lexington Avenue, New York, New York 10016. 1980. n.p.

Handbook for Educational Fund Raising: A Guide to Successful Principles and Practices for Colleges, Universities and Schools. Francis C. Pray, editor. Jossey-Bass, Inc., 433 California Street, San Francisco, California 94104. 1981. 422p.

Handbook of Special Events for Nonprofit Organizations: Tested Ideas for Fund Raising and Public Relations. Edwin R. Leibert and Bernice E. Sheldon. Taft Group, 5125 MacArthur Boulevard, N.W., Suite 300, Washington, D.C. 20016. 1972. 224p.

Handbook of Successful Fund-raising. Paul C. Carter. E. P. Dutton, Two Park Avenue, New York, New York 10016. 1970. various pagings.

Handicapped Funding Directory. Burton J. Eckstein. Research Grant Guides, Box 357, Oceanside, New York 11572. Biennial.

Happy to Be Here ("The Fund Raiser as Damon Runyon Character"). Garrison Keillor. Penguin Books, Inc., 625 Madison Avenue, New York, New York 10022. 1983. 276p.

How to Build a Big Endowment. Public Management Institute, 358 Brannan Street, San Francisco, California 94107. 1980. 590p.

How to Get Money for: Conservation and Community Development. Human Resources Network. Chilton Book Company, Chilton Way, Radnor, Pennsylvania 19089. 1975. various pagings.

How to Get Money for Research. Mary Rubin and the Business and Professional Women's Foundation. The Feminist Press, Box 334, Old Westbury, New York 11568. 1983. 96p.

How to Organize and Raise Funds for Small Non-Profit Organizations. David F. Long. Groupwork Today, Inc., Box 258, South Plainfield, New Jersey 07080. 1979. 283p.

How to Raise Money: Special Events for Arts Organizations. Ellen S. Daniels, editor. American Council for the Arts, 570 Seventh Avenue, New York, New York 10018. 1981. 32p.

How to Solicit Big Gifts. Daniel Lynn Conrad. Public Management Institute, 358 Brannan Street, San Francisco, California 94107. 1979. 257p.

How to Succeed in Fund Raising Today. Helen Knowles. Cumberland Press, 136 Main Street, Freeport, Maine 04032. 1975. 256p.

How to Write for Development. Henry L. Gayley. Council for Advancement and Support of Education, 11 Dupont Circle, Suite 400, Washington, D.C. 20036. 1981. 49p.

How to Write Successful Corporate Appeals/With Full Examples. James P. Sinclair. Public Service Materials Center, 111 North Central Avenue, Hartsdale, New York 10530. 1982. 110p.

How to Write Successful Foundation Presentations. Joseph Dermer. Public Service Materials Center, 111 North Central Avenue, Hartsdale, New York 10530. 1980. 80p.

Ideas Plus Dollars: Research Methodology and Funding. Second edition. Harold Zallen and Eugenia Zallen. Academic World, Inc., Drawer 2790, Norman, Oklahoma 73069. 1980. 387p.

An Introduction to Annuity, Charitable Remainder Trust, and Bequest Programs. William Dunseth. Council for Advancement and Support of Education, 11 Dupont Circle, Suite 400, Washington, D.C. 20036. 1982. 37p.

An Introduction to Fund Raising: The Newcomers' Guide to Development. Paula Faust, editor. Council for Advancement and Support of Education, 11 Dupont Circle, Suite 400, Washington, D.C. 20036. 1983. 92p.

Introduction to Planned Giving. Daniel W. Vecchitto, editor. Taft Group, 5125 MacArthur Boulevard, N.W., Suite 300, Washington, D.C. 20016. 1982. 179p.

The KRC Aide and Advisor for Fundraising Copywriters. Mitchell Keller. KRC Development Council. Available from Public Service Materials Center, 111 North Central Avenue, Hartsdale, New York 10530. 1981. 60p.

The KRC Computer Book for Fund Raisers. Liston Tatum. KRC Development Council. Available from Public Service Materials Center, 111 North Central Avenue, Hartsdale, New York 10530. 1975. 368p.

The KRC Desk Book for Fund Raisers/With Model Forms and Records. Lisa Pulling Semple. KRC Development Council. Available from Public Service Materials Center, 111 North Central Avenue, Hartsdale, New York 10530. 1980. 184p.

KRC Fund Raiser's Manual: A Guide to Personalized Fund Raising. Paul Blanshard, Jr. KRC Development Council, 431 Valley Road, New Canaan, Connecticut 06840. 1974. 246p.

The KRC Guide to Direct Mail Fund Raising. Mitchell Keller, editor. KRC Development Council. Available from Public Service Materials Center, 111 North Central Avenue, Hartsdale, New York 10530. 1977. 205p.

The KRC Handbook of Fund-raising Principles and Practices with Sample Forms and Records. KRC Development Council, 431 Valley Road, New Canaan, Connecticut 06840. 1982. 118p.

The KRC Portfolio of Fund Raising Letters. Richard H. Crohn and Mitchell Keller. KRC Development Council. Available from Public Service Materials Center, 111 North Central Avenue, Hartsdale, New York 10530. 1973. 245p.

Management Reporting Standards for Educational Institutions: Fund Raising and Related Activities. Cosponsored by CASE and the National Association of College and University Business Officers. Council for Advancement and Support of Education, 11 Dupont Circle, Suite 400, Washington, D.C. 20036. 1983. 18p.

Matching Gift Details 1983. Compiled by Elizabeth S. Hall. Council for Advancement and Support of Education, 11 Dupont Circle, Suite 400, Washington, D.C. 20036. 1983. 174p.

The Money Game: Financing Collegiate Athletics. Robert H. Atwell, et al. American Council on Education, One Dupont Circle, Washington, D.C. 20036. 1980. 72p.

The Money Givers. Joseph C. Goulden. Random House, Inc., 201 East 50th Street, New York, New York 10022. 1971. 341p.

Money Makers: A Systematic Approach to Special Events Fund Raising. Nike B. Whitcomb, Charles Alberti, and George Macko. Nike B. Whitcomb Associates, 1113 Lee Street, Evanston, Illinois 60202. 1982. Looseleaf.

The New How to Raise Funds from Foundations. Third edition. Joseph Dermer. Public Service Materials Center, 111 North Central Avenue, Hartsdale, New York 10530. 1979. 96p.

New York City Resources for the Arts and Artists: A Listing of Services and Support Available through the Agencies and Institutions of New York City. New York City Cultural Council. Cultural Council Foundation, 175 Fifth Avenue, New York, New York 10010. 1973. 95p.

Nonprofit Organization Handbook: A Guide to Fund Raising, Grants, Lobbying, Membership Building, Publicity and Public Relations. Patricia V. Gaby and Daniel M. Gaby. Prentice-Hall, Inc., Englewood Cliffs, New Jersey 07632. 1979. 333p.

Paying for the Piper. Ontario Federation of Symphony Orchestras, 56 the Esplanade, Toronto, Ontario M5E 1A7, Canada. 1983. 76p.

Philanthropy and Marketing: New Strategies for Fund Raising. James Gregory Lord. The Third Sector Press, 2000 Euclid Avenue, Box 18044, Cleveland, Ohio 44118. 1981. Looseleaf.

Planned Giving Ideas. Virginia L. Carter and Catherine S. Garigan, editors. Council for Advancement and Support of Education, 11 Dupont Circle, Suite 400, Washington, D.C. 20036. 1979. 30p.

Playing the Funding Game. Gregory C. Horgen. Human Services Development Center. Available from Robert D. Anderson Publishing Company, 7000 Franklin Boulevard, Suite 820, Box 22324, Sacramento, California 95822. 1981. 351p.

Promoting Fund Raising. Roy Evanson. Groupwork, Inc., Box 258, South Plainfield, New Jersey 07080. 1975. n.p.

Prospecting: Searching out the Philanthropic Dollar. Elizabeth Koochoo. Taft Group, 5125 MacArthur Boulevard, N.W., Suite 300, Washington, D.C. 20016. 1979. 69p.

Public/Private Cooperation: Funding for Small and Emerging Arts Programs. Foundation Center, 888 Seventh Avenue, New York, New York 10106. 1983. 60p.

Public Relations and Fund Raising for Hospitals. Harold P. Kurtz. Charles C. Thomas Publishers, 2600 South First Street, Springfield, Illinois 62717. 1980. 208p.

Raising Funds from America's 2,000,000 Overlooked Corporations. Aldo C. Podesta. Available from CRG Publications, Box 42120, N.W. Station, Washington, D.C. 20015. 1984. 119p.

Raising Money from Grants and Other Sources. Second edition. Tyler G. Hicks. International Wealth Success, Inc., 24 Canterbury Road, Rockville Centre, New York 11570. 1983. 496p.

Raising Money through Gift Clubs: A Survey of Techniques at 42 Institutions. Compiled by Robert D. Sweeney. Council for Advancement and Support of Education, 11 Dupont Circle, Suite 400, Washington, D.C. 20036. 1982. 71p.

The Raising of Money: Thirty-five Essentials. James Gregory Lord. Third Sector Press, 2000 Euclid Avenue, Box 18044, Cleveland, Ohio 44118. 1983. 128p.

Research and Project Funding for the Uninitiated. Robert E. McAdam, Michael Maker, and John F. McAteer. Charles C. Thomas Publishers, 2600 South First Street, Springfield, Illinois 62717. 1982. 72p.

Resource Directory for the Funding and Managing of Non-Profit Organizations. Ingrid Lemaire. The Edna McConnel Clark Foundation, 250 Park Avenue, Room 900, New York, New York 10017. 1977. 127p.

Stalking the Large Green Grant: A Fundraising Manual for Youth Serving Agencies. Third edition. Publications Office, National Youth Work Alliance, 1346 Connecticut Avenue, N.W., Washington, D.C. 20036. 1980. 78p.

Successful Community Fundraising: A Complete How-To Guide. Sheila W. Petersen. Caroline House Publishers, Inc., 920 West Industrial Drive, Aurora, Illinois 60506. 1979. 167p.

Successful Fundraising: A Handbook of Proven Strategies and Techniques. William K. Grasty and Kenneth G. Sheinkopf. Charles Scribner's Sons, 597 Fifth Avenue, New York, New York 10017. 1982. 318p.

Successful Fund Raising Techniques. Daniel Lynn Conrad. Public Management Institute, 358 Brannan Street, San Francisco, California 94107. 1976. 356p.

Support for the Arts: A Survey of Possible Sources for State University of New York. Susan G. Sorrels, editor. New York State University, Washington Office, 1730 Rhode Island Avenue, N.W., Suite 500, Washington, D.C. 20036. 1973. 164p.

Tested Ways to Successful Fund Raising. George A. Brakeley, Jr. American Management Association, Inc., 135 West 50th Street, New York, New York 10020. 1980. 176p.

The Thirteen Most Common Fund-raising Mistakes and How to Avoid Them. Paul H. Schneiter and Donald T. Nelson. Taft Group, 5125 MacArthur Boulevard, N.W., Suite 300, Washington, D.C. 20016. 1982. 95p.

Trustees in Fund Raising. Council for Advancement and Support of Education, 11 Dupont Circle, Suite 400, Washington, D.C. 20036. 1971. 40p.

United Arts Fundraising. American Council for the Arts, 570 Seventh Avenue, New York, New York 10018. Annual.

United Arts Fundraising Manual. Robert Porter, editor. American Council for the Arts, 570 Seventh Avenue, New York, New York 10018. 1980. 77p.

United Arts Fundraising Policy Book. American Council for the Arts, 570 Seventh Avenue, New York, New York 10018. Looseleaf.

Up Your Accountability: How to Up Your Serviceability and Funding Credibility by Upping Your Accounting Ability. Paul Bennett. Taft Group, 5125 MacArthur Boulevard, N.W., Suite 300, Washington, D.C. 20016. 1973. 66p.

Washington and the Arts: A Guide and Directory to Federal Programs and Dollars for the Arts. Janet English Gracey and Sally Gardner, special editors. American Council for the Arts, 570 Seventh Avenue, New York, New York 10018. 1971. 176p.

What Volunteers Should Know for Successful Fundraising. Maurice G. Gurin. Stein and Day, 122 East 42nd Street, New York, New York 10168. 1982. 144p.

Where to Get Money for Everything: A Complete Guide to Today's Money Sources. Paula Nelson. William Morrow and Company, Inc., 105 Madison Avenue, New York, New York 10016. 1982. 298p.

Winning Techniques in Athletic Fund Raising. Patricia L. Alberger. Council for Advancement and Support of Education, 11 Dupont Circle, Suite 400, Washington, D.C. 20036. 1981. 97p.

Winning the Money Game: A Guide to Community-based Library Fundraising. Baker and Taylor Company, 1515 Broadway, New York, New York 10036. 1979. 136p.

The Woman's Day Book of Fund Raising. Perri Ardman and Harvey Ardman. St. Martin's Press, 175 Fifth Avenue, New York, New York 10010. 1980. 313p.

GRANTSMANSHIP AND PROPOSAL WRITING

The Grantsmanship Center is the paramount resource in the area of grantsmanship and proposal writing. Frequent references throughout this text to its bimonthly *Grantsmanship Center News* attest to the up-to-date practicality and authenticity of the information it disseminates.

See the **Basic Fund-raising Library**, Section III, for more details as to its services and publications, as well as for information about Continuing Education Publications, Marquis Professional Publications, and the Plenum Press, among others.

About Foundations: How to Find the Facts You Need to Get a Grant. Judith B. Margolin. Foundation Center, 888 Seventh Avenue, New York, New York 10106. 1975. 38p.

Action Grants: Revitalizing and Conserving Cities. Wallace Katz. U.S. Department of Housing and Urban Development, Office of Community Planning and Development, Washington, D.C. 20410. 1980. 59p.

The Art of Winning Corporate Grants. Howard Hillman. Vanguard Press, Inc., 424 Madison Avenue, New York, New York 10017. 1980. 180p.

The Art of Winning Foundation Grants. Howard Hillman and Karin Abarbanel. Vanguard Press, Inc., 424 Madison Avenue, New York, New York 10017. 1975. 188p.

The Art of Winning Government Grants. Howard Hillman and Kathryn Natale. Vanguard Press, Inc., 424 Madison Avenue, New York, New York 10017. 1977. 246p.

The Art of Writing Business Reports and Proposals. Howard Hillman. Vanguard Press, Inc., 424 Madison Avenue, New York, New York 10017. 1981. 230p.

A Basic Guide to Proposal Development. Third edition. John C. Morrow. Business Publishers, Inc., Silver Spring, Maryland 20900. 1977. 25p.

The Basic Handbook of Grants Management. Robert Lefferts. Basic Books, Inc., 10 East 53rd Street, New York, New York 10022. 1983. 292p.

A Casebook of Grant Proposals in the Humanities. William Coleman, David Keller, and Arthur Pfeffer. Neal-Schuman Publishers, Inc., 23 Cornelia Street, New York, New York 10014. 1982. 248p.

Categorical Grants: Their Role and Design; The Intergovernmental Grant System: An Assessment and Proposed Policies. Advisory Commission on Intergovernmental Relations. Available from U.S. Government Printing Office, Washington, D.C. 20402. 1978. 319p.

The Challenge Grant Experience: Planning, Development, and Fundraising. Diane J. Gingold. Challenge Grant Program, National Endowment for the Arts, Washington, D.C. 20506. 1980. 115p.

Challenge Grant Recipient Study. Conducted for the National Endowment for the Arts by Leonard R. Vignola. National Foundation on the Arts and Humanities, National Endowment for the Arts, 806 15th Street, N.W., Washington, D.C. 20506. 1979. 74p.

Community Development: The Workings of a Federal-Local Block Grant; The Intergovernmental Grant System: An Assessment and Proposed Policies. Advisory Commission on Intergovernmental Relations. Available from U.S. Government Printing Office, Washington, D.C. 20402. 1977. 93p.

The Complete Grants Sourcebook for Higher Education. Public Management Institute. Available from American Council on Education, One Dupont Circle, Washington, D.C. 20036. 1980. 605p.

Consumerism, Federal Grants and You. Gaetane M. Larocque. Exposition Press, Inc., 325 Rabro Drive, Box 2120, Smithtown, New York 11787. 1974. 191p.

Developing Skills in Proposal Writing. Second edition. Mary Hall. Continuing Education Publications, 1633 S.W. Park, Portland, Oregon 97207. 1977. 339p.

The Dynamics of Funding: An Educator's Guide to Effective Grantsmanship. Paul B. Warren. Allyn and Bacon, Inc., Seven Wells Avenue, Newton, Massachusetts 02159. 1980. 366p.

Federal Grants: Course Manual. Lawrence R. Sidman and Leonard A. Zax. Federal Publications, 1120 20th Street, N.W., Washington, D.C. 20036. 1982. 476p.

Federal Grants and Cooperative Agreements: Law, Policy, and Practice. Richard B. Cappalli. Callaghan & Company, 3201 Glenview Road, Wilmette, Illinois 60091. 1983. Three volumes.

Federal Grants, Their Effects on State-Local Expenditures, Employment Levels, Wage Rates; The Intergovernmental Grant System: An Assessment and Proposed Policies. Advisory Commission on Intergovernmental Relations, Washington, D.C. 20575. 1977. 75p.

Federal Grants: Where in the Bureaucracy to Find Them. Second edition. Sara Case. American Library Association, Washington Office, 110 Maryland Avenue, N.W., Box 54, Washington, D.C. 20002. 1977. 27p.

Foundation Fundamentals: A Guide for Grant Seekers. Revised edition. Carol M. Kurzig. Foundation Center, 888 Seventh Avenue, New York, New York 10106. 1980. 148p.

The Funding Process: Grantsmanship and Proposal Development. Virginia A. Decker and Larry E. Decker. Community Collaborators, Box 5429, Charlottesville, Virginia 22905. 1978. 120p.

Getting a Grant in the Nineteen Eighties: How to Write Successful Grant Proposals. Second edition. Robert Lefferts. Prentice-Hall, Inc., Englewood Cliffs, New Jersey 07632. 1982. 168p.

Getting a Grant in the Nineteen Eighties: Readings in Cost and Managerial Accounting. Second edition. Alfred Rappaport, editor. Prentice-Hall, Inc., Englewood Cliffs, New Jersey 07632. 1982. 176p.

Getting Grants. Craig W. Smith and Erik W. Wkjei. Harper and Row Publishers, 10 East 53rd Street, New York, New York 10022. 1979. 288p.

Getting Yours: The Complete Guide to Government Money. Mathew Lesko. Penguin Books, Inc., 625 Madison Avenue, New York, New York 10022. 1982. 346p.

Government Contracts: Proposalmanship and Winning Strategies. Herman Holtz. Plenum Publishing Corporation, 233 Spring Street, New York, New York 10013. 1978. 302p.

Grant and Contract Funding Newsletters, Journals, Periodicals, and Newspapers: An Annotated Buyer's and Researcher's Bibliography. Tony W. Ott. Grant Administration Consultants, Box 234, Chesterfield, Missouri 63017. 1980. 125p.

Grant Budgeting and Finance: Getting the Most out of Your Grant Dollar. Frea E. Sladek and Eugene L. Stein. Plenum Publishing Corporation, 233 Spring Street, New York, New York 10013. 1981. 375p.

Grant Information System. William K. Wilson and Betty L. Wilson, editors. Oryx Press, 2214 North Central at Encanto, Phoenix, Arizona 85004. Annual.

Grant Money and How to Get It: A Handbook for Librarians. Richard W. Boss. R. R. Bowker Company, 1180 Avenue of the Americas, New York, New York 10036. 1980. 138p.

The Grant Proposal: A Guide for Preparation. Stewart A. Johnson. Marquis Academic Media, 200 East Ohio Street, Chicago, Illinois 60611. 1967. 12p.

Grant Proposals: A Practical Guide to Planning, Funding and Managing. Lawrence Blaine. Psyon Publications, 220 Redwood Highway, Number 102, Mill Valley, California 94941. 1981. 105p.

Grant Proposals That Succeed. Virginia P. White, editor. Plenum Press, 233 Spring Street, New York, New York 10013. 1983. 248p.

The Grant Writer's Handbook. Public Management Institute. Available from Gale Research Company, Book Tower, Detroit, Michigan 48226. 1980. 400p.

Grants: How to Find out About Them and What to Do Next. Virginia P. White. Plenum Publishing Corporation, 233 Spring Street, New York, New York 10013. 1975. 368p.

Grants Administration: A Systems Approach to Project Management. Public Management Institute. Available from Gale Research Company, Book Tower, Detroit, Michigan 48226. 1982. 563p.

Grants Administration Policies. U.S. Social and Rehabilitation Service. Available from U.S. Government Printing Office, Washington, D.C. 20402. 1972. 53p.

The Grants Economy and Collective Consumption. R. C. Matthews and B. Stafford. St. Martin's Press, 175 Fifth Avenue, New York, New York 10010. 1982. 338p.

Grants for the Arts. Virginia P. White. Plenum Publishing Company, 233 Spring Street, New York, New York 10013. 1980. 275p.

The Grants Game: How to Get Free Money. Lawrence Lee. Harbor Publishing, Inc., 1668 Lombard Street, San Francisco, California 94123. 1981. 224p.

Grants Register. Craig Alan Lerner, editor. Gale Research Company, Book Tower, Detroit, Michigan 48226. Biennial.

Grants Survival Library—1980. Donald Levitan and Daniel F. Donahue. Vance Bibliographies, Box 229, Monticello, Illinois 61586. 1980. 13p.

Grantsmanship: Money and How to Get It. Second edition. Marquis Academic Media, 200 East Ohio Street, Chicago, Illinois 60611. 1978. 47p.

Grantsmanship and Proposal Development Publications: An Annotated Buyer's and Researcher's Bibliography. Tony W. Ott. Grant Administration Consultants, Box 234, Chesterfield, Missouri 63017. 1980. 125p.

The Grantsmanship Center News. Grantsmanship Center, 1031 South Grand Avenue, Los Angeles, California 90015. Bimonthly.

A Guide to Grantsmanship. Donald M. Michaels and Lionel E. Mayrand, Jr., editors. New England Gerontology Center, New England Center for Continuing Education, 15 Garrison Avenue, Durham, New Hampshire 03824. 1977.

How to Get Corporate Grants. Daniel Lynn Conrad. Public Management Institute, 358 Brannan Street, San Francisco, California 94107. 1981. 351p.

How to Get Federal Contracts. Public Management Institute. Available from Gale Research Company, Book Tower, Detroit, Michigan 48226. 1980. 118p.

How to Get Federal Grants. Second edition. Daniel Lynn Conrad. Public Management Institute. Available from Gale Research Company, Book Tower, Detroit, Michigan 48226. 1979. 400p.

How to Get Government Grants. Philip Des Marais. Public Service Materials Center, 111 North Central Avenue, Hartsdale, New York 10530. 1975. 160p.

How to Write for Development. Henry T. Gayley. Council for Advancement and Support of Education, 11 Dupont Circle, Suite 400, Washington, D.C. 20036. 1981. 49p.

How to Write Successful Foundation Presentations. Joseph Dermer. Public Service Materials Center, 111 North Central Avenue, Hartsdale, New York 10530. 1975. 80p.

Improving Federal Grants Management: The Intergovernmental Grant System: An Assessment and Proposed Policies. Advisory Commission on Intergovernmental Relations, Washington, D.C. 20575. 1977. 287p.

The Individual's Guide to Grants. Judith B. Margolin. Plenum Publishing Corporation, 233 Spring Street, New York, New York 10013. 1983. 314p.

Influence of Federal Grants: Public Assistance in Massachusetts. Martha Derthick. Harvard University Press, 79 Garden Street, Cambridge, Massachusetts 02138. 1970. 285p.

Inside Grant and Project Writing: How to Write Projects That Get Funded. Thomas A. Adamson. Pam Publishers, 234 Abbott Street, Salinas, California 93901. 1979. 209p.

The Intergovernmental Grant System: An Assessment and Proposed Policies. Advisory Commission on Intergovernmental Relations, Washington, D.C. 20575. 1978. 29p.

The Intergovernmental Grant System as Seen by Local, State, and Federal Officials; The Intergovernmental Grant System: An Assessment and Proposed Policies. Advisory Commission on Intergovernmental Relations. Available from U.S. Government Printing Office, Washington, D.C. 20402. 1977. 287p.

Models for Money: Obtaining Government and Foundation Grants and Assistance. Second edition. Louis Urgo. Suffolk University Management Center, 41 Temple Street, Boston, Massachusetts 02114. 1978. 187p.

Money Business: Grants and Awards for Creative Artists. Revised edition. Rita K. Roosevelt, Anita M. Granoff, and Karen P. K. Kennedy. The Artists Foundation, Inc., 110 Broad Street, Boston, Massachusetts 02110. 1982. unpaged.

National Directory of Grants and Aid to Individuals in the Arts, International. Fifth edition. Daniel Millsaps, editor. Washington International Arts Letter, Box 9005, Washington, D.C. 20003. 1983.

The New Grants Planner. Daniel Lynn Conrad. Public Management Institute, 358 Brannan Street, San Francisco, California 94107. 1979. 397p.

Nonprofit Organization Handbook: A Guide to Fund Raising, Grants, Lobbying, Membership Building, Publicity and Public Relations. Patricia V. Gaby and Daniel M. Gaby. Prentice-Hall, Inc., Englewood Cliffs, New Jersey 07632. 1979. 333p.

Patterns of Concentration in Large Foundations' Grants to U.S. Colleges and Universities. Richard Colvard and A. M. Bennett. Research and Development Division, American College Testing Program, 2201 North Dodge Street, Box 168, Iowa City, Iowa 52243. 1974. 30p.

The Politics of Federal Grants. Marian Palley and George E. Hale. Congressional Quarterly, Inc., 1414 22nd Street, N.W., Washington, D.C. 20037. 1981. 225p.

A Preface to Grants Economics: The Economy of Love and Fear. Kenneth E. Boulding. Praeger Publishers, 521 Fifth Avenue, New York, New York 10175. 1981. 160p.

The Process of Grantsmanship and Proposal Development. John D. Callen, James C. Marillo, and Joseph T. Nocerno. Century Planning Associates, Inc., Vienna, Virginia 22180. 1976. v.p.

Program Planning and Proposal Writing. Grantsmanship Center, 1031 South Grand Avenue, Los Angeles, California 90015. n.d. 48p.

Proposal Development Handbook. American Association of State Colleges and Universities, One Dupont Circle, Washington, D.C. 20036. 1982. 12p.

Proposal Preparation and Management Handbook. Roy J. Loring and Harold Kerzner. Van Nostrand Reinhold, 135 West 50th Street, New York, New York 10020. 1982. 416p.

Proposal Preparation Manual. William F. Brown. U.S. Department of Transportation. Available from U.S. Government Printing Office, Washington, D.C. 20402. 1983. 87p.

Proposal Writer's Swipe File III. Taft Group, 5125 MacArthur Boulevard, N.W., Suite 300, Washington, D.C. 20016. 1981. 162p.

The Quick Proposal Workbook. Daniel Lynn Conrad. Public Management Institute, 358 Brannan Street, San Francisco, California 94107. n.d. 120p.

Raising Money from Grants and Other Sources. Second edition. Tyler G. Hicks. International Wealth Success, Inc., 24 Canterbury Road, Rockville Centre, New York 11570. 1983. 496p.

Recent Trends in Federal and State Aid to Local Governments. Advisory Commission on Intergovernmental Relations, Washington, D.C. 20575. 1980. 95p.

Redistribution through the Financial System: The Grants Economics of Money and Credit. Kenneth E. Boulding and Thomas F. Wilson, editors. Praeger Publishers, 521 Fifth Avenue, New York, New York 10175. 1978. 301p.

The Rich Get Richer and the Poor Write Proposals. Nancy Mitiguy. Prepared for the Citizen Involvement Training Project. University of Massachusetts, Amherst, Massachusetts 01003. 1978. 147p.

Selected Bibliography on Grantsmanship. Don Levitan. CPL Bibliographies, 1313 East 60th Street, Merriam Center, Chicago, Illinois 60637. 1974. 15p.

The States and Intergovernmental Aids: The Intergovernmental Grant System: An Assessment and Proposed Policies. Advisory Commission on Intergovernmental Relations, Washington, D.C. 20575. 1977. 83p.

While You're Up, Get Me a Grant: A Basic Bibliography on Grants. Bay Area Social Responsibilities Round Table, 2745 Stuart, #3, Berkeley, California 94705. 1976. 10p.

LAW AND TAXATION

The law and taxes are always with us, especially in charitable endeavors. Tax exemptions and allowable deductions are, of course, a consideration of major investigation in fund raising. Knowledge of the tax aspects of charitable giving, of the provisions of trusts and wills, the expectations of grantors and beneficiaries, and the legal status of foundations and not-for-profit organizations is a necessity.

The looseleaf tax publications of the Commerce Clearing House are invaluable in this regard.

Analysis of the Economic Recovery Program's Direct Significance for Philanthropic and Voluntary Organizations and the People They Serve. Independent Sector, 1828 L Street, N.W., Washington, D.C. 20036. 1982. n.p.

Audits of Certain Nonprofit Organizations. American Institute of Certified Public Accountants, Subcommittee on Nonprofit Organizations, 1211 Avenue of the Americas, New York, New York 10036. 1981. 171p.

California Taxation. Matthew Bender, 245 East 45th Street, New York, New York 10017. Looseleaf service basis.

Charitable Giving and Solicitation. Sue S. Stern, Jon L. Schumacher, and Patrick D. Martin. Prentice-Hall, Inc., Information Services Division, Englewood Cliffs, New Jersey 07632. Looseleaf service basis.

Charitable Giving and Tax-exempt Organizations: The Impact of the 1981 Tax Act. Bruce R. Hopkins. Ronald Press, 605 Third Avenue, New York, New York 10158. 1982. 166p.

Charitable Lead Trusts—Explanation, Specimen Agreements, Reporting Forms. Conrad Teitell. Taxwise Giving, 13 Arcadia Road, Box 299, Old Greenwich, Connecticut 06870. Looseleaf. Supplemented and revised annually.

Contributors Income Tax Deduction Guide. J. K. Lasser Tax Institute, Larchmont, New York 10538. 1981. 98p.

The Costs and Benefits of Deferred Giving. Norman S. Fink and Howard C. Metzler. Columbia University Press, 562 West 113th Street, New York, New York 10025. 1982. 224p.

Deferred Giving—Explanation, Specimen Agreements, Reporting Forms. Conrad Teitell. Taxwise Giving, 13 Arcadia Road, Box 299, Old Greenwich, Connecticut 06870. 1982. Two volumes.

Exempt Organizations Reports. Commerce Clearing House, Inc., 4025 West Peterson Avenue, Chicago, Illinois 60646. Looseleaf service basis.

The Federal Budget and the Nonprofit Sector. Lester M. Salamon and Alan J. Abramson. The Urban Institute, 2100 M Street, N.W., Washington, D.C. 20036. 1982. 116p.

Federal Grants and Cooperative Agreements: Law, Policy and Practice. Richard B. Cappalli. Callaghan & Company, 3201 Glenview Road, Wilmette, Illinois 60091. 1983. Three volumes.

Federal Income, Gift and Estate Taxation. Jacob Rabkin and Mark H. Johnson. Matthew Bender and Company, Inc., 245 East 45th Street, New York, New York 10017. Looseleaf service basis.

Federal Income Taxation of Corporations and Shareholders. Fourth edition. Boris I. Bittker and James Eustace. Warren, Gorham & Lamont, Inc., 210 South Street, Boston, Massachusetts 02111. 1971. Annual supplements.

Federal Tax Coordinator 2d. Research Institute of America, 589 Fifth Avenue, New York, New York 10017. Looseleaf service basis.

Federal Taxation of Trusts, Grantors and Beneficiaries. John L. Peschel and Edward D. Spurgeon. Warren, Gorham & Lamont, Inc., 210 South Street, Boston, Massachusetts 02111. 1978. Kept current through periodic supplements.

Fund-raising and Grant-aid: A Practical and Legal Guide for Charities and Voluntary Organizations. Ann Darnbrough and Derek Kinrade. State Mutual Book and Periodical Service, Ltd., 521 Fifth Avenue, New York, New York 10017. 1980. 160p.

Guide to the Administration of Charitable Remainder Trusts. Fourth edition. Winton Smith. Council for Advancement and Support of Education, 11 Dupont Circle, N.W., Suite 400, Washington, D.C. 20036. 1984. 350p.

A Guide to the California Non-Profit Public Benefit Corporation Law. James E. Topinka. The Management Center, 150 Post Street, Suite 640, San Francisco, California 94108. 1981. 136p.

Innovative Tax Strategies for Colleges and Universities. National Education Industry Group of Coopers and Lybrand, One Post Office Square, Boston, Massachusetts 02109. 1983. 19p.

An Introduction to Annuity, Charitable Remainder Trust, and Bequest Programs. Second edition. William B. Dunseth. Council for Advancement and Support of Education, 11 Dupont Circle, N.W., Suite 400, Washington, D.C. 20036. 1982. 37p.

The Law of Tax-exempt Organizations. Fourth edition. Bruce R. Hopkins. John Wiley and Sons, Inc., 605 Third Avenue, New York, New York 10158. 1983. 748p.

Legal Handbook for Nonprofit Organizations. Marc J. Lane. American Management Association, Inc., 135 West 50th Street, New York, New York 10020. 1981. 320p.

Nonprofit Organizations: Laws and Regulations Affecting Establishment and Operation. Howard E. Fischer. The Center for Nonprofit Organizations, Inc., 203 West 25th Street, Third Floor, New York, New York 10001. 1982. 11p.

Non-Profit Tax Exempt Corporations: The Alternative Tax Shelter: All You Need to Know about Setting Up and Maintaining a Non-Profit Corporation without a Lawyer. Ted Nicholas. Enterprise Publishing, Inc., 725 Market Street, Wilmington, Delaware 19801. 1983. 143p.

Patrons Despite Themselves: Taxpayers and Arts Policy. Alan L. Feld and Michael O'Hare. Twentieth Century Fund. New York University Press. Distributed by Columbia University Press, 562 West 113th Street, New York, New York 10025. 1983. 246p.

Rights and Remedies under Federal Grants. Richard B. Cappalli, Bureau of National Affairs, Inc., 1231 25th Street, N.W., Washington, D.C. 20037. 1979. 414p.

Standard Federal Tax Reports. Commerce Clearing House, Inc., 4025 West Peterson Avenue, Chicago, Illinois 60646. Looseleaf service basis.

Tax Aspects of Charitable Giving. Commerce Clearing House, Inc., 4025 West Peterson Avenue, Chicago, Illinois 60646. 1983. 64p.

Tax Economics of Charitable Giving. Eighth edition. Arthur Andersen and Company, 69 West Washington Street, Chicago, Illinois 60602. 1982. 141p.

Tax Exempt Organizations. Prentice-Hall, Inc., Information Service Division, Englewood Cliffs, New Jersey 07632. Looseleaf service basis.

Tax Techniques for Foundations and Other Exempt Organizations. Stanley S. Weithorn. Matthew Bender and Company, Inc., 245 East 45th Street, New York, New York 10017. Looseleaf service basis.

Tax-exempt Charitable Organizations. Second edition. Paul E. Treusch and Norman A. Sugarman. American Law Institute, 4025 Chestnut Street, Philadelphia, Pennsylvania 19104. 1983. 726p.

The Unrelated Business Income Tax. Joseph M. Galloway. Ronald Press, 605 Third Avenue, New York, New York 10158. 1982. 200p.

NOT-FOR-PROFIT ORGANIZATIONS AND AGENCIES

This section has been included as a convenient guide to the literature by subject. The arts, civic causes, education, hospitals and health care, libraries, religion, research, and social welfare titles are included.

Once again, we refer you to the basic library, Section III, especially to the *Annual Register of Grant Support* of the Marquis Professional Publications, and to the entries for Continuing Education Publications and the Plenum Press.

Accounting and Financial Reporting: A Guide for United Ways and Not-for-Profit Human Service Organizations. Russy D. Sumariwalla. United Way of America, 801 North Fairfax Street, Alexandria, Virginia 22314. 1974. 95p.

Accounting for Culture: A Primer for Non-Accountants. Second edition. Metropolitan Cultural Alliance, 250 Boylston Street, Boston, Massachusetts 02116. 1980. 34p.

Accounting for Librarians and Other Not-for-Profit Managers. G. Stevenson Smith. American Library Association, 50 East Huron Street, Chicago, Illinois 60611. 1983. 470p.

Accounting for Non-Profit Organizations. Second edition. Emerson O. Henke. Wadsworth Publishing Company, 10 Davis Drive, Belmont, California 94002. 1977. 211p.

Administration in the Arts: An Annotated Bibliography of Selected References. E. Arthur Prieve and Daniel J. Schmidt. Center for Arts Administration, Graduate School of Business, University of Wisconsin, Madison, Wisconsin 53706. 1977. 127p.

Art Marketing Handbook. Calvin J. Goodman. Florence J. Goodman, editor. Gee Tee Bee, 11901 Sunset Boulevard, Suite 102B, Los Angeles, California 90049. 1978. 502p.

Arts Administration: How to Set Up and Run a Successful Nonprofit Arts Organization. Tem Horwitz. Chicago Review Press, 215 West Ohio Street, Chicago, Illinois 60610. 1979. 256p.

Arts Administration Compensation: 1978 Survey. Mitchell B. Smith. American Council for the Arts, 570 Seventh Avenue, New York, New York 10018. 1980. 139p.

The Arts Administrator—Job Characteristics. Association of College, University and Community Arts Administrators, 6225 University Avenue, Madison, Wisconsin 53705. 1983. 79p.

The Arts and the World of Business: A Selected Bibliography. Second edition. Charlotte Georgi. Scarecrow Press, 52 Liberty Street, Box 656, Metuchen, New Jersey 08840. 1979. 188p.

Arts Management: An Annotated Bibliography. Revised edition. Stephen Benedict and Linda C. Coe. Center for Arts Information, 625 Broadway, New York, New York 10012. 1980. 47p.

The Arts Management Reader. Alvin H. Reiss. Marcel Dekker, 270 Madison Avenue, New York, New York 10016. 1979. 686p.

Arts Money: Raising It, Saving It, and Earning It. Joan Jeffri. Neal-Schuman Publishers, Inc., 23 Cornelia Street, New York, New York 10014. 1983. 240p.

Artsfax '81: A Report on the Finances, Personnel and Programs of Bay Area Arts Organizations. Virginia H. Baer. The San Francisco Foundation, 425 California Street, Suite 1600, San Francisco, California 94104. 1981. 161p.

Asking and Giving: A Report on Hospital Philanthropy. Robert Maris Cunningham. American Hospital Association, 840 North Lakeshore Drive, Chicago, Illinois 60611. 1980. 148p.

Audits of Certain Nonprofit Organizations. American Institute of Certified Public Accountants, Subcommittee on Nonprofit Organizations, 1211 Avenue of the Americas, New York, New York 10036. 1981. 171p.

Audits of Voluntary Health and Welfare Organizations. American Institute of Certified Public Accountants, 1211 Avenue of the Americas, New York, New York 10036. 1974. 51p.

A Bibliography on Arts Administration. Victoria E. Levene and William J. Buckley. State University of New York at Binghamton, School of Management, School of Arts and Sciences, Binghamton, New York 13901. 1977. 30p.

Boards of Directors: A Study of Current Practices in Board Management and Board Operations in Voluntary Hospitals, Health and Welfare Organizations. Nelly Hartogs and Joseph Weber. Sponsored by the Greater New York Fund, Inc. Oceana Publications, 75 Main Street, Dobbs Ferry, New York 10522. 1974. 266p.

Bookkeeping for Nonprofits. Public Management Institute, 358 Brannan Street, San Francisco, California 94107. 1979. 221p.

Box Office Guidelines. Revised edition. Foundation for the Extension and Development of the American Professional Theatre. Drama Book Publishers, 821 Broadway, New York, New York 10003. 1977. 66p.

Budgeting for Nonprofits. Second edition. V. Srikanth and Lyn Levy. Public Management Institute, 358 Brannan Street, San Francisco, California 94107. 1980. 321p.

Budgeting Procedures for Hospitals. Second edition. Truman H. Esmond, Jr. American Hospital Association, 840 North Lakeshore Drive, Chicago, Illinois 60611. 1982. 92p.

Building Voluntary Support for the Two-Year College. John E. Bennett, editor. Council for Advancement and Support of Education, 11 Dupont Circle, Suite 400, Washington, D.C. 20036. 1979. 142p.

The Capital Campaign. Council for Advancement and Support of Education, 11 Dupont Circle, Suite 400, Washington, D.C. 20036. 1979. 64p.

Capital Financing for Hospitals. American Hospital Association, 840 North Lakeshore Drive, Chicago, Illinois 60611. 1974. 60p.

College and University Endowment: Status and Management. D. Kent Halstead. U.S. Office of Education. Available from U.S. Government Printing Office, Washington, D.C. 20402. 1977. 81p.

Commitment to Culture: Art Patronage in Europe, Its Significance for America. Frederick Dorian. University of Pittsburgh Press, 127 North Bellefield Avenue, Pittsburgh, Pennsylvania 15260. 1964. 521p.

A Communications Manual for Nonprofit Organizations. Lucille A. Maddalena. Advancement and Support of Education, 11 Dupont Circle, Suite 400, Washington, D.C. 20036. 1982. 321p.

The Community College Foundation. W. Harvey Sharron, Jr., editor. Council for Advancement and Support of Education, 11 Dupont Circle, Suite 400, Washington, D.C. 20036. 1982. 321p.

The Community Orchestra: A Handbook for Conductors, Managers and Boards. James Van Horn. Greenwood Press, 51 Riverside Avenue, Westport, Connecticut 06880. 1979. 127p.

The Complete Grants Sourcebook for Higher Education. Public Management Institute. Available from American Council on Education, One Dupont Circle, Washington, D.C. 20036. 1980. 605p.

Computer Resource Guide for Nonprofits. Second edition. Kenneth Gilman. Public Management Institute, 358 Brannan Street, San Francisco, California 94107. 1984. 691p.

Computers for Nonprofits. Second edition. Kenneth Gilman. Public Management Institute, 358 Brannan Street, San Francisco, California 94107. 1982. 600p.

Corporate Planning for Nonprofit Organizations. James M. Hardy. Association Press, 291 Broadway, New York, New York 10007. 1973. 119p.

Corporate Support. Council for Advancement and Support of Education, 11 Dupont Circle, Suite 400, Washington, D.C. 20036. 1981. 56p.

Corporate Support of Higher Education, 1979. Council for Financial Aid to Education, 680 Fifth Avenue, New York, New York 10019. 1980. 20p.

The Corporation and the Campus. Robert H. Connery, editor. Praeger Publishers, 521 Fifth Avenue, New York, New York 10175. 1970. 187p.

Critical Issues Involved in the Review of Research Proposals at Universities. Arthur B. Jebens, Eugene J. Millstein, and David A. Wearley. University of California, Berkeley, California 94720. 1975. 52p.

Cost Effective Analysis in Fund Raising for Colleges and Universities. Warren Heeman. Jossey-Bass, 433 California Street, San Francisco, California 94104. 1979. 342p.

Cultural Directory II: Federal Funds and Services for the Arts and Humanities. Linda C. Coe, Rebecca Denny, and Anne Rogers. Prepared for the Federal Council on the Arts and Humanities. Smithsonian Institution Press, Room 2280, Arts and Industries Building, Washington, D.C. 20560. 1980. 270p.

Decision Making for Library Management. Michael R. W. Bommer and Ronald W. Chorba. Knowledge Industry Publications, Inc., 701 Westchester Avenue, White Plains, New York 10604. 1982. 178p.

Developing an Older Volunteers Program: A 10-Step Guide for Hospitals. American Hospital Association, 840 North Lakeshore Drive, Chicago, Illinois 60611. 1981. 46p.

Development Today: A Guide for Non-Profit Organizations. Jeffrey L. Lant. Robert D. Anderson Publishing Company, 7000 Franklin Boulevard, Suite 820, Box 22324, Sacramento, California 95882. 1980. 200p.

Dollars and Sense: A Community Fundraising Manual for Women's Shelters and Other Non-Profit Organizations. Western States Shelter Network, 870 Market Street, Suite 1058, San Francisco, California 94102. 1982. 135p.

The Dynamics of Funding: An Educator's Guide to Effective Grantsmanship. Paul B. Warren. Allyn and Bacon, Inc., Seven Wells Avenue, Newton, Massachusetts 02159. 1980. 366p.

Education and the Business Dollar: A Study of Corporate Contributions Policy and American Education. Kenneth Gilbert Patrick and Richard Eells. Macmillan Publishing Company, Inc., 866 Third Avenue, New York, New York 10022. 1969. 313p.

Educational Volunteerism: A New Look. Susanne E. Taranto and Simon O. Johnson. Charles C. Thomas Publishers, 2600 South First Street, Springfield, Illinois 62717. 1984. 129p.

Educational Volunteerism: A State of the Art Summary with Implications for Vocational Education. U.S. Department of Education, Office of Vocational and Adult Education, Washington, D.C. 20202. 1980. 26p.

The Encyclopedia of the Music Business. Harvey Rachlin. Harper and Row, Inc., 10 East 53rd Street, New York, New York 10022. 1981. 524p.

Enterprise in the Nonprofit Sector. James C. Crimmins and Mary Keil. Partners for Livable Places. Available from Publishing Center for Cultural Resources, 625 Broadway, New York, New York 10012. 1983. 141p.

Factbook on Higher Education. American Council on Education, One Dupont Circle, Washington, D.C. 20036. 1977. v.p.

Federal Support to Universities, Colleges and Selected Nonprofit Institutions: Fiscal Year 1980. Available from U.S. Government Printing Office, Washington, D.C. 20402. 1982. 174p.

Financial Grants for Writers/Artists. H.T. Jackson Enterprises, Box 438, Chicago, Illinois 60606. n.d.

Financial Management for Arts Organizations. Mary M. Wehle. Arts Administration Research Institute, 75 Sparks Street, Cambridge, Massachusetts 02138. 1975. 163p.

Financial Management for the Arts. Revised edition. Frederick J. Turk. American Council for the Arts, 570 Seventh Avenue, New York, New York 10018. 1982. 102p.

Financial Practice for Performing Arts Companies: A Manual. Mary M. Wehle. Available from Publishing Center for Cultural Resources, 625 Broadway, New York, New York 10012. 1977. 163p.

Financing the Nonprofit Organization for Recreation and Leisure Services. Harry E. Moore, Jr. Groupwork, Inc., Box 258, South Plainfield, New Jersey 07080. 1981. 24p.

Foundation Guide for Religious Grant Seekers. Peter S. Robinson, editor. Scholars Press, 101 Salem Street, Box 2268, Chico, California 95927. 1979. 98p.

Fund Raising: A Guide for Non-Profit Corporations. Othniel Alsop Pendleton. Prentice-Hall, Inc., Englewood Cliffs, New Jersey 07632. 1981. 207p.

Fund Raising for Non-Profit Groups. Second edition. Joyce Young. Self Counsel Press, Inc., 1303 North Northgate Way, Seattle, Washington 98133. 1981. 102p.

Fund Raising in ARL Libraries. Systems and Procedures Exchange Center. Association of Research Libraries, Office of Management Studies, 1527 New Hampshire Avenue, N.W., Washington, D.C. 20036. 1983. 103p.

The Fund Raising Manual: Strategies for Non-Profit Organizations. Thomas W. Tenbrunsel. Prentice-Hall, Inc., Englewood Cliffs, New Jersey 07632. 1982. 192p.

Funding Sources and Technical Assistance for Museums and Historical Agencies: A Guide to Public Programs. Hedy A. Hartman. American Association for State and Local History, 708 Berry Road, Nashville, Tennessee 37204. 1979. 144p.

Glossary of Tools and Concepts for Nonprofit Managers. Barbara Schilling. The Management Center, 150 Post Street, Suite 640, San Francisco, California 94108. 1980. 22p.

Grant Money and How to Get It: A Handbook for Librarians. Richard W. Boss. R. R. Bowker Company, 1180 Avenue of the Americas, New York, New York 10036. 1980. 138p.

Grants and Awards Available to American Writers. PEN, 47 Fifth Avenue, New York, New York 10003. Biennial.

Grants for Libraries: A Guide to Public and Private Funding Programs and Proposal Writing Techniques. Emmett Corry. Libraries Unlimited, Box 263, Littleton, Colorado 80160. 1982. 240p.

Grants for the Arts. Virginia P. White. Plenum Publishing Corporation, 233 Spring Street, New York, New York 10013. 1980. 275p.

Growth in the Eighties: A Manager's Guide to Financial Productivity for Non-Profit Organizations. The Not for Profit Group, Chemical Bank, 1212 Sixth Avenue, New York, New York 10036. n.d. n.p.

Guide to Government Resources for Economic Development—A Handbook for Non-Profit Agencies and Municipalities. Compiled by Northeast Midwest Institute. Public Service Materials Center, 111 North Central Avenue, Hartsdale, New York 10530. Annual.

Handbook for Educational Fund Raising: A Guide to Successful Principles and Practices for Colleges, Universities and Schools. Francis C. Pray, editor. Jossey-Bass, 433 California Street, San Francisco, California 94104. 1981. 422p.

Handbook of Special Events for Nonprofit Organizations: Tested Ideas for Fund Raising and Public Relations. Edwin R. Leibert and Bernice E. Sheldon. Taft Group, 5125 MacArthur Boulevard, N.W., Suite 300, Washington, D.C. 20016. 1972. 224p.

Handicapped Funding Directory. Burton J. Eckstein. Research Grant Guides, Box 357, Oceanside, New York 11572. Biennial.

How to Do Theatre Publicity. Nancy McArthur. Good Ideas Company, Box 296, Berea, Ohio 44017. 1978. 247p.

How to Get Money for: Conservation and Community Development. Human Resources Network. Chilton Book Company, Chilton Way, Radnor, Pennsylvania 19089. 1975. various pagings.

How to Manage a Non-Profit Organization. John Fisher. Management and Fund Raising Centre. Available from Public Service Materials Center, 111 North Central Avenue, Hartsdale, New York 10530. 1978. 214p.

How to Organize and Raise Funds for Small Non-Profit Organizations. David F. Long. Groupwork Today, Inc., Box 258, South Plainfield, New Jersey 07080. 1979. 283p.

How to Raise Money: Special Events for Arts Organizations. Edited by Ellen S. Daniels. American Council for the Arts, 570 Seventh Avenue, New York, New York 10018. 1981. 32p.

How to Run a Small Box Office. Kirsten Beck. Available from Drama Book Publishers, 821 Broadway, New York, New York 10003. 1980. 96p.

How to Sell Your Art Work: A Complete Guide for Commercial and Fine Artists. Milton Berlye. Prentice-Hall, Inc., Englewood Cliffs, New Jersey 07632. 1978. 269p.

Innovative Tax Strategies for Colleges and Universities. National Education Industry Group of Coopers and Lybrand, One Post Office Square, Boston, Massachusetts 02109. 1983. 19p.

Inside the Music Publishing Industry. Paul Dranov. Knowledge Industry Publications, Inc., 701 Westchester Avenue, White Plains, New York 10604. 1980. 185p.

Insurance and the Performing Arts. Thomas Moon. Concert Society of California, Box 1831, Garden Grove, California 92642. 1983. 80p.

International Awards in the Arts: For Graduate and Professional Study. Institute of International Education, 809 United Nations Plaza, New York, New York 10017. 1969. 105p.

The Library and Information Manager's Guide to Online Services. Ryan E. Hoover, editor. Knowledge Industry Publications, Inc., 701 Westchester Avenue, White Plains, New York 10604. 1980. 270p.

The Library Manager's Guide to Automation. Second edition. Richard W. Boss. Knowledge Industry Publications, Inc., 701 Westchester Avenue, White Plains, New York 10604. 1983. 165p.

Management Assistance for the Arts: A Survey of Programs. Compiled by Ellen Thurston. Stephen Benedict, editor. Center for Arts Information, 625 Broadway, New York, New York 10012. 1980. 51p.

Management Control in Nonprofit Organizations. Revised edition. Robert N. Anthony and Regina E. Herzlinger. Richard D. Irwin, Inc., 1818 Ridge Road, Homewood, Illinois 60430. 1980. 600p.

Management Control in Nonprofit Organizations: Text and Cases. Kavasseri V. Ramanathan. John Wiley and Sons, Inc., 605 Third Avenue, New York, New York 10158. 1982. 612p.

The Management of Small History Museums. Second edition. Carl E. Guthe. American Association for State and Local History, 708 Berry Road, Nashville, Tennessee 37204. 1964. 80p.

Management of Visual Arts, Museums and Galleries: A Selected Bibliography. Anthony G. White. Vance Bibliographies, Box 299, Monticello, Illinois 61856. 1979. 8p.

Management Principles for Non-Profit Agencies and Organizations. Gerald Zaltman. American Management Association, Inc., 135 West 50th Street, New York, New York 10020. 1979. 584p.

Management Reporting Standards for Educational Institutions: Fund Raising and Related Activities. Cosponsored by CASE and the National Association of College and University Business Officers. Council for Advancement and Support of Education, 11 Dupont Circle, Suite 400, Washington, D.C. 20036. 1983. 18p.

Managing Nonprofit Agencies for Results: A Systems Approach to Long-Range Planning. Paul Hennessey. Public Management Institute, 358 Brannan Street, San Francisco, California 94107. 1979. 250p.

Managing Nonprofit Organizations. Diane Borst and Patrick J. Montana. American Management Association, Inc., 135 West 50th Street, New York, New York 10020. 1977. 328p.

Managing Staff for Results. Joanne Pugh. Public Management Institute. Available from Gale Research Company, Book Tower, Detroit, Michigan 48226. 1980. 411p.

Marketing for Non-Profit Organizations. Second edition. Philip Kotler. Prentice-Hall, Inc., Englewood Cliffs, New Jersey 07632. 1982. 592p.

Marketing Higher Education: A Practical Guide. Robert S. Topor. Council for Advancement and Support of Education, 11 Dupont Circle, Suite 400, Washington, D.C. 20036. 1983. 90p.

Marketing in Nonprofit Organizations. Patrick J. Montana, editor. American Management Association, Inc., 135 West 50th Street, New York, New York 10020. 1978. 302p.

Marketing in Nonprofit Organizations. Benson P. Shapiro. Marketing Science Institute, 14 Story Street, Cambridge, Massachusetts 02138. 1972. 47p.

Marketing the Arts. Michael P. Mokwa, William M. Dawson, and E. Arthur Prieve, editors. Praeger Publishers, 521 Fifth Avenue, New York, New York 10175. 1980. 304p.

Marketing the Arts: A Selected and Annotated Bibliography. Kent Nakamoto and Kathi Levin. Association of College, University and Community Arts Administrators, Box 2137, Madison, Wisconsin 53701. 1978. 18p.

Marketing the Arts in a Rural Environment: The Monadnock Arts Study. George Miaolis and David Lloyd. Wright State University, 7751 Colonel Glenn Highway, Dayton, Ohio 45431. 1979. 66p.

Marketing the Library. Benedict A. Leerburger. Knowledge Industry Publications, Inc., 701 Westchester Avenue, White Plains, New York 10604. 1982. 124p.

Marketing Your Hospital: A Strategy for Survival. Norman H. McMillan. American Hospital Association, 840 North Lakeshore Drive, Chicago, Illinois 60611. 1981. 128p.

Matching Gift Details 1983. Compiled by Elizabeth S. Hall. Council for Advancement and Support of Education, 11 Dupont Circle, Suite 400, Washington, D.C. 20036. 1983. 174p.

MBO for Nonprofit Organizations. Dale D. McConkey. American Management Association, Inc., 135 West 50th Street, New York, New York 10020. 1975. 223p.

Media Handbook for the Arts. Richard M. Cottam and Martin Umansky. Association of Community Arts Councils of Kansas, 112 West Sixth Street, Topeka, Kansas 66603. 1979. 28p.

Money Business: Grants and Awards for Creative Artists. Revised edition. Rita K. Roosevelt, Anita M. Granoff, and Karen P. K. Kennedy. The Artists Foundation, Inc., 110 Broad Street, Boston, Massachusetts 02110. 1982. unpaged.

The Money Game: Financing Collegiate Athletics. Robert H. Atwell, et al. American Council on Education, One Dupont Circle, Washington, D.C. 20036. 1980. 72p.

Museum Accounting Handbook. William H. Daughtrey and Malvern J. Gross. American Association of Museums, 1055 Thomas Jefferson Street, N.W., Washington, D.C. 20007. 1978. 158p.

Museum Public Relations. G. Donald Adams. American Association for State and Local History, 708 Berry Road, Nashville, Tennessee 37204. 1983. 300p.

National Directory of Arts and Education Support by Business Corporations. Second edition. Daniel Millsaps, editor. Washington International Arts Letter, Box 9005, Washington, D.C. 20003. 1982. 229p.

National Directory of Arts Support by Private Foundations. Fifth edition. Daniel Millsaps, editor. Washington International Arts Letter, Box 9005, Washington, D.C. 20003. 1983. 336p.

National Directory of Grants and Aid to Individuals in the Arts, International. Fifth edition. Daniel Millsaps, editor. Washington International Arts Letter, Box 9005, Washington, D.C. 20003. 1983.

National Directory of Nonprofit Management Support Organizations. Support Center, 1709 New Hampshire Avenue, N.W., Washington, D.C. 20009. Biennial.

New Dimensions for the Arts: 1971-1972. National Foundation on the Arts and Humanities, National Endowment for the Arts, Washington, D.C. 20506. 1973. 135p.

New Partnerships: Higher Education and the Non-Profit Sector. Elinor Miller Greenberg, editor. Jossey-Bass, 433 California Street, San Francisco, California 94104. 1983. 113p.

New York City Resources for the Arts and Artists: A Listing of Services and Support Available through the Agencies and Institutions of New York City. New York City Cultural Council. Cultural Council Foundation, 175 Fifth Avenue, New York, New York 10010. 1973. 95p.

Nonprofit Arts Organizations: Formation and Maintenance. Eric Peterson. Bay Area Lawyers for the Arts, Fort Mason Center, Building 310, San Francisco, California 94123. 1977. 175p. Supplement, 1978.

Nonprofit Corporations, Organizations and Associations. Fourth edition. Howard L. Oleck. Prentice-Hall, Inc., Englewood Cliffs, New Jersey 07632. 1980. 1,221p.

Nonprofit Financial Management. Christian P. Frederiksen. Public Management Institute, 358 Brannan Street, San Francisco, California 94107. 1979. 232p.

Nonprofit Management Skills for Women Managers. Public Management Institute. Available from Gale Research Company, Book Tower, Detroit, Michigan 48226. 1980. 280p.

Nonprofit Organization Handbook. Tracy D. Connors, editor. McGraw-Hill Book Company, 1221 Avenue of the Americas, New York, New York 10020. 1979. 740p.

Nonprofit Organization Handbook: A Guide to Fund Raising, Grants, Lobbying, Membership Building, Publicity and Public Relations. Patricia V. Gaby and Daniel M. Gaby. Prentice-Hall, Inc., Englewood Cliffs, New Jersey 07632. 1979. 333p.

Nonprofit Organization Participation in the Federal Aid System. U.S. Senate, Committee on Governmental Affairs, Washington, D.C. 20510. 1980. Two volumes.

The Nonprofit Secretary Handbook. Susan Fox and Stephen Hitchcock. Public Management Institute, 358 Brannan Street, San Francisco, California 94107. 1983.

On TAP (*Technical Assistance Programs*): A Directory of Resources for New York City Nonprofit Organizations. Public Interest Public Relations, 225 West 34th Street, New York, New York 10001. 1979. 200p.

On the Dotted Line: The Anatomy of a Contract. Joseph Golden. Available from the Alliance of New York State Arts Councils, 18 West Carver Street, Huntington, New York 11743. 1979. 77p.

Organizational Survival in the Performing Arts: The Making of the Seattle Opera. Mahmoud Salem. Praeger Publishers, 521 Fifth Avenue, New York, New York 10175. 1976. 210p.

Organizing the Library's Support: Donors, Volunteers, Friends. Donald W. Krummel, editor. Graduate School of Library Science, University of Illinois, Publications Office, 249 Armory Building, 505 East Armory Street, Champaign, Illinois 61820. 1980. 119p.

Partners: A Practical Guide to Corporate Support of the Arts. Cultural Assistance Center. Available from American Council for the Arts, 570 Seventh Avenue, New York, New York 10018. 1982. 112p.

Patrons Despite Themselves: Taxpayers and Arts Policy. Alan L. Feld and Michael O'Hare. Twentieth Century Fund. New York University Press, New York, New York 10025. 1983. 246p.

Patterns of Concentration in Large Foundations' Grants to U.S. Colleges and Universities. Richard Colvard and A. M. Bennett. Research and Development Division, American College Testing Program, 2201 North Dodge Street, Box 168, Iowa City, Iowa 52243. 1974. 30p.

Personnel Policies for Museums: A Handbook for Management. Ronald L. Miller. American Association of Museums, 1055 Thomas Jefferson Street, N.W., Washington, D.C. 20007. 1980. 164p.

Persuade and Provide: The Story of the Arts and Education Council in St. Louis. Michael Newton and Scott Hadley. American Council for the Arts, 570 Seventh Avenue, New York, New York 10018. 1970. 249p.

Presenting Performances: A Handbook for Sponsors. Fourth edition. Thomas Wolf. American Council for the Arts, 570 Seventh Avenue, New York, New York 10018. 1981. 164p.

Principles of Accounting and Financial Reporting for Nonprofit Organizations. Malvern J. Gross and Stephen F. Jablonsky. John Wiley and Sons, Inc., 605 Third Avenue, New York, New York 10158. 1979. 415p.

Public Media Manual for Museums. John Anderson and Diana Sperberg. Texas Association of Museums, Box 13353, Capitol Station, Austin, Texas 78711. 1979. 79p.

Public/Private Cooperation: Funding for Small and Emerging Arts Programs. Foundation Center, 888 Seventh Avenue, New York, New York 10106. 1983. 60p.

Public Relations and Fund Raising for Hospitals. Harold P. Kurtz. Charles C. Thomas Publishers, 2600 South First Street, Springfield, Illinois 62717. 1980. 208p.

Raising Money through Gift Clubs: A Survey of Techniques at 42 Institutions. Robert D. Sweeney, compiler. Council for Advancement and Support of Education, 11 Dupont Circle, Suite 400, Washington, D.C. 20036. 1982. 71p.

Readings in Public and Nonprofit Marketing. Christopher H. Lovelock and Charles B. Weinberg. Scientific Press, The Stanford Barn, Palo Alto, California 94303. 1978. 304p.

The Reluctant Patron: The United States Government and the Arts, 1943-1965. Gary O. Larson. University of Pennsylvania, Philadelphia, Pennsylvania 19104. 1983. 320p.

Resource Directory for the Funding and Managing of Non-Profit Organizations. Ingrid Lemaire. The Edna McConnel Clark Foundation, 250 Park Avenue, Room 900, New York, New York 10017. 1977. 127p.

Selected Information Resources on Scholarships, Fellowships, Grants and Loans. Compiled by John Henry Hass. U.S. Library of Congress, Science and Technology Division, National Referral Center, Washington, D.C. 20540. 1977. 17p.

Self-Portrait with Donors: Confessions of an Art Collector. John Walker. Little, Brown and Company, 34 Beacon Street, Boston, Massachusetts 02106. 1974. 320p.

The Small College Advancement Program: Managing for Results. Wesley K. Willmer. Council for Advancement and Support of Education, 11 Dupont Circle, Suite 400, Washington, D.C. 20036. 1981. 145p.

The Small Theatre Handbook: A Guide to Management and Production. Joann Green. Harvard Common Press, 535 Albany Street, Boston, Massachusetts 02172. 1982. 163p.

Sold Out: A Publicity and Marketing Guide. Kate MacIntyre. Theatre Development Fund, 1501 Broadway, New York, New York 10036. 1980. 48p.

Stalking the Large Green Grant: A Fundraising Manual for Youth Serving Agencies. Third edition. Publications Office, National Youth Work Alliance, 1346 Connecticut Avenue, N.W., Washington, D.C. 20036. 1980. 78p.

Subscribe Now! Building Arts Audiences through Dynamic Subscription Promotion. Third edition. Danny Newman. Theatre Communications Group, Inc., 355 Lexington Avenue, New York, New York 10017. 1977. 288p.

Support for the Arts: A Survey of Possible Sources for State University of New York. Susan G. Sorrels, editor. New York State University, Washington Office, 1730 Rhode Island Avenue, N.W., Suite 500, Washington, D.C. 20036. 1973. 164p.

A Survey of Arts Administration Training 1982-83. Fourth edition. American Council for the Arts, 570 Seventh Avenue, New York, New York 10018. 1982. 82p.

Symphony Orchestra Program. National Foundation on the Arts and Humanities, National Endowment for the Arts, Washington, D.C. 20506. 1975. 16p.

Theater Market Place. Lawrence Epstein. Facts on File, Inc., 119 West 57th Street, New York, New York 10019. 1982. unpaged.

Theatre Management in America: Principle and Practice: Producing for the Commercial, Stock, Resident, College and Community Theatre. Revised edition. Stephen Langley. Drama Book Publishers, 821 Broadway, New York, New York 10003. 1980. 490p.

Theatre Profiles/2: An Informational Handbook of Nonprofit Professional Theatres in the United States. Lindy Zesch, editor; Marsue Cumming, associate editor. Theatre Communications Group, Inc., 355 Lexington Avenue, New York, New York 10017. 1975. 219p.

Theatre Program. National Foundation on the Arts and Humanities, National Endowment for the Arts, Washington, D.C. 20506.

This Business of Art. Diane Cochrane. Watson-Guptill Publications, One Astor Plaza, 1515 Broadway, New York, New York 10036. 1978. 256p.

This Business of Music. Fourth edition. Sidney Shemel and M. William Krasilovsky. Billboard Publications, 2160 Patterson Street, Cincinnati, Ohio 45214. 1979. 596p.

United Arts Fundraising. American Council for the Arts, 570 Seventh Avenue, New York, New York 10018. Annual.

United Arts Fundraising Manual. Robert Porter, editor. American Council for the Arts, 570 Seventh Avenue, New York, New York 10018. 1980. 77p.

United Arts Fundraising Policy Book. American Council for the Arts, 570 Seventh Avenue, New York, New York 10018. Looseleaf.

Visual Arts Program. National Foundation on the Arts and Humanities, National Endowment for the Arts, Washington, D.C. 20506.

Voluntary Support for Public Higher Education, 1977-78. Brakely, John Price Jones, Inc., 6 East 43rd Street, New York, New York 10017. 1980. 24p.

Voluntary Support of Education. Council for Financial Aid to Education, Inc., 680 Fifth Avenue, New York, New York 10019. Annual.

Washington and the Arts: A Guide and Directory to Federal Programs and Dollars for the Arts. Janet English Gracey and Sally Gardner, special editors. American Council for the Arts, 570 Seventh Avenue, New York, New York 10018. 1971. 176p.

Winning Techniques in Athletic Fund Raising. Patricia L. Alberger. Council for Advancement and Support of Education, 11 Dupont Circle, Suite 400, Washington, D.C. 20036. 1981. 97p.

Winning the Money Game: A Guide to Community-based Library Fundraising. Baker and Taylor Company, 1515 Broadway, New York, New York 10036. 1979. 136p.

PUBLICITY AND PUBLIC RELATIONS

Successful fund raising depends largely upon effective public relations, popularly known as "PR." Publicity has to be sought in person, by telephone and direct mail, and through the media. *Lesly's Public Relations Handbook,* third edition, Prentice-Hall, 1983, and the *Ayer Public Relations and Publicity Style Book*, revised seventh edition, IMS Press, 1983, are the two standard works on the subject.

Ayer Public Relations and Publicity Style Book. Revised seventh edition. Curtis Risley, editor. IMS Press, 426 Pennsylvania Avenue, Fort Washington, Pennsylvania 19034. 1983. n.p.

Communication and Moneymaking: A Guide for Using Public Relations to Improve Fundraising Success. Don Bates. Heladon Press, Box 2827, Grand Central Station, New York, New York 10017. 1980. 20p.

Fund Raising Consultancy and Public Relations. Andrew DeMille. State Mutual Book and Periodical Service, Ltd., 521 Fifth Avenue, New York, New York 10017. 1981. 292p.

Getting in Ink and on the Air: A Publicity Handbook. Metropolitan Cultural Alliance, 250 Boylston, Boston, Massachusetts 02116. 1973. 48p.

Getting Publicity. Martin Bradley Winston. John Wiley and Sons, Inc., 605 Third Avenue, New York, New York 10158. 1983. 193p.

Handbook of Public Relations. Second edition. Howard Stephenson. McGraw-Hill Book Company, 1221 Avenue of the Americas, New York, New York 10020. 1971. 836p.

Handbook of Special Events for Nonprofit Organizations: Tested Ideas for Fund Raising and Public Relations. Edwin R. Leibert and Bernice E. Sheldon. Association Press, 291 Broadway, New York, New York 10007. 1972. 224p.

How to Do Theatre Publicity. Nancy McArthur. Good Ideas Company, Box 296, Berea, Ohio 44017. 1978. 247p.

"How-To" Guides for Publicity Chairpersons. Cleveland Area Arts Council, 510 The Arcade, Cleveland, Ohio 44114. 1973. 25p.

How to Publicize Yourself, Your Family and Your Organization. J. Sutherland Gould. Prentice-Hall, Inc., Englewood Cliffs, New Jersey 07632. 1983. 216p.

If You Want Air Time: A Publicity Handbook. National Association of Broadcasters, 1771 N Street, N.W., Washington, D.C. 20036. 1979. 18p.

A Layman's Guide to Successful Publicity. Oscar Leiding. Ayer Press, One Bala Avenue, Bala Cynwyd, Pennsylvania 19004. 1976. 158p.

Lesly's Public Relations Handbook. Third edition. Philip Lesly, editor. Prentice-Hall, Inc., Englewood Cliffs, New Jersey 07632. 1983. 718p.

Managing Your Public Relations: Guidelines for Nonprofit Organizations. National Communication Council for Human Services and Public Relations Society of America. Public Relations Society of America, 845 Third Avenue, New York, New York 10022. 1977. Set of six guides: *Making the Most of Special Events* (Harold N. Weiner, 20p.); *Measuring Potential and Evaluating Results* (Alice Norton, 20p.); *Planning and Setting Objectives* (Frances E. Koestler, 22p.); *Using Publicity to Best Advantage* (Frances Schmidt, 20p.); *Using Standards to Strengthen Public Relations* (Anne L. New and Don Bates, 18p.); and *Working with Volunteers* (Dorothy Ducas, 16p.).

Media Handbook for the Arts. Richard M. Cottam and Martin Umansky. Association of Community Arts Councils of Kansas, 112 West Sixth Street, Topeka, Kansas 66603. 1979. 28p.

Museum Public Relations. G. Donald Adams. American Association for State and Local History, 708 Berry Road, Nashville, Tennessee 37204. 1983. 300p.

Nonprofit Organization Handbook: A Guide to Fund Raising, Grants, Lobbying, Membership Building, Publicity and Public Relations. Patricia V. Gaby and Daniel M. Gaby. Prentice-Hall, Inc., Englewood Cliffs, New Jersey 07632. 1979. 333p.

O'Dwyer's Directory of Public Relations Firms. J. R. O'Dwyer Company, Inc., 271 Madison Avenue, New York, New York 10016. Annual.

PR Blue Book. PR Publishing Company, Inc., Box 600, Exeter, New Hampshire 03833. Annual.

Practical Publicity: How to Boost Any Cause. David Tedone. Harvard Common Press, 535 Albany Street, Boston, Massachusetts 02172. 1983. 179p.

The Practice of Public Relations. Fraser P. Seitel. Charles E. Merrill Publishing Company, 1300 Alum Creek Drive, Columbus, Ohio 43216. 1980. 333p.

Printing and Promotion Handbook: How to Plan, Produce and Use Printing, Advertising and Direct Mail. Third edition. Daniel Melcher and Nancy Larrick. McGraw-Hill Book Company, 1221 Avenue of the Americas, New York, New York 10020. 1966. 451p.

Professional's Guide to Public Relations Services. Fourth edition. Richard Weiner. Prentice-Hall, Inc., Englewood Cliffs, New Jersey 07632. 1980. 390p.

Professional's Guide to Publicity. Third edition. Richard Weiner. Taft Group, 5125 MacArthur Boulevard, N.W., Suite 300, Washington, D.C. 20016. 1982. 176p.

Public Media Manual for Museums. John Anderson and Diana Sperberg. Texas Association of Museums, Box 13353, Capitol Station, Austin, Texas 78711. 1979. 79p.

Public Relations and Fund Raising for Hospitals. Howard P. Kurtz. Charles C. Thomas Publishers, 2600 South First Street, Springfield, Illinois 62717. 1980. 208p.

Public Relations Handbook. Second edition, revised. Richard W. Darrow and Dan J. Forrestal. Dartnell Corporation, 4660 Ravenswood Avenue, Chicago, Illinois 60640. 1979. 1,115p.

Public Relations Practices: Case Studies. Allen H. Center. Prentice-Hall, Inc., Englewood Cliffs, New Jersey 07632. 1975. 376p.

Public Relations Register. Public Relations Society of America, 845 Third Avenue, New York, New York 10022. Annual.

Publicity for Volunteers: A Handbook. Virginia Borton. Walker and Company, 720 Fifth Avenue, New York, New York 10019. 1981. 128p.

Sold Out: A Publicity and Marketing Guide. Kate MacIntyre. Theatre Development Fund, 1501 Broadway, New York, New York 10036. 1980. 48p.

Subscribe Now! Building Arts Audiences through Dynamic Subscription Promotion. Third edition. Danny Newman. Theatre Communications Group, Inc., 355 Lexington Avenue, New York, New York 10017. 1977. 288p.

Successful Public Relations Techniques. Public Management Institute, 358 Brannan Street, San Francisco, California 94107. 1980. 449p.

United States Publicity Directory. National Register Publishing Company, Inc., 5201 Old Orchard Road, Skokie, Illinois 60077. Annual. Five volumes covering periodicals, newspapers, communications services, radio, television, and business-financial publicity outlets.

What Happens in Public Relations. Gerald J. Voros and Paul Alvarez. American Management Association, Inc., 135 West 50th Street, New York, New York 10020. 1982. 232p.

Writing for Public Relations. George A. Douglas. Charles E. Merrill Publishing Company, 1300 Alum Creek Drive, Columbus, Ohio 43216. 1980. 192p.

VOLUNTEERISM

As Susan Rice writes in her Foreword to this volume, fund raising is an enterprise which is predominantly dependent upon people, functioning in four basic categories: developmental planning and promotion leadership, paid staff, donors, and volunteers. Each group has its role; each group is important.

Volunteers, in particular, make a vital contribution in that their spontaneous enthusiasm is indispensable to a successful program. *America's Voluntary Spirit: A Book of Readings*, a 1983 publication of the Foundation Center, is recommended as an interesting and informative book on the subject.

An Accounting Manual for Voluntary Social Welfare Organizations. Child Welfare League of America. Family Service Association of America, 44 East 23rd Street, New York, New York 10010. 1971. 67p.

Alternatives in Public Service Delivery: Volunteers in Federal Agencies. Prepared for the Subcommittee on Intergovernmental Relations of the Committee on Government Affairs, U.S. Senate, by U.S. Library of Congress, Congressional Research Service. Available from Committee on Government Affairs, U.S. Senate, Washington, D.C. 20570.

Americans Volunteer—1981. Independent Sector, 1828 L Street, N.W., Washington, D.C. 20036. 1981. 14p.

America's Voluntary Spirit: A Book of Readings. Brian O'Connell. Foundation Center, 888 Seventh Avenue, New York, New York 10106. 1983. 450p.

Applied Volunteerism in Community Development. Richard E. Hardy and John G. Cull. Charles C. Thomas Publishers, 2600 South First Street, Springfield, Illinois 62717. 1973. 227p.

Audits of Voluntary Health and Welfare Organizations. American Institute of Certified Public Accountants, 1211 Avenue of the Americas, New York, New York 10036. 1974. 51p.

Becoming a Volunteer: Resources for Individuals, Libraries and Organizations. U.S. Library of Congress, National Library Service for the Blind and Physically Handicapped, Washington, D.C. 20540. 1981. 17p.

Boards of Directors: A Study of Current Practices in Board Management and Board Operations in Voluntary Hospitals, Health and Welfare Organizations. Nelly Hartogs and Joseph Weber. Sponsored by the Greater New York Fund, Inc. Oceana Publications, 75 Main Street, Dobbs Ferry, New York 10522. 1974. 266p.

Business Voluntarism, Prospects for 1982. E. Patrick McGuire and Nathan Weber. The Conference Board, Inc., 845 Third Avenue, New York, New York 10022. 1982. 7p.

Citizen Boards at Work: New Challenges to Effective Action. Harleigh B. Trecker. Association Press, 291 Broadway, New York, New York 10007. 1970. 288p.

Clearinghouse Greensheets. Volunteer: The National Center for Citizen Involvement, Box 4179, Boulder, Colorado 80306. Annual.

Community Resource Tie Line. Four-One-One, 7304 Beverly Street, Annandale, Virginia 22003. Annual. (Includes *Green Sheets, Training Blue Book,* and *Program Profiles.*)

Developing an Older Volunteers Program: A 10-Step Guide for Hospitals. American Hospital Association, 840 North Lakeshore Drive, Chicago, Illinois 60611. 1981. 46p.

Directory of Agencies: U.S. Voluntary, International Voluntary, Intergovernmental. National Association of Social Workers, 1425 H Street, Suite 600, Washington, D.C. 20005. 1980. 104p.

Directory of Volunteer Bureaus and Voluntary Action Centers. Jean V. Varney, editor. Association of Volunteer Bureaus, 801 North Fairfax Street, Alexandria, Virginia 22314. Annual.

Educational Volunteerism: A New Look. Susanne E. Taranto and Simon O. Johnson. Charles C. Thomas Publishers, 2600 South First Street, Springfield, Illinois 62717. 1984. 129p.

Educational Volunteerism: A State of the Art Summary with Implications for Vocational Education. U.S. Department of Education, Office of Vocational and Adult Education, Washington, D.C. 20202. 1980. 26p.

The Effective Coordination of Volunteers. Lorraine Lafota. National Clearinghouse on Domestic Violence, Box 2309, Rockville, Maryland 20852. 1980. 133p.

Effective Leadership in Voluntary Organizations: How to Make the Greatest Use of Citizen Service and Influence. Brian O'Connell. Association Press, 291 Broadway, New York, New York 10007. 1976. 202p.

Effective Leadership of Voluntary Organizations. Newel W. Comish. Anna Publishing, Inc., 2090-A Aloma Avenue, Winter Park, Florida 32792. 1976. 205p.

The Effective Management of Volunteer Programs. Marlene Wilson. Volunteer Management Associates, 279 South Cedar Brook Road, Boulder, Colorado 80302. 1976. 197p.

The Effective Voluntary Board of Directors: What It Is and How It Works. Revised edition. William Conrad and William Glenn. Swallow Press. Ohio University Press, Scott Triangle, Athens, Ohio 45701. 1983. 244p.

Encouraging Voluntarism and Volunteers. Lucille A. Maddalena, editor. Available from Council for Advancement and Support for Education, 11 Dupont Circle, Suite 400, Washington, D.C. 20036. 1980. 95p.

Final Report of the Institute for Community Service. Lutheran Social Services of Minnesota, 2414 Park Avenue, Minneapolis, Minnesota 55404. 1973. 64p.

Funding Volunteer Services—Potential Sources of Dollars to Expand Agency Programs. Federation of Protestant Welfare Agencies, 281 Park Avenue South, New York, New York 10010. 1981. 24p.

Fund-raising and Grant-aid: A Practical and Legal Guide for Charities and Voluntary Organizations. Ann Darnbrough and Derek Kinrade. State Mutual Book and Periodical Service, Ltd., 521 Fifth Avenue, New York, New York 10017. 1980. 160p.

The Future of Voluntary Organizations: Report of the Wolfenden Committee. Biblio Distribution Centre, 81 Adams Drive, Totowa, New Jersey 07512. 1978. 286p.

Handbook for Agency Coordinators for Volunteer Programs. Voluntary Action Center for New York City, Mayor's Office for Volunteers, 51 Chambers, New York, New York 10007. 1972. 20p.

Helping People Volunteer. Judy Rauner. Available from American Council for the Arts, 570 Seventh Avenue, New York, New York 10018. 1980. 95p.

Helping the Volunteer Get Started: The Role of the Volunteer Center. Ruby Sills Miller. Volunteer: The National Center for Citizen Involvement, Box 4179, Boulder, Colorado 80306. 1972. 90p.

Institute for Community Service Manual: A Process for Developing Agency-based Volunteer Social Work Staff. Lutheran Social Services of Minnesota, 2414 Park Avenue, Minneapolis, Minnesota 55404. 1973. 122p.

The International Directory of Voluntary Work. State Mutual Book and Periodical Service, Ltd., 521 Fifth Avenue, New York, New York 10017. 1981. 175p.

International Who's Who in Community Service. Available from Biblio Distribution Centre, 81 Adams Drive, Totowa, New Jersey 07512. Annual.

Involving Volunteers in Your Advancement Programs. Edited by Virginia Carter Smith and Patricia L. Alberger. Council for Advancement and Support of Education, 11 Dupont Circle, Suite 400, Washington, D.C. 20036. 1983. 112p.

Let's Plan: A Guide to the Planning Process for Voluntary Organizations. John C. DeBoer. Pilgrim Press, 132 West 31st Street, New York, New York 10001. 1970. 181p.

Making Things Happen: A Guide for Members of Volunteer Organizations. Joan Wolfe. Brick House Publishing Company, 34 Essex Street, Andover, Massachusetts 01810. 1981. 96p.

Managing Volunteers for Results. Audrey Richards. Public Management Institute, 358 Brannan Street, San Francisco, California 94107. 1979. 354p.

Model Volunteer Program. Association of Volunteer Centers, c/o Mary Louise Gilkes, 812 West Paseo del Prado, Green Valley, Arizona 85614. Annual.

The New Volunteerism: A Community Connection. Barbara Feinstein and Catherine Cavanaugh. Schenkman Publishing Company, Inc., 3 Mt. Auburn Place, Cambridge, Massachusetts 02138. 1979. 208p.

Planning, Implementing, Evaluating a Workshop for Directors of Volunteers. Tessie Okin and Carolyn Wiener. Volunteer: The National Center for Citizen Involvement, Box 4179, Boulder, Colorado 80306. 1973. 68p.

Recruiting, Training and Motivating Volunteer Workers. Arthur R. Pell. Pilot Books, 347 Fifth Avenue, New York, New York 10016. 1977. 63p.

Salary Study and Survey. Association of Volunteer Centers, c/o Mary Louise Gilkes, 812 West Paseo del Prado, Green Valley, Arizona 85614. Annual.

The Successful Volunteer Organization: Getting Started and Getting Results in Nonprofit, Charitable, Grassroots and Community Groups. Joan Flanagan. Contemporary Books, Inc., 180 North Michigan Avenue, Chicago, Illinois 60601. 1981. 376p.

Training Volunteer Leaders: A Handbook to Train Volunteers and Other Leaders of Program Groups. Research and Development Division, Young Men's Christian Associations of the United States, 101 North Wacker Drive, Chicago, Illinois 60606. 1974. 189p.

Voluntarism and the Business Community. Harold L. Wattel, editor. Hofstra University, 1000 Fulton Avenue, Hempstead, New York 11550. 1971. 589p.

Voluntarism at the Crossroads. Gordon Manser and Rosemary Higgins Cass. Family Service Association of America, 44 East 23rd Street, New York, New York 10010. 1976. 262p.

Voluntarism in America: Promoting Individual and Corporate Responsibility: Hearing Before the Subcommittee on Aging, Family and Human Services of the Committee on Labor and Human Resources. U.S. Senate, Committee on Labor and Human Resources, Washington, D.C. 20510. 1982. 147p.

Voluntary Action Research. D. C. Heath Company, 125 Spring Street, Lexington, Massachusetts 02173. Annual.

Voluntary Associations: Perspectives on the Literature. Constance Smith and Anne Freedman. Harvard University Press, 79 Garden Street, Cambridge, Massachusetts 02138. 1972. 250p.

Voluntary Associations in Change and Conflict—A Bibliography. James Nwannukwu Kerri. CPL Bibliographies, 1313 East 60th Street, Merriam Center, Chicago, Illinois 60637. 1974. 13p.

Voluntary Non-Profit Sector: An Economic Analysis. Burton A. Weisbrod. Lexington Books, 125 Spring Street, Lexington, Massachusetts 02173. 1977. 208p.

Voluntary Organizations. Renouf USA, Inc., Old Post Road, Brookfield, Vermont 05036. 1980. 191p.

Voluntary Social Services Directory of Organizations and Handbook of Information. National Council of Social Service, London. International Publications Service, 114 East 32nd Street, New York, New York 10016. 1973. 153p.

The Volunteer and Community Agencies. Thomas A. Routh. Charles C. Thomas Publishers, 2600 South First Street, Springfield, Illinois 62717. 1972. 92p.

The Volunteer Community: Creative Use of Human Resources. Eva Schindler-Rainman and Ronald Lippitt. University Associates, 8517 Production Avenue, Box 26240, San Diego, California 92126. 1975. 176p.

Volunteer Management. Chicago Metropolitan Board YMCA. Edited by Beth Broadway. YMCA of the USA, 6400 Shafer Court, Rosemont, Illinois 60018. 1981. 105p.

Volunteer Training and Development: A Manual for Community Groups. Revised edition. Anne K. Stenzel and Helen M. Feeney. Continuum Publishing Company, 575 Lexington Avenue, New York, New York 10017. 1976. 204p.

Volunteer Workers: A Bibliography. Mary A. Vance. Vance Bibliographies, Box 229, Monticello, Illinois 61856. 1982. 27p.

Volunteerism: An Emerging Profession. John G. Cull and Richard E. Hardy. Charles C. Thomas Publishers, 2600 South First Street, Springfield, Illinois 62717. 1974. 220p.

Volunteerism in the Eighties: Fundamental Issues in Voluntary Action. John D. Harman, editor. University Press of America, 4720 Boston Way, Lanham, Maryland 20706. 1982. 292p.

Volunteers in Human Services. U.S. Department of Health and Human Services, Washington, D.C. 20201. 1980. 31p.

Volunteers Today. Harriet Naylor. Dryden Associates, Dryden, New York 13053. 1973. 195p.

What Volunteers Should Know for Successful Fundraising. Maurice G. Gurin. Stein and Day, 122 East 42nd Street, New York, New York 10168. 1982. 151p.

Your Volunteer Program. Des Moines Area Community College, Project Motivate, 2006 South Ankeny Boulevard, Ankeny, Iowa 50317. 1970. 300p.

Section III:
A Basic
Fund-raising
Library

This third section was the most fun to do. The most pleasant part of the work was the selecting of the very best titles from the plethora of citations for this basic recommended library. The best resources are those by publishers specializing in materials on fund-raising, grants and foundations. For that reason the material is arranged by publisher. The listing is alphabetical by the name of the publisher, 14 of them, citing representative recommended titles from their respective catalogs.

The authors suggest writing to get on their mailing lists for advertising flyers and announcements.

American Association of Fund Raising Counsel.25 West 43rd Street, New York, New York 10036.

The annual AAFRC report, *Giving USA*, "A Compilation of Facts and Trends on American Philanthropy," is without question the authoritative statistical compendium in the entire field of fund raising, grants, and foundations. The AAFRC also publishes a bimonthly newsletter, *The Fund Raising Review*. A $49.50 annual membership fee includes both the newsletter and the yearly *Giving USA* report, which is $25.00 if sold separately.

Continuing Education Publications. 1633 Southwest Park, Portland, Oregon 97207.

Mary Hall, vice-president and general manager of the Weyerhaeuser Company Foundation, is the author of one of the standard books on proposal writing. *Developing Skills in Proposal Writing* (1977, $14.00) is written in lively, informative style, featuring clearly written, step-by-step descriptions of how to write a proposal, together with illustrative examples.

Council on Foundations. 1828 L Street, N.W., Washington, D.C. 20036.

The Council publishes a biweekly newsletter, an annual report, and various handbooks and monographs. Its major publication is its bimonthly *Foundation News*, "The Magazine of Philanthropy" ($24.00 a year). Its articles are directed to foundation administrators and to new grantseekers who want to find out about trends in thinking, current developments, and reviews of recent publications in the field.

The Foundation Center. 888 Seventh Avenue, New York, New York 10106. Toll-free telephone number: (800) 424-9836.

The Foundation Center, founded in 1956, has for 28 years been the single most authoritative source of information about philanthropic giving in the United States. The Center represents some 22,000 active foundations.

In addition to its New York City address, it maintains offices in Cleveland, San Francisco, and Washington, D.C. It provides a national network of 130 cooperating libraries which offer free public access to all of the Center's publications as well as to a collection of other books, journals, services, and documents relating to the subject. For the name and address of the Foundation Center cooperating collection nearest you, call the toll-free number above.

The Center also offers the Associates Program to fund raisers who need continuing information about grants and foundations. An annual fee of $250.00 entitles members to toll-free telephone reference and research service, access to the Center's three computerized databases, and photo or microfilm copying of needed materials.

A most important part of its services is its publications program. Among the Center's many uniquely superb reference publications are:

The Foundation Directory (ninth edition, 1983, $60.00) includes over 4,000 corporate, community, and independent foundations making a total of $3.5 billion in grants annually.

The Foundation Grants Index Annual (twelfth edition, 1983, $35.00) describes over 27,000 grants of over $5,000. The grants are indexed by subject, geographical location, names of recipient organizations, and by keyword.

The Foundation Grants Index Bimonthly (6 issues a year, $20.00) updates the *Foundation Grants Index Annual.* It describes over 2,000 recent grants in each number and includes bibliographical essays on subjects of interest as well as a bibliographical information service.

The National Data Directory (1984, two volumes, $50.00) includes all currently active grantmaking foundations in the United States. It gives names, addresses, and fiscal data for approximately 22,000 foundations making grants exceeding a total of $3.9 billion annually.

Foundation Grants to Individuals (1982, $15.00) gives full information about programs for individuals of some 950 foundations which give a total of more than $96 million annually.

Sourcebook Profiles (quarterly, $250.00 a year) is the complete fund-raising research service. It covers the 1,000 largest foundations in a two-year publishing cycle, analyzing 500 each year in comprehensive detail. Cumulative volumes for 1982 and 1983 are available at $200.00 each; all three, including 1984, for $500.00.

Comsearch Broad Topics. Comsearch Printouts: Geographic. Comsearch Printouts: Special Topics. Comsearch Printouts: Subjects. Comsearch Broad Topics covers funds given in eleven broad subject areas: (1) Grants for Arts and Cultural Programs; (2) Grants for Business and Employment; (3) Grants for Children and Youth; (4) Grants for Higher Education; (5) Grants for Hospitals and Medical Care Programs; (6) Grants for Museums; (7) Grants for Science Programs; (8) Grants for Social Science Programs; (9) Grants for Women and Girls; (10) Grants for International and Foreign Programs; (11) Grants for Minorities. The computer-produced guides to foundation giving, the *Comsearch Printouts* by geographic location, special topics, and subject are described in detail in the section "bibliographies" in the text preceding.

Foundation Center Computer Databases Online, available through *DIALOG,* Lockheed Information Retrieval Service, Marketing Department, 3460 Hillview Avenue, Palo Alto, California 94304. The Center offers three of its important sources of information online: *The Foundation Directory,* the *Foundation Grants Index,* and the *National Data Book.* Searches of these databases can provide comprehensive and timely answers to an unlimited variety of questions.

Finally, two specific publications are especially recommended: *Foundation Fundamentals: A Guide for Grantseekers,* by Carol Kurzig (revised edition, 1981, $6.50), and *America's Voluntary Spirit: A Book of Readings,* by Brian

O'Connell, with a foreword by John W. Gardner (1983, $19.95 hardbound; $14.95 paperbound).

Government Publications. Order from Superintendent of Documents, Government Printing Office, Washington, D.C. 20402, unless another address is given. (Payment must be received in advance of shipment for all publications ordered. Orders may also be charged to MasterCard or VISA accounts.)

The United States Government Printing Office (GPO) is probably the largest publisher in the world. It is responsible for the printing and binding of all congressional records, reports, bills, and other legislative publications, as well as those of all the departments and other establishments of the federal government.

It sends selected publications to libraries throughout the United States on its depository library program. A list of these libraries is available from the Superintendent of Documents.

The GPO sells its publications via mail order and some 16,000 popular government documents may be purchased at GPO bookstores located in the following cities:

Washington, D.C. area:
  Main Bookstore, 710 N. Capitol St. Phone, 202-275-2091.
  Commerce Department, 14th and E Sts. NW. Phone, 202-377-3527.
  HHS, 330 Independence Ave. SW. Phone, 202-472-7478.
  Retail Sales Branch, 8660 Cherry Lane, Laurel, Md. Phone, 301-953-7974.
  Pentagon Building, Main Concourse. Phone 703-557-1821.
  State Department, 21st and C Sts. NW. Phone, 202-632-1437.

Atlanta, Ga., Federal Bldg., 275 Peachtree St. NE. Phone 404-221-6947.

Birmingham, Ala., 9220-B Parkway East, Roebuck Shopping City. Phone, 205-254-1056.

Boston, Mass., John F. Kennedy Federal Bldg., Sudbury St. Phone, 617-223-6071.

Chicago, Ill., Everett McKinley Dirksen Bldg., 219 S. Dearborn St. Phone, 312-353-5133.

Cleveland, Ohio, Federal Office Bldg., 1240 E. 9th St. Phone, 216-522-4922.

Columbus, Ohio, Federal Office Bldg., 200 N. High St. Phone, 614-469-6956.

Dallas, Tex., Federal Bldg.-U.S. Courthouse, 1100 Commerce St. Phone, 214-767-0076.

Denver, Colo., Federal Bldg., 1961 Stout St. Phone, 303-837-3964.

Detroit, Mich., Patrick V. McNamara Federal Bldg., 477 Michigan Ave. Phone, 313-226-7816.

Houston, Tex., 45 College Center, 9319 Gulf Freeway. Phone, 713-229-3515.

Jacksonville, Fla., Federal Bldg., 400 W. Bay St. Phone, 904-791-3801.

Kansas City, Mo., Federal Office Bldg., 601 E. 12th St. Phone, 816-374-2160.

Los Angeles, Calif., ARCO Plaza, 505 S. Flower St. Phone, 213-688-5841.

Milwaukee, Wis., Federal Bldg., 519 E. Wisconsin Ave. Phone, 414-291-1304.

New York, N.Y., 26 Federal Plaza. Phone, 212-264-3825.

Philadelphia, Pa., Federal Office Bldg., 600 Arch St. Phone, 215-597-0677.

Pittsburgh, Pa., Federal Bldg., 1000 Liberty Ave. Phone, 412-644-2721.

Pueblo, Colo., 720 N. Main Majestic Bldg. Phone, 303-544-3142.

San Francisco, Calif., Federal Office Bldg., 450 Golden Gate Ave. Phone, 415-556-0643.

Seattle, Wash., Federal Office Bldg., 915 Second Ave. Phone, 206-442-4270.

Three publications are available to assist the public in keeping posted of current titles and of information for ordering. The *Monthly Catalog of U.S. Government Publications* ($215.00 a year) is the most comprehensive listing of the publications of the departments and agencies of the federal government. There are two other free catalogs of new or popular titles in print: *U.S. Government Books*, listing 1,000 bestselling items, and *New Books*, a bimonthly list of all government publications placed on sale in the preceding two months. The following publications are recommended as having information particularly useful for fund raising by way of grants and foundations:

Catalog of Federal Domestic Assistance ($32.00 a year) is the "Bible" for detailed information on federal domestic assistance programs. Issued annually, it describes federal grant programs, giving deadlines, names to contact, telephone numbers, funding levels, eligibility, et al. This information is also available online by way of the *Federal Assistance Program Retrieval System* (FAPRS).

The Congressional Directory (biennial, $12.00 paperbound; $16.00 hardbound; $20.00 thumb-indexed) lists the names of all legislators and congressional committees. It is useful to have this information since committees may be considering legislation of interest to grantseekers.

The United States Government Organization Manual (annual, $9.00) as the official handbook of the United States Government, lists every department, agency, commission, and quasi-governmental organization, giving the names of key personnel, addresses, and telephone numbers, together with a brief description of the functions of each.

For additional titles, see section on "Government Publications" in the text preceding.

The Grantsmanship Center. 1031 South Grand Avenue, Los Angeles, California 90015. Toll-free telephone number: (800) 421-9512.

Now in its twelfth year, The Grantsmanship Center is the oldest and largest fund-raising training organization in the country. It offers a program of more than 250 workshops conducted in over 75 cities annually.

The Center has published, since 1973, the bimonthly *Grantsmanship Center News* ($28.00 a year) which has over 100,000 readers. This excellent magazine offers lively and authoritative how-to articles, case studies, and significant information about new developments in the field. There are regular columns on current publications, selected GAO reports, federal regulations and deadlines, et al.

Among its many well-written and useful reprint articles for sale, the following are especially recommended:

The Basic Grantsmanship Library (sixth edition, 1982, $3.00) is a fine basic library, to which *this* "Basic Fund Raising Library" is very much indebted. Federal sources of funding and government publications are especially emphasized.

How Foundations Review Proposals and Make Grants (revised, 1978, $2.00) offers suggestions and guidelines for the preparation of grant applications and provides a list of reasons why proposals are often turned down.

Program Planning and Proposal Writing (expanded version, 1979, $3.25) is probably the best 48 pages of information for $3.25 that can be found on the subject. It is so good, in fact, that the *Annual Register of Grant Support* (see below) reprints it with permission in its introductory materials. The booklet, written by Norton J. Kiritz, president of The Grantsmanship Center, describes the form and contents of a good proposal, giving guidelines, checklists, and examples. It would seem that if one followed the advice given, one could really hope to be successful in getting a grant.

Hoke Communications. 224 Seventh Avenue, Garden City, Long Island, New York 11530.

Although there are few commercial magazines in the fund-raising field, *Fund Raising Management* (bimonthly, $30.00 a year), can be recommended wholeheartedly, and not just by default for lack of competition. It features popularly written articles, book notes, and a plethora of advertisements on how to raise money effectively, especially by direct mail campaigns and by the use of volunteers, together with suggestions for the recognition of donors. Hoke also publishes *FRM Weekly*.

Marquis Professional Publications. 200 East Ohio Street, Chicago, Illinois 60611.
 Toll-free telephone number: (800) 428-3898.

Of the many directories in the field, if only one could be chosen, it should
probably be the *Annual Register of Grant Support* (17th edition, 1983/84,
$67.50). It is the most complete and comprehensive of the specialized direc-
tories, listing 2,587 entries including corporate, private, public, and nontradi-
tional sources of grant support.

Other directories which should be mentioned, aside from the publications
of The Foundation Center and Taft Corporation described elsewhere, are the
Corporate 500: The Directory of Corporate Philanthropy (third edition, 1984,
Public Management Institute, 358 Brannan Street, San Francisco, California
94107, $245.00); *DRG: Directory of Research Grants* (annual, The Oryx Press,
2214 North Central at Encanto, Suite 103, Phoenix, Arizona 85004, $52.50);
and the *Grants Register* (biennial, St. Martin's Press, 175 Fifth Avenue, New
York, New York 10010, $32.50).

For detailed, authoritative reviews of these titles, as well as of other
reference tools cited throughout this text, see the *American Reference Books
Annual* (Libraries Unlimited, Inc., Box 263, Littleton, Colorado 80160, $65.00
per volume).

The Plenum Press. 233 Spring Street, New York, New York 10013.

The Plenum Press is the publisher of Virginia P. White's excellent books,
Grants Proposals That Succeed (1983, $22.50), *Grants: How to Find Out
about Them and What to Do Next* (1975, $19.50), and *Grants for the Arts*
(1980, $19.50); of Judith Margolin's *The Individual's Guide to Grants* (1983,
$15.95); and of the quarterly *Grants Magazine: The Journal of Sponsored
Research and Other Programs* ($65.00 a year or $27.00 to individual subscribers
certifying journal is for their personal use only). The Plenum Press is indis-
putably the most prestigious press in the field of grants literature.

Public Service Materials Center. 111 North Central Avenue, Hartsdale, New York
 10530.

With a catalog of some fifty titles, the Public Service Materials Center is
the leading commercial publisher of books in the area of fund raising. Among
their most recent publications are *Raising Funds from America's 2,000,000
Overlooked Corporations* (Aldo C. Podesta, 1983, $24.00); *How to Write
Successful Corporate Appeals/With Full Examples* (James P. Sinclair, 1984,
$19.75); and *The Complete Guide to Corporate Fund Raising* (Joseph Dermer
and Stephen Wertheimer, editors, 1984, $16.75).

Taft Corporation. 5125 MacArthur Boulevard, N.W., Suite 300, Washington,
 D.C. 20016. Toll-free telephone number: (800) 424-3761.

For over a decade, the Taft Corporation has been the authority on "Profit Thinking for Nonprofit Organizations." The complete Taft Information System is expensive, but individual titles may be purchased separately.

The Taft Foundation Information System ($347.00 a year) includes the annual *Taft Foundation Reporter* ($250.00), a directory of the largest private foundations, the monthly newsletter, *Foundation Giving Watch* ($150.00 a year), and the monthly *Foundation Updates.*

The Taft Corporate Information Service ($347.00 a year) includes the annual *Taft Corporate Directory* ($250.00) which covers the major corporate foundations which have given a total of over a half billion dollars in charitable contributions during the last year, the monthly newsletter, *Corporate Giving Watch* ($150.00 a year), and the monthly *Corporate Updates.* Both systems together, as Taft Basic II, sell for $577.00—a considerable savings.

The Taft Corporation publishes the *Taft Trustees of Wealth,* an annual biographical directory of private corporate foundation officers ($120.00), as well as several other highly useful titles, among which are *The Proposal Writer's Swipe File III* (1982, $12.95), and the monthly action newsletter for nonprofit management professionals, *The Nonprofit Executive* ($77.00 a year).

The Third Sector Press. 2000 Euclid Avenue, Box 18044, Cleveland, Ohio 44118.

The publication of James Gregory Lord's *Philanthropy and Marketing: New Strategies for Fund Raising* (1981, looseleaf, $47.50) has been greeted by an unprecedented avalanche of critical acclaim. This is hardly surprising when one looks at the author's credentials: 14 years as a staff member of Cleveland's United Way, as well as several years in public relations, journalism, and editorial work in radio, television, and newspapers. This looseleaf volume is spare of text but long on practical and innovative techniques for fund raising. Mr. Lord's latest book, just published, is *The Raising of Money: Thirty-five Essentials* (1984, $34.50). It capsulizes the essential ideas of fund-raising.

Washington International Arts Letter. 325 Pennsylvania Avenue, S.E., Washington, D.C. 20003. (Address orders to Box 9005, Washington, D.C. 20003)

The *Arts Patronage Series* (APS), edited by Daniel Millsaps, is comprised of several directories that have appeared over the past two decades and which are kept current in between new or revised editions in the *Washington International Arts Newsletter* (10 issues a year; $24.50 to individuals; $48.00 a year to institutions).

Among the most recent of these directories are the *National Directory of Arts and Education Support by Business Corporations* (APS No. 10, second edition, 1982, $75.00); *National Directory of Grants and Aid to Individuals in the Arts* (APS No. 11, fifth edition, 1983, $79.95); and *National Directory of Arts Support by Private Foundations* (APS No. 12, fifth edition, 1983, $79.95). For complete reviews of these titles, see the *American Reference Books Annual* (Libraries Unlimited, Inc., Box 263, Littleton, Colorado 80160. $65.00 per volume).

John Wiley & Sons. 605 Third Avenue, New York, New York 10158.

One of the largest, oldest, and most respected of commercial publishers, the Wiley catalog of business publications is outstanding, especially in the field of accounting. Two of their publications recommended for not-for-profit institutions are the *Financial and Accounting Guide for Nonprofit Organizations* (Malvern J. Gross and William Warshauer, third revised edition, 1983, $49.95), and *Principles of Accounting and Financial Reporting for Nonprofit Organizations,* by Malvern J. Gross and Stephen J. Jablonsky (1979, $39.95).

Index

Abarbanel, Karin, 100, 118
Abels, David M., 55
*About Foundations: How to Find the
    Facts You Need to Get a Grant,*
    100, 118
Abramson, Alan J., 127
Abt, Clark C., 98
ACA Update, 4, 60
Academy of Political Science, 107
*Accounting and Financial Reporting:
    A Guide for United Ways and
    Not-for-Profit Human Service
    Organizations,* 18, 71, 130
*Accounting and Reporting Practices of
    Private Foundations: A Critical
    Evaluation,* 71, 100
*Accounting for Culture: A Primer for
    Non-Accountants,* 130
*Accounting for Librarians and Other
    Not-for-Profit Managers,* 71, 130
Accounting for Non-Accountants, 71
*Accounting for Non-Profit Organiza-
    tions,* 71, 130
*Accounting Fundamentals for Non-
    Accountants,* 71
*Accounting Handbook for Non-
    Accountants,* 47, 72
*Accounting Manual for Voluntary Social
    Welfare Organizations,* 47, 72,
    151
Ackerman, Robert W., 98
*Action Grants: Revitalizing and Con-
    serving Cities,* 39, 118
*Action in the Action Grants: A Select
    Bibliography on the Urban
    Development Action Grant
    Program,* 20
Adams, G. Donald, 140, 148
Adamson, Thomas A., 123
*Administration in the Arts: An
    Annotated Bibliography of
    Selected References,* 20, 130
*Administrative Policies and Information
    Sources Relating to Federal
    Domestic Assistance Programs,*
    39
*Administrative Procedures for the
    Electronic Office,* 86

Advancement Analysis, 60
Advisory Commission on Intergovern-
    mental Relations, 24, 39, 40, 41,
    42, 43, 44, 45, 119, 120, 123,
    125
Advisory Committee on Endowment
    Management, 77
*Advisory Panels of the National Endow-
    ment for the Arts,* 24
Affordable Word Processing, 87
Akey, Denise, 26
Albanese, Robert, 95
Alberger, Patricia L., 117, 146, 154
Alberti, Charles, 114
Alfred, Richard L., 107
Allen, Herb, 32, 106
Alliance of New York State Arts Coun-
    cils, 142
*Alternatives in Public Service Delivery:
    Volunteers in Federal Agencies,*
    39, 151
Alvarez, Paul, 150
American Artist Business Letter, 60
American Arts, 4, 60
American Association for State and
    Local History, 3, 76, 110, 136,
    138, 140, 148
American Association of Fund Raising
    Counsel, 4, 60, 63, 94, 105, 111,
    161
*American Association of Fund Raising
    Counsel Bulletin,* 60
American Association of Museums, 140,
    143
American Association of State Colleges
    and Universities, 48, 51, 124
American Business History, 89
American Business Values in Transition,
    89
American Council for the Arts, 4, 28,
    30, 53, 60, 74, 93, 94, 96, 103,
    107, 112, 117, 119, 131, 133,
    135, 137, 142, 143, 145, 146,
    154
American Council on Education, 5, 24,
    62, 64, 79, 107, 135, 140
American Enterprise Institute for Public
    Policy Research, 95

American Hospital Association, 72, 78, 89, 106, 131, 132, 134, 140, 152
American Institute of Certified Public Accountants, 126, 131, 151
American Law Institute, 129
American Library Association, 24, 27, 71, 105, 120, 130
American Reference Books Annual, 166, 167
American Society of Directors of Volunteer Services, 5, 67
American Society of Directors of Volunteer Services Membership Roster, 5
Americans Volunteer—1981, 13, 151
America's Most Successful Fund Raising Letters, 105
America's Voluntary Spirit: A Book of Readings, 151, 162
America's Wealthiest People: Their Philanthropic and Nonprofit Affiliations, 89
Analysis of the Economic Recovery Program's Direct Significance for Philanthropic and Voluntary Organizations and the People They Serve, 126
Anatomy of an Art Auction; a Vital Guide for Organization Fundraisers, 105
Anderson, John, 51, 143, 149
Andrews, Francis S., 110
Andrews, Frank Emerson, 97, 101
Anglo-American Conference on the Role of Philanthropy in the 1980's, 97
Annual Fund, 105
Annual Fund Ideas, 105
Annual Index Foundation Reports (Maryland), 34
Annual Register of Grant Support, 24, 130, 166
Annual Report (National Endowment for the Arts), 15
Annual Survey of Corporate Contributions, 89
Anshen, Melvin, 92
Anthony, Robert N., 76, 138
Apple Computer, 83
Applied Volunteerism in Community Development, 151
Ardman, Harvey, 117
Ardman, Perri, 117
Art Index, 58
Art Marketing Handbook, 130
Art of Asking: A Handbook for Successful Fund Raising, 47, 105
Art of Fund Raising, 105
Art of Winning Corporate Grants, 89, 118

Art of Winning Foundation Grants, 100, 118
Art of Winning Government Grants, 118
Art of Writing Business Reports and Proposals, 118
Arthur Andersen and Company, 129
Artists Foundation, Inc., ix, 6, 124, 140
Arts Administration Compensation, 131
Arts Administration: How to Set Up and Run a Successful Nonprofit Arts Organization, 131
Arts Administration Research Institute, 74, 135
Arts Administrator—Job Characteristics, 131
Arts and Business Council, 6, 61
Arts and the World of Business: A Selected Bibliography, x, 20, 131
Arts Business, 60
Arts in Education Sourcebook, 4
Arts Management, 61
Arts Management: An Annotated Bibliography, 20, 131
Arts Management Reader, 131
Arts Money: Raising It, Saving It, and Earning It, 105, 131
Arts Patronage Series, 167
Arts Reporting Service, 61
Artsfax '81: A Report on the Finances, Personnel and Programs of Bay Area Arts Organizations, 72, 131
Aschner, Katherine, 88
Asking and Giving: A Report on Hospital Philanthropy, 89, 131
Associated Grantmakers of Massachusetts, 35, 52
Association for Volunteer Administration, 7, 64
Association for Volunteer Administration Membership Directory, 7
Association for Volunteer Administration Newsletter/Bulletin, 7, 61
Association of College, University, and Community Arts Administrators, 131, 139
Association of Community Arts Councils of Kansas, 34, 50, 140, 148
Association of Research Libraries, 108, 109, 136
Association of Voluntary Action Scholars, 7, 61, 64
Association of Voluntary Action Scholars Newsletter, 7
Association of Volunteer Bureaus, 152
Association of Volunteer Centers, 8, 26, 61, 154, 155
Association of Volunteer Centers Notebook, 8, 61

Atlanta Public Library, 33
Atwell, Robert H., 79, 114, 140
Audits of Certain Nonprofit Organiza-
tions, 126, 131
Audits of Voluntary Health and Welfare
Organizations, 131, 151
Auerbach Publications, 86
Automated Office/Office of the Future,
87
A-V Connection, 24, 105
AVA in the Marketplace, 7
Awakening the Slumbering Giant: Inter-
governmental Relations and
Federal Law, 39
Awards, Honors & Prizes: An Interna-
tional Directory of Awards and
Their Donors, 24
Ayer Fund-Raising Dinner Guide, 106
Ayer Public Relations and Publicity
Style Book, 147

Baer, Virginia H., 72, 131
Bahnuik, Margaret Hilton, 86
Bakal, Carl, 106
Baker, C. R., 80
Bank of America, 22, 91, 92
Bank of America Corporate Responsibil-
ity Report, 91
Barclay, Shelley, 32
Basic Funding Development, 106
Basic Grantsmanship Library, 165
Basic Guide to Proposal Development,
118
Basic Handbook of Grants Management,
47, 119
Bates, Don, 78, 107, 147, 148
Bauer, Raymond A., 92
Bay Area Committee for Responsive
Philanthropy, 32
Bay Area Lawyers for the Arts, 141
Bay Area Social Responsibilities Round
Table, 23, 125
BCA News, 8, 61
Beck, Kirsten, 137
Becoming a Volunteer: Resources for
Individuals, Libraries and Organi-
zations, 39, 151
Before You Give Another Dime, 106
Beginner's Guide to Buying a Personal
Computer, 83
Belzer, Jack, 84
Benedict, Stephen, 20, 76, 131, 138
Bennett, A. M., 103, 124, 143
Bennett, John E., 132
Bennett, Paul, 81, 117
Benson, George C., 90
Berger, Renee A., 98
Berlye, Milton, 137

Bertsch, Kenneth A., 92
Better Giving: The New Needs of Amer-
ican Philanthropy, 89
Bibliographic Retrieval Service (BRS),
57, 60
Bibliography of Fund Raising and
Philanthropy, 15, 20, 90, 106
Bibliography of U.S. Government Docu-
ments Pertaining to Government
Support of the Arts, 1963-1972,
21
Bibliography on Arts Administration,
21, 132
Bibliography on Fundraising, 21, 106
Bibliography on Historical Organization
Practices, 3
Big Foundations, 100
Big Gift, 106
Birkin, Stanley J., 83
Bittker, Boris I., 127
Blaine, Lawrence, 75, 121
Blanshard, Paul, Jr., 50, 113
Blomstrom, Robert L., 90
Blume, Hilary, 48, 108
Blumenthal, Susan, 85
Boards of Directors: A Study of Current
Practices in Board Management
and Board Operations in Volun-
tary Hospitals, Health and Welfare
Organizations, 132, 152
Bommer, Michael R. W., 73, 134
Bonney, Clara A., 23
Bookkeeping for Nonprofits, 72, 132
Boone, Susan, 36
Borst, Diane, 77, 139
Borton, Virginia, 52, 150
Boss, Richard W., 48, 54, 88, 121, 136,
138
Boulding, Kenneth E., 124, 125
Bowers, John Z., 96
Bowker/Bantam 1984 Complete Source-
book of Personal Computing, 84
Box Office Guidelines, 132
Bradshaw, Thornton, 93
Brakeley, George A., Jr., 116
Brannon, Gerard M., 73
Braunstein, Susan, 107
Bread Game: The Realities of Founda-
tion Fund Raising, 106
Breaking Even: Financial Management in
Human Service Organizations, 72
Broadway, Beth, 156
Broce, Thomas E., 37, 109
Brookings Institution, 80
Brown, Marjorie J., 56
Brown, William, 96
Brown, William F., 51, 125
Brownrigg, W. Grant, 93, 107
BRS, 57, 60

BRS Database Catalog, 57
Brysh, Janet F., 34
Buckley, William J., 21, 132
Budgeting: A Guide for United Ways and Other Not-for-Profit Human Services Organizations, 18, 72
Budgeting for Nonprofits, 72, 132
Budgeting Procedures for Hospitals, 72, 132
Building Voluntary Support for the Two-Year College, 132
Buildings and the Income Tax, 73
Buntaine, Norman, 96
Bureau of National Affairs, 128
Burns, Michael, 33
Business and Professional Women's Foundation, 112
Business and Society: A Managerial Approach, 90
Business and Society: Concepts and Policy Issues, 90
Business and Society: Environment and Responsibility, 90
Business and Society: Managing Corporate Social Impact, 90
Business and Society: Managing Corporate Social Performance, 90
Business and Society: 1976-2000, 90
Business and Society Review, 61
Business and Society: Strategies for the 1980's, 90
Business Committee for the Arts, 8, 60, 61, 93
Business Ethics: Concepts and Cases, 90
Business Ethics in America, 90
Business, Government and Society: A Managerial Perspective, 89, 91
Business in the Humane Society, 91
Business Index, 58
Business Periodicals Index, 58
Business Publications Index and Abstracts, 58
Business Voluntarism, Prospects for 1982, 152
Business Volunteers for the Arts, 6, 61
Butners, Astrida, 96
Byte, 85

Caldwell Public Library, 34
California Nonprofit Corporation Handbook, 47, 72
California Office of Planning and Research, 40
California Taxation, 126
Callen, John J., 124
Capital Campaign, 106, 132
Capital Financing for Hospitals, 72, 106, 132

Capital Ideas: Step-by-Step—How to Solicit Major Gifts from Private Sources, 106
Cappalli, Richard B., 120, 127, 128
Carroll, Archie B., 90
Carter, Paul C., 49, 112
Carter, Virginia L., 105, 115
Case, Sara, 27, 120
Case Currents, 10, 61
Case Placement Letter, 61
Casebook in Business, Government and Society, 91
Casebook of Grant Proposals in the Humanities, 119
Cass, Rosemary Higgins, 155
Catalog of Federal Domestic Assistance, 40, 164
Catalog of Federal Grant-in-Aid Programs to State and Local Governments, 24, 40
Catalog of State Services (California), 40
Categorical Grants: Their Role and Design; the Intergovernmental Grant System: An Assessment and Proposed Policies, 40, 119
Cavanagh, Gerald F., 89
Cavanaugh, Catherine, 155
Center, Allen H., 149
Center for Arts Information, 20, 76, 131, 138
Center for Non-Profit Organizations, 9, 128
Challenge Grant Experience: Planning, Development, and Fundraising, 119
Challenge Grant Program, 119
Challenge Grant Recipient Study, 40, 119
Chamberlain, Neil W., 95, 99
Changing Position of Philanthropy in the American Economy, 91
Charitable Foundations Directory of Ohio, 36
Charitable Giving and Solicitation, 91, 106, 126
Charitable Giving and Tax-Exempt Organizations: The Impact of the 1981 Tax Act, 126
Charitable Lead Trusts—Explanation, Specimen Agreements, Reporting Forms, 126
Charitable Trust Directory (Washington), 37
Charities and Charitable Foundations, 100
Charity Auction Management Manual, 108
Charity Racket, 100, 106

Charity under Siege: Government Regulation of Fund Raising, 106
Charity U.S.A.: An Investigation into the Hidden World of the Multi-Billion Dollar Charity Industry, 106
Chemical Bank, 75, 94, 136
Chicago Corporate Connection: A Directory of Chicago Area Corporate Contributions, 34
Chicago Metropolitan Board YMCA, 156
Child Welfare League of America, 47, 72, 151
Chorafas, Dimitris N., 87
Chorba, Ronald W., 73, 134
Ciba Foundation, 96, 102
Cibbarelli and Associates, 55, 84
Citizen Boards at Work: New Challenges to Effective Action, 152
Citizen Involvement Training Project, 125
Citizen Participation and Voluntary Action Abstracts, 7, 61
Citizens Forum/NML, 91
Citizens' Scholarship Foundation of America, 61
Clark, Henry B., 108
Clearinghouse Greensheets, 18, 152
Cleveland Area Arts Council, 148
Clutterbuck, David, 94
Cmiel, Kenneth, 34
Cochrane, Diane, 145
Coe, Linda C. 20, 25, 107, 131, 134
Cohen, Lily, 110
Coldren, Sharon L., 107
Cole, Kathryn W., 29
Coleman, William, 28, 119
College and University Endowment: Status and Management, 72, 132
Colorado Foundation Directory, 32
Colvard, Richard, 103, 124, 143
Comish, Newel W., 153
Commerce Clearing House, 62, 127, 129
Commission on Foundations and Private Philanthropy, 102
Commitment to Culture: Art Patronage in Europe; Its Significance for America, 132
Committee for Economic Development, 98
Committee for Full Funding of Education Programs, 9, 62
Commodore Computer Systems, 83
Communicating and Moneymaking: A Guide for Using Public Relations to Improve Fundraising Success, 107, 147
Communications Manual for Nonprofit Organizations, 47, 73, 133

Community and the Bank, 91
Community College Foundation, 100, 133
Community Congress of San Diego, 32
Community Development: The Workings of a Federal-Local Block Grant: An Assessment and Proposed Policies, 40, 119
Community Focus, 18, 62
Community Orchestra: A Handbook for Conductors, Managers and Boards, 133
Community Resource Tie Line, 12, 152
Complete Fund Raising Guide, 107
Complete Grants Sourcebook for Higher Education, 24, 119, 133
Complete Guide to Corporate Fund Raising, 91, 107, 166
Complete Guide to Successful Fund-Raising, 107
Compu-Guide, 84
CompuServe, 56
Compute!, 85
Computer Basics for Nonprofit Organizations, 82
Computer Graphics: A Programming Approach, 82
Computer Publishers and Publications 1984, 82
Computer Readable Data Bases: A Directory and Data Sourcebook, 55
Computer Resource Guide for Nonprofits, 24, 84, 133
Computers and Information Processing in Business, 83
Computers and Management, 83
Computers and Management in a Changing Society, 83
Computers for Nonprofits, 83, 133
Computerworld, 86
Comsearch Printouts, 21, 25, 162
Concert Society of California, 138
Conference Board, 77, 89, 92, 94, 95, 152
Congressional Directory, 164
Congressional Research Service, 39, 151
Connecticut Foundation Directory, 33
Connell, Stephen, 87
Connery, Robert H., 93, 107, 133
Connors, Tracy D., 51, 79, 142
Conrad, Daniel Lynn, 94, 112, 116, 122, 124, 125
Conrad, William, 153
Constant Quest: Raising Billions through Capital Campaigns, 107
Consumerism, Federal Grants and You, 119

Contemporary Challenges in the Business-Society Relationship, 91
Continuing Education Publications, 161
Contributors Income Tax Deduction Guide, 127
Cook, Susan M., 33
Coopers and Lybrand International, Australia, 88
Coopers and Lybrand, National Education Industry Group, 64, 128, 137
Coping with Reduced Resources, 107
Corporate Community Involvement, 91
Corporate 500: The Directory of Corporate Philanthropy, 25, 91, 166
Corporate Foundation Profiles, 25, 100
Corporate Fund Raising: A Practical Plan of Action, 107
Corporate Fund Raising Directory, 25, 107
Corporate Giving in Chicago, 34
Corporate Giving Watch, 30, 167
Corporate Giving Yellow Pages, 91
Corporate Performance: The Key to Public Trust, 92
Corporate Philanthropic Public Service Activities, 92
Corporate Philanthropy, 11, 92
Corporate Philanthropy in the Eighties: Expert Advice for Those Who Give or Seek Funds, 92
Corporate Planning for Nonprofit Organizations, 73, 133
Corporate Power and Social Responsibility, 92
Corporate Responsibility for Social Problems: A Bibliography, 22, 92
Corporate Social Audit, 92
Corporate Social Responsibility, 92
Corporate Social Responsibility: Policies, Programs and Publications, 10, 92
Corporate Strategies for Social Performance, 92
Corporate Support, 92, 133
Corporate Support of Higher Education, 1979, 10, 93, 133
Corporate Updates, 30, 167
Corporation and the Campus, 93, 107, 133
Corporations and Their Critics: Issues and Answers to the Problems of Corporate Social Responsibility, 93
Corry, Emmett, 27, 136
Corson, John, 91, 95, 97
Cost Effective Analysis in Fund Raising for Colleges and Universities, 107, 134

Cost Principles Applicable to Grants and Contracts with State and Local Governments, 40, 73
Costs and Benefits of Deferred Giving, 107, 127
Cottam, Richard M., 50, 140, 148
Council for Advancement and Support of Education, 9, 49, 61, 75, 76, 78, 80, 92, 100, 104, 105, 106, 111, 112, 113, 114, 115, 117, 123, 128, 132, 133, 139, 140, 143, 144, 146, 153, 154
Council for Advancement and Support of Education Directory, 10
Council for Financial Aid to Education, 10, 92, 93, 98, 99, 133, 146
Council on Better Business Bureaus, 99
Council on Foundations, 10, 51, 63, 95, 96, 97, 104, 161
Courtade, Kay Carter, 38
Cover, Nelson, 111
Cox, Allan, 93
Cox Report on the American Corporation, 93
Creative Computing, 86
Creative Philanthropy: Carnegie Corporation in Africa, 1953-1974, 93
Crimmins, James C., 135
Critical Issues Involved in the Review of Research Proposals at Universities, 133
Crohn, Richard H., 114
Cronin, Jerry, 95
CSFA News, 61
Cuadra, Ruth N., 55
Cuadra Associates, 55
Cull, John G., 151, 156
Cultural Assistance Center, 96, 142
Cultural Council Foundation, 36, 114, 141
Cultural Directory II: Federal Funds and Services for the Arts and Humanities, 25, 107, 134
Cultural Post, 15, 62
Cultural Wasteland, 4
Culture and Management: Text and Readings in Comparative Management, 73
Cumerford, William R., 109
Cumming, Marsue, 52, 81, 145
Cumulative List of Organizations Described in Section 170 (c) of the Internal Revenue Code of 1954, 25, 40
Cuninggim, Merrimon, 104
Cunningham, Robert Maris, 89, 131
Current Contents/Arts and Humanities, 58
Current Index to Journals in Education, 59

Daedalus, 62
Dallas Public Library, 37
Daniels, Ellen S., 30, 112, 137
Darnbrough, Ann, 109, 127, 153
Darrow, Richard W., 51, 149
Dartnell Corporation, 51, 149
Data Base Alert, 56
Data Processing Management, 54
Datapro Automated Office Solutions,
    88
Datapro Directory of Online Services,
    56
Datapro Directory of Small Computers,
    86
Datapro Directory of Software, 56, 86
Datapro Reports on Microcomputers, 84
Datapro Reports on Office Systems, 88
Datapro Research Corporation, 56, 84,
    86, 88
Daughtrey, William H., 140
Davis, John H., 102
Davis, Keith, 90
Davis, King E., 109
Davis, William, 98
Dawson, William M., 78, 139
DeBettencourt, F. G., 38
DeBoer, John C., 154
*Decision Making for Library Manage-
    ment*, 73, 134
Decker, Larry E., 120
Decker, Virginia, 120
Deferred Gifts: How to Get Them, 107
*Deferred Giving—Explanation, Specimen
    Agreements, Reporting Forms*,
    127
Deferred Giving Newsletter, 11, 62
Delaware Foundations, 33
DeMille, Andrew, 109, 147
Denny, Rebecca, 25, 107, 134
Dermer, Joseph, 31, 91, 102, 103, 105,
    107, 113, 114, 123, 166
Derthick, Martha, 123
Des Marais, Philip, 123
Des Moines Area Community College,
    Project Motivate, 157
*Designs for Fund Raising: Principles,
    Patterns, Techniques*, 108
*Developing an Older Volunteers Pro-
    gram: A 10-Step Guide for Hos-
    pitals*, 134, 152
Developing Skills in Proposal Writing,
    119, 161
*Development Today: A Guide for Non-
    profit Organizations*, 73, 134
DIALOG, 57, 60, 162
DIALOG Database Catalog, 57
Dickinson, Frank G., 91
*Dictionary of Computers, Data Process-
    ing, and Telecommunications*, 84
Dieckman, Jeanette, 37

Digest of Selected Reports, 18, 59
Dimensions, 15, 62
Direct Mail Fund Raisers Association,
    11, 49, 111
*Direct Mail Fund Raisers Association
    Membership Directory*, 11
*Direct Mail Fund Raisers Association
    Newsletter*, 11, 62
Direct Mail Fund Raising, 108
*Directory of Agencies: U.S. Voluntary,
    International Voluntary, Inter-
    governmental*, 152
Directory of Associations in Canada, 25
*Directory of California Nonprofit Asso-
    ciations*, 25
*Directory of Charitable Funds in New
    Hampshire*, 35
*Directory of Connecticut Founda-
    tions*, 33
Directory of Directories, 25
*Directory of Fee-Based Information
    Services*, 55
*Directory of Foundations in Massachu-
    setts*, 35
Directory of Funded Projects, 40
*Directory of Grants for Children and
    Youth Programs*, 26
*Directory of Grants for Crime and
    Delinquency Prevention*, 26
*Directory of Grants for Energy and
    Environment*, 26
Directory of Grants for Health, 26
*Directory of Grants for Law and Advo-
    cacy*, 26
*Directory of Grants for Nonprofit
    Management Support*, 26
Directory of Grants for the Disabled, 26
*Directory of Historical Societies and
    Agencies in the U.S. and Canada*,
    3
Directory of Idaho Foundations, 34
*Directory of Information Management
    Software for Libraries, Informa-
    tion Centers and Record Centers*,
    55, 84
Directory of Kansas Foundations, 34
Directory of Maine Foundations, 34
*Directory of Massachusetts Founda-
    tions*, 35
*Directory of Montana and Wyoming
    Foundations*, 35, 38
Directory of Oklahoma Foundations, 37
Directory of Online Data Bases, 55
*Directory of Online Information
    Resources*, 55
Directory of Pennsylvania Foundations,
    37
Directory of Research Grants, 26, 166
Directory of Texas Foundations, 37

Directory of Volunteer Bureaus and
Voluntary Action Centers, 8, 26,
152
Do or Die: Survival for Nonprofits, 73
Dollars and Sense: A Community Fund-
raising Manual for Women's
Shelters and Other Non-Profit
Organizations, 47, 108, 134
Donahue, Daniel F., 22, 23, 35, 122
Donohue, Brian C., 85
Donors Forum of Chicago, 34
Dorian, Frederick, 132
Doswell, Andrew, 87
Dougan, Richard, 88
Douglas, George A., 150
Douglas M. Lawson Associates, 27, 101
Doyle, Alfreda, 21, 106, 111
Dranov, Paul, 138
Driscoll, Robert, 85
Drotning, Philip T., 108
Ducas, Dorothy, 78, 148
Dunseth, William, 113, 128
Dustan, Jane, 74, 101
Dynamics of Funding: An Educator's
Guide to Effective Grantsman-
ship, 119, 134

Eastern Connecticut State College
Foundation, 33, 35
Eastern Montana College Foundation,
35, 38
Eckstein, Burton J., 28, 102, 112, 137
Eckstein, Richard M., 102
Economic Factors in the Growth of
Corporate Giving, 73, 93
Edna McConnel Clark Foundation, 30,
80, 116, 144
Education and the Business Dollar: A
Study of Corporate Contribu-
tions Policy and American
Education, 134
Education Funding Research Council, 28
Education Index, 59
Educational Record: The Magazine of
Higher Education, 5, 62
Educational Volunteerism: A New Look,
134, 152
Educational Volunteerism: A State of
the Art Summary With Implica-
tions for Vocational Education,
41, 134, 152
Eells, Richard, 95, 134
Effect of Tax Deductibility on the Level
of Charitable Contributions and
Variations on the Theme, 73
Effective Coordination of Volunteers,
41, 153

Effective Corporate Fundraising, 93
Effective Leadership in Voluntary
Organizations: How to Make the
Greatest Use of Citizen Service
and Influence, 153
Effective Leadership of Voluntary
Organizations, 153
Effective Management of Volunteer
Programs, 153
Effective Nonprofit Executive Hand-
book, 48, 73
Effective Voluntary Board of Directors:
What It Is and What It Does, 153
Effort (Education Full Funding Report),
9, 62
Eischen, Martha, 84
Electronic Mail: A Revolution in Busi-
ness Communications, 87
Electronics Industries Association, 85
Electronics Industries Association,
Consumer Electronics Group, 85
ELHI Funding Sources Newsletter, 62
Elton, Martin C. J., 87
Encouraging Voluntarism and Volun-
teers, 153
Encyclopedia of Associations, 26
Encyclopedia of Computer Science and
Technology, 84
Encyclopedia of Fund Raising, 108
Encyclopedia of Information Systems
and Services, 55
Encyclopedia of the Music Business, 135
Encyclopedia of U.S. Government
Benefits, 27
Endangered Sector, 93
English, Raymond, 98
Enterprise in the Nonprofit Sector, 135
Epstein, Lawrence, 145
Escape from the Money Trap, 108
Esmond, Truman H., Jr., 72, 132
Ethics and Public Policy Center, 98
Ethics of Corporate Conduct, 93
Ethridge, James M., 25
Eustace, James, 127
Evaluating Development Performance,
108
Evaluation: A Systematic Approach, 73
Evaluation Handbook, 48, 74
Evanson, Roy, 115
Exempt Organizations Reports, 62,
127
External Fund Raising, 108

Factbook on Higher Education, 5, 135
FAPRS, 164
Farmer, Richard N., 92
Faust, Paula, 113

Federal Aid to States, 41
Federal Assistance Program Retrieval
    Service, 164
*Federal Budget and the Nonprofit
    Sector*, 127
*Federal Council on the Arts and Human-
    ities*, 25, 107, 134
Federal Funding Forum, 12, 108
Federal Funding Guide, 108
*Federal Funds for Research, Develop-
    ment and Other Scientific Activi-
    ties*, 27, 41
*Federal Grants and Contracts Weekly:
    Selected Project Opportunities
    for the Education Community*, 62
*Federal Grants and Cooperative Agree-
    ments: Law, Policy, and Practice*,
    120, 127
Federal Grants: Course Manual, 48, 120
*Federal Grants, Their Effects on State-
    Local Expenditures, Employment
    Levels, Wage Rates: The Intergov-
    ernmental Grant System*, 41, 120
*Federal Grants: Where in the Bureau-
    cracy to Find Them*, 27, 120
*Federal Income, Gift and Estate Taxa-
    tion*, 127
*Federal Income Taxation of Corpora-
    tions and Shareholders*, 127
Federal Procurement Data System, 41
*Federal Support to Universities, Colleges
    and Selected Nonprofit Institu-
    tions: Fiscal Year 1980*, 41, 135
Federal Tax Coordinator 2d, 127
*Federal Taxation of Trusts, Grantors and
    Beneficiaries*, 127
Federation of Protestant Welfare Agen-
    cies, 11, 62, 63, 153
*Federation of Protestant Welfare Agen-
    cies Newsletter*, 11, 63
*Fee-Based Information Services: A
    Study of a Growing Industry*, 54
Feeney, Helen M., 53, 156
Feinstein, Barbara, 155
Feld, Alan L., 128, 142
Fenn, Dan H., Jr., 92
Filer, John F., 90
Filer Report, 90
*Final Report of the Institute for Com-
    munity Service*, 153
*Financial and Accounting Guide for
    Nonprofit Organizations*, 71, 74,
    168
*Financial Aspects of Administration of
    Grants-In-Aid, Loans and Con-
    tracts with Program Participants*,
    41, 74
Financial Grants for Writers/Artists, 135

*Financial Management for Arts Organiza-
    tions*, 74, 135
Financial Management for the Arts,
    74, 135
Financial Management of Federal Aid,
    41, 74
*Financial Practice for Performing Arts
    Companies: A Manual*, 135
*Financing the Nonprofit Organization
    for Recreation and Leisure
    Services*, 74, 135
Fink, Norman S., 107, 127
*First Five Years: Fiscal 1966 through
    Fiscal 1970*, 101
First Seminar on National Develop-
    ment Foundations, 103
Fisch, Edith, 100
Fischer, Howard E., 128
Fisher, John, 75, 137
501 (c) (3) Group, 96
*Five Hundred Ways for Small Charities
    to Raise Money*, 108
*5,123 Examples of How BCA Companies
    Supported the Arts*, 8, 93
Flanagan, Joan, 111, 155
Fogel, David, 93
Ford Foundation, 77
*Ford Foundation at Work: Philanthropic
    Choices, Methods and Styles*, 101
Ford Foundation Report, 101
Forrestal, Dan J., 51, 149
Forster, Cynthia, 26
Fosler, R. Scott, 98
*Foundation Administrator: A Study of
    Those Who Manage America's
    Foundations*, 74, 101
Foundation Center, ix, 12, 21, 25, 27,
    29, 56, 59, 95, 97, 100, 101, 103,
    115, 118, 120, 143, 151, 161,
    166
Foundation Center Computer Data-
    bases, 56, 162
Foundation Center National Data Book,
    27, 56, 162
*Foundation Center National Data
    Directory. See Foundation Cen-
    ter National Data Book*
*Foundation Center Source Book Pro-
    files*, 27, 162
Foundation Directory, 27, 56, 100, 162
Foundation 500, 27, 101
Foundation for the Extension and
    Development of American Pro-
    fessional Theater, 78, 132
*Foundation Fundamentals: A Guide for
    Grant Seekers*, 101, 120, 162
Foundation Gamesmanship, 101
Foundation Giving Watch, 167

Foundation Grants Index, 56, 162
Foundation Grants Index Annual, 59,
    162
Foundation Grants Index Bimonthly,
    162
Foundation Grants to Individuals, 27,
    162
Foundation Guide for Religious Grant
    Seekers, 101, 135
Foundation Handbook: A Private
    Foundation Approach to Fund
    Raising at State Colleges and
    Universities, 48
Foundation News: The Journal of
    Philanthropy, 11, 63, 161
Foundation Primer, 101
Foundation Updates, 167
Foundation Watcher, 101
Foundations and Fund Raising: A
    Bibliography of Books to 1980,
    22, 102, 108
Foundations and Government; State and
    Federal Law and Supervision, 102
Foundations in New Jersey, 36
Foundations in Wisconsin, 38
Foundations, Private Giving, and Public
    Policy: Report and Recommenda-
    tions, 102
Foundations That Send Their Annual
    Report, 27
Foundations: Their Use and Abuse, 101
Foundations: Twenty Viewpoints, 101
Four-One-One, 15, 65, 108, 152
Fox, Susan, 51, 79, 142
Frederick, William C., 90
Frederiksen, Christian P., 79, 141
Freed, Doris Jonas, 100
Freedman, Anne, 156
Freeman, David F., 49, 102
Freeman, Howard E., 73
Freeman, Robert J., 74
Fremont-Smith, Marion, 97, 102
FRI Annual Giving Book, 48
FRI Monthly Portfolio, 63
FRM Weekly, 63, 165
Fubini, Carol, 35
Fund Accounting: Theory and Practice,
    74
"Fund Raiser as Damon Runyon
    Character," 112
Fund Raiser's Exchange, 63
Fund Raiser's Guide, 63
Fund-raising: A Comprehensive Hand-
    book, 48, 108
Fund Raising: A Guide for Nonprofit
    Corporations, 108, 135
Fund Raising: A Guide for Research
    on Individuals, 109
Fund Raising: A Professional Guide, 109

Fund-raising and Grant-aid:A Practical
    and Legal Guide to Charities and
    Voluntary Organizations, 109,
    127, 153
Fund Raising by Computer, 83, 109
Fund Raising Consultancy and Public
    Relations, 109, 147
Fund Raising for Non-Profit Groups,
    109, 136
Fund Raising for Philanthropy, 93, 109
Fund Raising for Small Charities and
    Organizations, 109
Fund Raising Forum, 15, 63
Fund Raising in ARL Libraries, 109, 136
Fund Raising in the Black Community:
    History, Feasibility, Conflict, 109
Fund Raising Institute, 48, 63, 83, 101,
    106, 107, 108, 109, 110
Fund Raising Letter Collection, 110
Fund Raising Letters: A Comprehensive
    Study Guide to Raising Money by
    Direct Response Marketing, 110
Fund Raising Management, 63, 105, 165
Fund Raising Manual: Strategies for
    Nonprofit Organizations, 48, 110,
    136
Fund Raising—Marketing for Human
    Needs, 110
Fund Raising Practices of United Way
    Agencies in New York City, 110
Fund Raising Resource Manual, 48,
    110
Fund Raising Review, 4, 63, 161
Fund Raising Techniques, 110
Fund Raising: The Guide to Raising
    Money from Private Sources, 109
Funding Center, 110
Funding in Aging: Public, Private and
    Voluntary, 110
Funding Process: Grantsmanship and
    Proposal Development, 120
Funding Sources and Technical Assis-
    tance for Museums and Historical
    Agencies, 3, 110, 136
Funding Volunteer Services—Potential
    Sources of Dollars to Expand
    Agency Programs, 153
Funding Workbook, 110
Future of Philanthropic Foundations,
    102
Future of Voluntary Organizations:
    Report of the Wolfenden Com-
    mittee, 153
Future Role of Business in Society, 94

Gaby, Daniel M., 51, 114, 124, 142, 148
Gaby, Patricia V., 51, 114, 124, 142,
    148

Galambos, Louis B., 98
Galbraith, Ian A., 87
Galloway, Joseph M., 129
Gardner, Sally, 30, 117, 146
Garigan, Catherine E., 97, 115
Gary W. Phillips and Associates, 109
Gayley, Henry L., 49, 112, 123
Geographic Distribution of Federal Funds: A Report of the Federal Government's Impact by State, County, and Large City, 42
Georgi, Charlotte, 20, 131
Georgia Foundation Directory, 33
Gerardi, Kathleen Hamilton, 110
Getting a Grant in the Nineteen Eighties: How to Write Successful Grant Proposals, 120
Getting a Grant in the Nineteen Eighties: Readings in Cost and Managerial Accounting, 74, 120
Getting Grants, 120
Getting in Ink and on the Air: A Publicity Handbook, 147
Getting Publicity, 147
Getting Your Share: An Introduction to Fund Raising, 110
Getting Yours: The Complete Guide to Government Money, 111, 120
Gilbert, Charles, 89
Gilman, Kenneth, 24, 83, 84, 133
Gingold, Diane J., 119
Giovanni Agnelli Foundation, 28
Give! Who Gets Your Charity Dollar?, 94, 111
Giving and Getting: A Chemical Bank Study of Charitable Contributions 1983 through 1988, 94
Giving and Taking: Across the Foundation Desk, 102
Giving U.S.A.: Annual Report, ix, 4, 94, 105, 111, 161
Gladstone, M., 21
Glenn, William, 153
Glossary of Tools and Concepts for Nonprofit Managers, 75, 136
Goheen, Robert F., 51, 104
Golden, Joseph, 142
Golf Tournament Management Manual, 108
Gonzales, Rosy B., 20, 90, 106
Goodman, Calvin J., 130
Goodman, Florence J., 130
Gould, J. Sutherland, 148
Goulden, Joseph C., 95, 114
Government Contracts: Proposalmanship and Winning Strategies, 120
Gracey, Janet English, 30, 117, 146
Granoff, Anita M., 124, 140

Grant and Contract Funding Newsletters, Journals, Periodicals and Newspapers, 22, 121
Grant Budgeting and Finance: Getting the Most out of Your Grant Dollar, 75, 121
Grant Information System, 63, 121
Grant Money and How to Get It: A Handbook for Librarians, 48, 121, 136
Grant Proposal: A Guide for Preparation, 121
Grant Proposals: A Practical Guide to Planning, Funding and Managing, 75, 121
Grant Proposals That Succeed, 121, 166
Grant Writer's Handbook, 48, 121
Grants Administration: A Systems Approach to Project Management, 121
Grants Administration Manual, 42, 48
Grants Administration Policies, 42, 121
Grants and Assistance News, 14, 121
Grants and Awards, 42
Grants and Awards Available to American Writers, 27, 136
Grants Economy and Collective Consumption, 122
Grants for Libraries: A Guide to Public and Private Funding Programs and Proposal Writing Techniques, 27, 136
Grants for the Arts, 122, 136, 166
Grants Game: How to Get Free Money, 122
Grants: How to Find Out About Them and What to Do Next, 27, 121, 166
Grants-in-Aid: A Bibliography of Selective References, 1861-1960, 22
Grants in the Humanities: A Scholar's Guide to Funding Sources, 28
Grants Magazine: The Journal of Sponsored Research and Other Programs, 63, 166
Grants Policy Statement, 42
Grants Register, 28, 122, 166
Grants Resource Manual, 22, 35
Grants Survival Library—1980, 22, 122
Grantseekers Guide: A Directory for Social and Economic Justice Projects, 28
Grantsmanship and Proposal Development Publications: An Annotated Buyer's and Researcher's Bibliography, 22, 122
Grantsmanship Center, ix, 64, 122, 124, 165

Grantsmanship Center News, 64, 82, 118, 122, 165

Grantsmanship: Money and How to Get It, 122

Grassroots Fundraising Book: How to Raise Money in Your Community, 111

Grassroots Fundraising Journal, 64

Grasty, William K., 52, 116

Greater New York Fund, 132, 152

Greater New York Fund/United Way, 110

Green, Jenny, 88

Green, Joann, 52, 80, 144

Greenberg, Elinor Miller, 141

Greenwald, Harry, 30

Grisham, Roy A., 27

Gross, Malvern J., 74, 80, 140, 143, 168

Growth in the Eighties: A Manager's Guide to Financial Productivity for Non-Profit Organizations, 75, 136

GSM Library Guides, 83, 87

Guggenheims, 102

Guide for Fundraisers, 111

Guide for Preparing a Statement of Accountability, 15, 75

Guide for State and Local Government Agencies: Cost Principles and Procedures for Establishing Cost Allocation Plans and Indirect Cost Rates for Grants and Contracts with the Federal Government, 42, 75

Guide to Arkansas Private Foundations, 32

Guide to California Foundations, 32

Guide to Charitable Foundations in the Greater Akron Area, 36

Guide to Charitable Trusts and Foundations in the State of Hawaii, 33

Guide to Corporate Giving in Connecticut, 33

Guide to Corporate Giving in the Arts, 4, 28, 94

Guide to Creative Giving, 94

Guide to European Foundations, 28

Guide to Federal Assistance, 28

Guide to Federal Funding for Education, 28

Guide to Foundations in Florida, 33

Guide to Foundations in Georgia, 33

Guide to Government Resources for Economic Development—A Handbook for Non-Profit Agencies and Municipalities, 28, 42, 136

Guide to Grants: Governmental and Nongovernmental, 23

Guide to Grantsmanship, 122

Guide to Minnesota Foundations, 35

Guide to Oregon Foundations, 37

Guide to Successful Fund Raising, 111

Guide to Successful Fund Raising: For Authentic Charitable Purposes, 111

Guide to Successful Phonathons, 111

Guide to Texas Foundations, 37

Guide to the Administration of Charitable Remainder Trusts, 10, 75, 128

Guide to the California Non-Profit Public Benefit Corporation Law, 128

Guide to the Electronic Office, 87

Guide to the National Endowment for the Arts, 28

Guide to Washington, D.C. Foundations, 38

Gurin, Maurice G., 117, 157

Guthe, Carl E., 76, 138

Hadley, Scott, 103, 143

Hale, George E., 124

Hall, Elizabeth S., 114, 140

Hall, James L., 56

Hall, Mary, 119, 161

Halstead, D. Kent, 72, 132

Handbook for Agency Coordinators for Volunteer Programs, 48, 154

Handbook for Development Officers at Independent Schools, 49

Handbook for Direct Mail Fundraising, 49, 111

Handbook for Educational Fund Raising: A Guide to Successful Principles and Practices for Colleges, Universities and Schools, 49, 111, 137

Handbook of Corporate Social Responsibility: Profiles of Involvement, 49, 94

Handbook of Federal Assistance: Financing, Grants, Technical Aids, 49

Handbook of Public Relations, 49, 147

Handbook of Special Events for Nonprofit Organizations: Tested Ideas for Fund Raising and Public Relations, 49, 111, 137, 147

Handbook of Successful Fund-Raising, 49, 112

Handbook on Private Foundations, 11, 49, 102

Handicapped Funding Directory, 28, 112, 137

Happy to Be Here, 112

Hardy, James M., 73, 133

Hardy, Richard E., 151, 156
Harman, John D., 157
Harrington, Steven, 82
Harris, James F., 92
Hartman, Hedy A., 110, 136
Hartner, Elizabeth P., 54
Hartogs, Nelly, 132, 152
Hass, John Henry, 23, 45, 144
Hayes, Frederick, 76
Hayes, R. S., 80
Health Funds Development Letter,
        64
Heeman, Warren, 107, 134
Helping People Volunteer, 154
Helping the Volunteer Get Started:
        The Role of the Volunteer
        Center, 18, 154
Henke, Emerson O., 71, 130
Hennessey, Paul, 77, 139
Herzlinger, Regina E., 76, 138
HEW Catalog of Assistance, 42
Hicks, Tyler G., 115, 125
Higher Education and National Affairs,
        5, 64
Higher Education Management News-
        letter, 64
Highlights (Arts and Business Coun-
        cil), 6
Hillman, Howard, 89, 100, 118
Hitchcock, Stephen, 25, 48, 51, 73,
        79, 142
Hodson, H. V., 29
Hodson, Harry V., 97
Hogue, W. Dickerson, 92
Hoke Communications, 165
Holloway, George T., 20, 90, 106
Holtz, Herman, 120
Holzman, Albert G., 84
Hooper, William T., 37
Hoover, Ryan E., 54, 138
Hopkins, Bruce R., 106, 126, 128
Hopwood, Susan, 38
Horgen, Gregory C., 115
Horwitz, Tim, 131
Hospital Fund Raising Newsletter, 64
Hospitals, 5
How Foundations Review Proposals
        and Make Grants, 165
How to Be a Good Corporate Citizen:
        A Manager's Guide to Making
        Social Responsibility Work—and
        Pay, 94
How to Be an Effective Board Member,
        75
How to Build A Big Endowment, 112
How to Buy a Home Computer: A Guide
        for Consumers, 85
How to Buy an Office Computer or
        Word Processor, 85

How to Create New Ideas for Corporate
        Profit and Personal Success, 94
How to Do Theatre Publicity, 137, 148
How to Get Corporate Grants, 94, 122
How to Get Federal Contracts, 122
How to Get Federal Grants, 122
How to Get Government Grants, 123
How to Get Money for: Conservation
        and Community Development,
        112, 137
How to Get Money for Research, 112
How to Get Your Fair Share of Founda-
        tion Grants, 102
"How-To" Guides for Publicity Chair-
        persons, 148
How to Manage a Non-Profit Organiza-
        tion, 75, 137
How to Organize and Raise Funds for
        Small Non-Profit Organizations,
        112, 137
How to Publicize Yourself, Your Family
        and Your Organization, 148
How to Raise Money: Special Events for
        Arts Organizations, 112, 137
How to Run a Small Box Office, 137
How to Secure and Manage Foundation
        and Federal Funds in the 1980's,
        75, 102
How to Sell Your Art Work: A Complete
        Guide for Commercial and Fine
        Artists, 137
How to Solicit Big Gifts, 112
How to Succeed in Fund Raising Today,
        112
How to Write for Development, 49,
        112, 123
How to Write Successful Corporate
        Appeals/With Full Examples, 94,
        112, 166
How to Write Successful Foundation
        Presentations, 102, 113, 123
Huber, John P., 33, 35
Human Resources Network, 49, 94, 112,
        137
Human Services Development Center,
        115
Humanities, 64
Humphries, H. R., 109
Huntsinger, Jerry, 110
Hutler, Albert A., 111
Hyslop, David, 87

IBM, 83
Ideas Plus Dollars: Research Methodol-
        ogy and Funding, 113
If You Want Air Time: A Publicity
        Handbook, 50, 148

Improving Federal Grants Management,
42, 123
*Improving the Financial Management
and Auditing of Federal Assis-
tance Programs: The "Single-
Audit" Concept*, 43, 76
Independent Sector, 13, 64
Independent Sector Update, 13, 64
Index to Legal Periodicals, 59
Indiana Foundations: A Directory, 34
Individual's Guide to Grants, 123, 166
*Influence of Federal Grants: Public
Assistance in Massachusetts*, 123
Information Industry Association, 84
*Information Industry Market Place: An
International Directory of Infor-
mation Products and Services*, 55
Information Sources, 84
*Innovative Tax Strategies for Colleges
and Universities*, 128, 137
*Inside Grant and Project Writing: How
to Write Projects That Get
Funded*, 123
Inside the Music Publishing Industry,
138
Instant Foundation Telephone Index,
102
*Institute for Community Service
Manual: A Process for Developing
Agency-Based Volunteer Social
Work Staff*, 50, 154
Insurance and the Performing Arts, 138
Interface Age, 86
*Intergovernmental Grant System: An
Assessment and Proposed Policies*,
43, 123
*Intergovernmental Grant System as Seen
by Local, State, and Federal
Officials*, 43, 123
International Association of Business
Communicators, 79
*International Awards in the Arts: For
Graduate and Professional Study*,
28, 138
*International Business Philanthropy:
Papers from a Symposium
Cosponsored by the National
Council on Philanthropy and
Seven Springs Center, an Affiliate
of Yale University*, 94
International Council on United Fund
Raising, 13, 67
*International Directory of Data Bases
Relating to Companies*, 56
*International Directory of Voluntary
Work*, 154
International Foundation Directory, 29
International Fund Raising Association,
13

*International Philanthropy: A Compila-
tion of Grants by U.S. Founda-
tions*, 29, 95, 103
*International Who's Who in Community
Service*, 154
*Introduction to Annuity, Charitable
Remainder Trusts, and Bequest
Programs*, 113, 128
*Introduction to Automated Literature
Searching*, 54
Introduction to Fund Accounting, 76
*Introduction to Fund Raising: The
Newcomer's Guide to Develop-
ment*, 113
*Introduction to Online Information
Systems*, 54
Introduction to Planned Giving, 113
Investment Policies of Foundations, 103
Investor Responsibility Research Cen-
ter, 92
*Involving Volunteers in Your Advance-
ment Programs*, 154
Irregular Serials and Annuals, 60
Issues in Business and Society, 95

J. K. Lasser Tax Institute, 127
Jablonsky, Stephen F., 80, 143, 168
Jackson, H. T., 135
Jacobsen, Julia M., 38
Jacoby, Neil H., 92
Jebens, Arthur B., 133
Jeffri, Joan, 105, 131
Johnson, Mark H., 127
Johnson, Simon O., 134, 152
Johnson, Stewart A., 121
Joseph Rowntree Memorial Trust,
97
Josiah Macy, Jr., Foundation, 96
Journal of Arts Management and Law,
64
Journal of Student Financial Aid, 14,
64
Journal of Voluntary Action Research,
7, 64
Journal of Volunteer Administration, 7
64
Junior League of Denver, 32
Junkin, Daniel P., 37

Kahn, Herman, 96
Kasik, Mary, 25
Katz, Harvey, 94, 111
Katz, Wallace, 39, 118
Katzan, Harry, 88
Kay, Lillian W., 94
Keens, Martha, 29, 95, 103
Keil, Mary, 135

Keillor, Garrison, 112
Keller, David, 119
Keller, Mitchell, 29, 50, 113, 114
Kennedy, Karen P. K., 124, 140
Kennedy Center News, 65
Kent, Allen, 84
Kerri, James Nwannukwu, 23, 156
Kerzner, Harold, 51, 80, 125
King , George V., 107
Kinrade, Derek, 109, 127, 153
Kiritz, Norton J., 165
Kirstein, George C., 89
Klein, Thomas A., 99
Klepper, Anne, 92
Kletzien, S. Damon, 37
Knowles, Helen, 112
Knox, Frank M., 87
Knudsen, Raymond B., 96
Koch, Frank, 96
Koester, Frances E., 78, 148
Koochoo, Elizabeth, 98, 115
Koskoff, David E., 103
Kotler, Philip, 78, 139
Krasilovsky, M. William, 145
KRC Aide and Advisor for Fund Raising Copywriters, 50, 113
KRC Computer Book for Fund Raisers, 113
KRC Desk Book for Fund Raisers/With Model Forms and Records, 50, 113,
KRC Development Council, 29, 50, 65, 113, 114
KRC Fund Raiser's Manual: A Guide to Personalized Fund Raising, 50, 113
KRC Guide to Direct Mail Fund Raising, 29, 113
KRC Handbook of Fund Raising Principles and Practices with Sample Forms and Records, 50, 114
KRC Letter, 65
KRC Portfolio of Fund Raising Letters, 114
Kroos, Herman E., 89
Krummel, Donald W., 79, 142
Kruzas, Anthony T., 55
Kurtz, Harold P., 115, 143, 149
Kurzig, Carol, 27, 101, 120, 162

Lafota, Lorraine, 41, 153
Lane, Marc J., 50, 128
Langley, Stephen, 145
Lant, Jeffrey L., 73, 134
Larocque, Gaetane M., 119
Larrick, Nancy, 51, 149
Larson, Gary O., 144
Law of Tax-exempt Organizations, 128

Lawe, Theodore M., 75, 102
Laws and Regulations Concerning Nonprofit Organizations Explained for Laymen, 9
Lawson, Douglas M., 27
Layman's Guide to Successful Publicity, 148
Lee, James C., 73
Lee, Lawrence, 122
Leerburger, Benedict A., 78, 140
Lefever, Ernest W., 98
Lefferts, Robert, 47, 119, 120
Legal Handbook for Nonprofit Organizations, 50, 128
Leibert, Edwin R., 49, 111, 137, 147
Leiding, Oscar, 148
Lemaire, Ingrid, 30, 80, 116
Lemish, Donald L., 48
Lerner, Craig Alan, 28, 122
Lesko, Mathew, 111, 120
Lesly, Philip, 50, 148
Lesly's Public Relations Handbook, 50, 148
Let's Plan: A Guide to the Planning Process for Voluntary Organizations, 154
Levene, Victoria E., 21, 132
Levin, Kathi, 23, 139
Levitan, Donald, 22, 23, 35, 122, 125
Levy, Lyn, 72, 132
Levy, Susan, 34
Library and Information Manager's Guide to Online Services, 54, 138
Library Manager's Guide to Automation, 88, 138
Limits of Corporate Responsibility, 95
Linkages: Improving Financial Management in Local Government, 76
Lippitt, Ronald, 156
List of Organizations Filing as Private Foundations, 29
Liston, Robert A., 100, 106
Lloyd, David, 78, 139
Lock-In Problem for Capital Gain: An Analysis of the 1970-71 Experience, 73
Lockheed Information Retrieval Service (DIALOG), 57, 162
Lohman, Roger A., 72
Long, David F., 112, 137
Longley, Dennis, 84
Lord, Benjamin, 91
Lord, James Gregory, 80, 97, 115, 116, 167
Loring, Roy J., 51, 80, 125
Lovelock, Christopher H., 78, 80, 143
Lutheran Social Services of Minnesota, 50, 153, 154
Lynn, Edward S., 74, 76

MacIntyre, Kate, 144, 150
Macko, George, 114
Maddalena, Lucille A., 47, 73, 133, 153
Magat, Richard, 101
*Major Sources of Grant and Contract
Program Information: An Anno-
tated Buyer's and Researcher's
Guide*, 23
Maker, Michael, 116
Making the Most of Special Events, 77,
148
*Making Things Happen: A Guide for
Members of Volunteer Organiza-
tions*, 154
Management and Fund Raising Center,
75, 137
*Management Assistance for the Arts:
A Survey of Programs*, 76, 138
Management Center, 75, 128, 136
*Management Control in Nonprofit
Organizations*, 76, 138
*Management Control in Nonprofit
Organizations: Text and Cases*,
76, 138
*Management of American Foundations:
Administration, Policies, and
Social Role*, 76, 103
Management of Small History Museums,
76, 138
*Management of Visual Arts, Museums
and Galleries: A Selected Bibliog-
raphy*, 23, 138
*Management Principles for Non-Profit
Agencies and Organizations*, 76,
138
*Management Reporting Standards for
Educational Institutions: Fund
Raising and Related Activities*,
76, 114, 139
*Management: Toward Accountability for
Performance*, 95
*Managing a Business Contributions Pro-
gram*, 95
Managing Corporate Contributions, 77,
95
*Managing Educational Endowments:
Report to the Ford Foundation*,
77
*Managing Federal Assistance in the
1980's: A Report to the Congress
of the United States*, 43, 77
*Managing Federal Assistance in the
1980's: A Study of Federal
Assistance Management*, 43, 77
*Managing Nonprofit Agencies for
Results: A Systems Approach to
Long-Range Planning*, 77, 139
Managing Nonprofit Organizations, 77,
139

*Managing Paperwork: The Key to
Productivity*, 87
*Managing Smaller Corporate Giving
Programs*, 95
Managing Staff for Results, 77, 139
Managing the Data Resource Function,
55
Managing Volunteers for Results, 77,
154
*Managing Your Public Relations: Guide-
lines for Nonprofit Organizations*,
77, 148
Mandelson, Jennifer, 32
Manser, Gordon, 155
Mansfield, Richard, 83
Maranjian, Lorig, 54
Margolin, Judith B., 100, 118, 123, 166
Marillo, James C., 124
Market the Arts, 78
Marketing for Nonprofit Organizations,
78, 139
*Marketing for Public and Nonprofit
Managers*, 78
*Marketing Higher Education: A Practical
Guide*, 78, 139
Marketing in Nonprofit Organizations,
78, 139
Marketing the Arts, 78, 139
*Marketing the Arts: A Selected and
Annotated Bibliography*, 23, 139
*Marketing the Arts in a Rural Environ-
ment: The Monadnock Arts
Study*, 78, 139
Marketing the Library, 78, 140
*Marketing Your Hospital: A Strategy
for Survival*, 78, 140
Marquette University Memorial Library,
38
Marquis Professional Publications, 166
Martel, Leon, 96
Martin, Patrick D., 91, 106, 126
Massachusetts Foundation Directory, 35
Matching Gift Details 1983, 114, 140
Matthew Bender, 126, 127, 129
Matthews, R. C., 122
Mayrand, Lionel E., Jr., 122
MBO for Nonprofit Organizations,
79, 140
McAdam, Robert E., 116
McArthur, Nancy, 137, 148
McAteer, John F., 116
McConaughy, Paul D., 27
McConkey, Dale D., 79, 140
McGlynn, Daniel R., 85
McGrath, Richard A., 87
McGuire, E. Patrick, 152
McIlhaney, William H., 104
McMillan, Norman H., 78, 140

Measuring Business's Social Performance: The Corporate Social Audit, 95
Measuring Potential and Evaluating Results, 77, 148
Media Handbook for the Arts, 50, 140, 148
Medical Research Funding Bulletin, 65
Meeting Human Needs: Toward a New Public Philosophy, 95
Megna, Ralph J., 82
Melcher, Daniel, 51, 149
Melillo, Joseph V., 78
Mellons, 103
Memorandum on Corporate Giving, 11, 95
Metropolitan Cultural Alliance, 130, 147
Metropolitan Philadelphia Philanthropy Study, 37
Metzler, Howard C., 107, 127
Meyer, Jack A., 95
Miaolis, George, 78, 139
Michaels, Donald M., 122
Michigan Foundation Directory, 35
Michigan League for Human Services, 35
Microcomputer Market Place 1983, 85
Microcomputer User's Handbook, 1983-84, 84
Microcomputing, 86
Miletich, John J., 22, 102, 108
Miller, Myron D., 83
Miller, Ronald L., 143
Miller, Ruby Sills, 154
Millsaps, Daniel, 29, 96, 124, 140, 141, 167
Millstein, Eugene J., 133
Minnesota Council on Foundations, 35
Minority Organizations: A National Directory, 29
Mirkin, Howard R., 107
Mirror-on-Volunteerism, 12, 65
Mitchell, Janet, 36
Mitchell Guide to Long Island Foundations, Corporations and Their Managers, 36
Mitchell Guide to New Jersey Foundations, Corporations and Their Managers, 36
Mitchell Guide to Upstate New York Foundations, Corporations and Their Managers, 36
Mitiguy, Nancy, 125
Model Volunteer Program, 8, 154
Models for Money: Obtaining Government and Foundation Grants and Assistance, 50, 103, 123

Mokwa, Michael P., 78, 139
Money Business: Grants and Awards for Creative Artists, ix, 6, 124, 140
Money Game: Financing Collegiate Athletics, 78, 114, 140
Money Givers, 95, 114
Money Makers: A Systematic Approach to Special Events Fund Raising, 114
Montana, Patrick J., 77, 78, 139
Monthly Catalog of United States Government Publications, 59, 164
Moon, Thomas, 138
Moore, Harry E., Jr., 74, 135
Moore, Wilbert E., 81
Morrow, John C., 118
Mosgrove, Stephen A., 71
Motivations for Charitable Giving: A Reference Guide, 96
Murphy, E. Jefferson, 93
Museum Accounting Handbook, 140
Museum Public Relations, 140, 148
Music Index, 59
Myer, John N., 71

Nakamoto, Kent, 23, 139
NASFAA Newsletter, 65
Nason, John W., 104
Natale, Kathryn, 118
National Assistance Management Association, 14, 63, 65
National Assistance Management Association Journal, 14, 65
National Assistance Management Association Membership Directory, 14
National Association of Broadcasters, 50, 148
National Association of College and University Business Officers, 76, 114, 139
National Association of Social Workers, 152
National Association of Student Financial Aid Administrators, 14, 64, 65
National Association of Student Financial Aid Administrators Newsletter, 14
National Bureau of Economic Research, 91
National Catholic Development Conference, 14, 20, 62, 63, 75, 90, 106
National Chamber Foundation, 92
National Clearinghouse on Domestic Violence, 41, 153
National Communication Council for Human Services, 77, 148

National Corporations: Analysis of Corporate and Employee Giving in 1981 United Way Campaigns, 96

National Council of Social Service, London, 156

National Council on the Arts, 101

National Development Foundations: A Private Sector Response to the Development Needs and Opportunities within Latin America, 103

National Directory of Arts and Education Support by Business Corporations, 29, 96, 140, 167

National Directory of Arts Support by Private Foundations, 29, 141, 167

National Directory of Corporate Charity (California Edition), 32, 96

National Directory of Grants and Aid to Individuals in the Arts, International, 29, 124, 141, 167

National Directory of Newsletters and Reporting Services, 60

National Directory of Nonprofit Management Support Organizations, 29, 141

National Endowment for the Arts, 15, 28, 39, 40, 43, 44, 45, 46, 62, 101, 119, 141, 145, 146

National Endowment for the Arts, Challenge Grant Program, 119

National Endowment for the Arts Guide to Programs, 15

National Endowment for the Humanities, 16, 64

National Foundation on the Arts and Humanities, 15, 40, 43, 44, 45, 46, 119, 141, 145, 146

National Society of Fund Raising Executives, 16, 29, 85

National Society of Fund Raising Executives—Directory of Membership, 16, 29

National Society of Fund Raising Executives Journal, 16, 65

National Society of Fund Raising Executives Newsletter, 16, 65

National Youth Work Alliance, 52, 116, 144

Naylor, Harriet, 157

Needs Assessment Handbook, 50, 79

Nelson, Donald T., 116

Nelson, Paula, 117

Nelson, Ralph L., 73, 93, 103

New, Anne L., 78, 148

New Awards, Honors & Prizes, 24

New Books (USGPO), 164

New Corporate Philanthropy: How Society and Business Can Profit, 96

New Dimensions for the Arts: 1971-1972, 43, 141

New England Gerontology Center, 122

New Grants Planner, 124

New How to Raise Funds from Foundations, 103, 114

New Information Systems and Services, 55

New Jersey Notes, 65

New Models for Creative Giving, 96

New Partnerships: Higher Education and the Non-Profit Sector, 141

New Philanthropy, 96

New Volunteerism: A Community Connection, 155

New Ways to Succeed with Foundations—A Guide for the Reagan Years, 103

New York City Cultural Council, 114, 141

New York City Resources for the Arts and Artists: A Listing of Services and Support Available through the Agencies and Institutions of New York City, 36, 114, 141

New York Notes, 65

New York Times Index, 59

New York Times Information Bank, 56

Newman, Danny, 144, 150

Newton, Michael, 103, 143

Next 200 Years, 96

Nicholas, Ted, 128

Nichols, Clark C., 106

Nickelsberg, Barry, 110

Nickerson, Clarence B., 47, 72

Nielson, Waldemar A., 93, 100

Nike B. Whitcomb Associates, 114

Nocerno, Joseph T., 124

Nolan, Richard L., 55

Nonprofit Arts Organizations: Formation and Maintenance, 141

Nonprofit CEOs Speak Out on Importance of Communication, 79

Nonprofit Corporations, Organizations and Associations, 79, 141

Nonprofit Executive/NPO Careers/Taft Report, 65, 167

Nonprofit Financial Management, 79, 141

Nonprofit Management Skills for Women Managers, 79, 141

Nonprofit Organization Handbook, 51, 79, 142

Nonprofit Organization Handbook: A Guide to Fund Raising, Grants, Lobbying, Membership Building, Publicity and Public Relations, 51, 114, 124, 142, 148

Nonprofit Organization Participation in the Federal Aid System, 43, 142

Nonprofit Organizations: Laws and Regulations Affecting Establishment and Operation, 128

Nonprofit Secretary Handbook, 51, 79, 142

Nonprofit Tax Exempt Corporations; The Alternative Tax Shelter: All You Need to Know about Setting Up and Maintaining a Non-Profit Corporation without a Lawyer, 128

Northeast Midwest Institute, 28, 136

Norton, Alice, 78, 148

Not for Profit Group, Chemical Bank, 75, 94, 136

NPO Resource Review, 65

NSF Factbook, 30

O'Brien, James A., 83

O'Connell, Brian, 151, 153, 163

O'Dwyer's Directory of Public Relations Firms, 149

Office, 88

Office Administration and Automation, 88

Office Automation, 87

Office Automation: A Manager's Guide, 88

Office Automation and Word Processing Buyer's Guide, 88

Office Automation and Word Processing Fundamentals, 87

Office Automation: The Productivity Challenge, 87

Office Management and Control: The Administrative Managing of Information, 87

O'Hare, Michael, 128, 142

Okin, Tessie, 155

Oleck, Howard L., 79, 141

On Online: An Introduction to Online, 55

On TAP (Technical Assistance Programs): A Directory of Resources for New York City Nonprofit Organizations, 36, 142

On the Dotted Line: The Anatomy of a Contract, 142

Online Bibliographic Databases, 56

Online, Inc., 85

Online Review, 56

Opera Program, 43

Oppedisano-Reich, Marie, 110

Opportunities for Philanthropy—1976: Report of an International Conference, 11, 96

ORBIT, 57

ORBIT Search Service Databases, 57

Organizational Survival in the Performing Arts: The Making of the Seattle Opera, 79, 142

Organizing the Library's Support: Donors, Volunteers, Friends, 79, 142

Ott, Tony, 22, 23, 121, 122

OUA/Data, 33

Oxbridge Directory of Newsletters, 60

PAIS Bulletin, 57, 59

Palley, Marian, 124

Paluszek, John L., 90

Pan American Development Foundation, 66, 103

Parkin, Andrew, 54

Partners: A Practical Guide to Corporate Support of the Arts, 96, 142

Partners for Livable Places, 135

Partners for Progress, 66

Partnerships Dataline USA, 91

Patillo, Manning, Jr., 102

Patrick, Kenneth Gilbert, 134

Patrons Despite Themselves: Taxpayers and Arts Policy, 128, 142

Patterns of Concentration in Large Foundations' Grants to U.S. Colleges and Universities, 103, 124, 143

Paying for the Piper, 115

Pell, Arthur R., 155

Peltu, Malcolm, 87

Pendleton, Othniel Alsop, 108, 135

Personal Computing, 86

Personnel Policies for Museums: A Handbook for Management, 143

Persuade and Provide: The Story of the Arts and Education Council in St. Louis, 103, 143

Peschel, John L., 127

Petersen, Sheila W., 116

Peterson, Eric, 141

Pfeffer, Arthur, 119

Philanthropic Digest, 66

Philanthropoids: Foundations and Society, Unsubsidized Anatomy of the Burden of Benevolence, 97, 104

Philanthropy and Marketing: New Strategies for Fund Raising, 80, 97, 115, 167

Philanthropy and the Business Corporation, 97

Philanthropy in the 70's: An Anglo-American Discussion, 11, 97

Philanthropy in the United States, 97

Philanthropy Monthly, 66

Phillips, Edgar H., 110

Phillips, Gary W., 109

Pittsburgh Jewish Publishing and Education Foundation, 93, 109

Place, Irene, 87

Planned Giving Idea Book, 97

Planned Giving Ideas, 97, 115

Planning and Setting Objectives, 78, 148

Planning, Implementing, Evaluating a Workshop for Directors of Volunteers, 18, 155

Playing the Funding Game, 115

Plenum Press, 166

Plessner, Gerald M., 108

Podesta, Aldo C., 115, 166

Politics of Federal Grants, 124

Porter, Robert, 28, 53, 94, 117, 145

Post, James E., 97

PR Bluebook, 149

PR Reporter, 66

Practical Guide to Small Computers for Business and Professional Use, 84

Practical Publicity: How to Boost Any Cause, 149

Practice of Public Relations, 149

Pray, Francis C., 49, 111, 137

Preface to Grants Economics: The Economy of Love and Fear, 124

Presenting Performances: A Handbook for Sponsors, 143

Preston, Lee E., 97

Prieve, E. Arthur, 20, 78, 130, 139

Principles of Accounting and Financial Reporting for Nonprofit Organizations, 80, 143

Printing and Promotion Handbook: How to Plan, Produce and Use Printing, Advertising and Direct Mail, 51, 149

Private and Foreign Aid, 11

Private Enterprise and Public Purpose, 97

Private Measurement and Public Policy: The Principle of Public Responsibility, 97

Private Money and Public Service: The Role of Foundations in American Society, 104

Private Philanthropy and Public Welfare: The Joseph Rowntree Memorial Trust, 1954-1979, 97

Process of Grantsmanship and Proposal Development, 124

Professional Secretary's Handbook: A Guide to the Electronic and Conventional Office, 88

Professional's Guide to Public Relations Services, 149

Professional's Guide to Publicity, 149

Profile of Corporate Contributions, 10, 98

Profiles of Financial Assistance Programs, 44

Profiles of Involvement, 49, 94

Program Announcement (National Endowment for the Humanities), 16, 44

Program Planning and Proposal Writing, 124, 165

Promoting Fund Raising, 115

Proposal Development Handbook, 51, 124

Proposal Preparation and Management Handbook, 51, 80, 125

Proposal Preparation Manual, 44, 51, 125

Proposal Writer's Swipe File III, 125, 167

Prospecting: Searching Out the Philanthropic Dollar, 98, 115

Public Accountability of Foundations and Charitable Trusts, 104

Public Affairs Information Service, 57, 59

Public Affairs Information Service Bulletin, 59

Public Image of Big Business in America, 1880-1940: A Quantitative Study in Social Change, 98

Public Information Handbook for Foundations, 11, 51, 104

Public Interest Public Relations, 36, 142

Public Management Institute, 24, 25, 26, 48, 50, 51, 72, 74, 75, 77, 79, 80, 83, 84, 91, 94, 108, 112, 116, 119, 121, 122, 124, 125, 132, 133, 139, 141, 142, 150, 154, 166

Public Media Manual for Museums, 51, 143, 149

Public/Private Cooperation: Funding for Small and Emerging Arts Programs, 115, 143

Public-Private Partnership: An Opportunity for Urban Communities, 98

Public-Private Partnership in American Cities: Seven Case Studies, 98

Public Relations and Fund Raising for Hospitals, 115, 143, 149
Public Relations Handbook, 51, 149
Public Relations Journal, 17, 66
Public Relations News, 66
Public Relations Practices: Case Studies, 149
Public Relations Quarterly, 66
Public Relations Register, 17, 149
Public Relations Society of America, 17, 66, 77, 148, 149
Public Service Materials Center, 25, 27, 28, 29, 30, 31, 42, 50, 91, 94, 97, 103, 105, 107, 108, 112, 113, 114, 123, 136, 137, 166
Publicity for Volunteers, 52, 150
Pugh, Joanne, 77, 139
Purcell, Elizabeth F., 96

Quick Proposal Workbook, 125

Rabkin, Jacob, 127
Rachlin, Harvey, 135
Radio Shack, 83
Raising Funds from America's 2,000,000 Overlooked Corporations, 115, 166
Raising Money from Grants and Other Sources, 115, 125
Raising Money through Gift Clubs: A Survey of Techniques at 42 Institutions, 115, 143
Raising of Money: Thirty-Five Essentials, 116, 167
Raitt, David, 54
Ramanathan, Kavasseri V., 76, 138
Rappaport, Alfred, 74, 120
Raudsepp, Eugene, 94
Rauner, Judy, 154
Readings in Public and Nonprofit Marketing, 80, 143
Recent Trends in Federal and State Aid to Local Governments, 44, 125
Records Management: Controlling Business Information, 87
Recruiting, Training and Motivating Volunteer Workers, 155
Redistribution through the Financial System: The Grants Economics of Money and Credit, 125
Regional Young Adult Project, 30, 96, 106
Reiss, Alvin H., 131
Reluctant Patron: The United States Government and the Arts, 1943-1965, 144
Report of the Wolfenden Committee, 153

Research and Project Funding for the Uninitiated, 116
Research, Demonstration, Training and Fellowship Awards, 44
Research in Corporate Social Performance and Policy, 98
Research Institute of America, 127
Research Program Guidelines, 44
Resource Directory for the Funding and Managing of Non-Profit Organizations, 30, 80, 116, 144
Resource Guide of State and Philanthropic Grants Information, 23
Restructuring Federal Assistance: The Consolidation Approach, 44
Review Guide, Grantees Financial Management Systems, 44
RF Illustrated, 66
Rice, Susan F., viii, x
Rich: A Study of the Species, 98
Rich Get Richer and the Poor Write Proposals, 125
Richards, Audrey, 26, 77, 154
Richman, Saul, 51, 104
Rights and Remedies under Federal Grants, 128
Rinder, Robert M., 84
Risley, Curtis, 147
Robinson, Peter S., 101, 135
Rockefeller Foundation, 66
Rogers, Anne, 25, 107, 134
Roosevelt, Rita K., 124, 140
Rosen, Arnold, 86
Rosenberg, Jerry M., 84
Ross, J. David, 104
Rossi, Peter H., 73
Routh, Thomas A., 156
Rubin, Mary, 112
Rudy, William H., 101
Russell, John M., 102

Salamon, Lester M., 127
Salary Study and Surveys (Association of Volunteer Centers), 8, 155
Salem, Mahmoud, 79, 142
San Diego County Foundation Directory, 32
San Francisco Foundation, 72, 131
San Francisco Public Library, 25
Sanders, Donald H., 83
Sawyer, George C., 90
Schachter, Esther R., 100
Schaevitz, Robert C., 49
Schilling, Barbara, 75, 136
Schindler-Rainman, Eva, 156
Schmidt, Daniel J., 20, 130
Schmidt, Frances, 78, 148
Schmittroth, John, 55
Schneiter, Paul H., 47, 105, 116

Scholars, Dollars, and Public Policy: New Frontiers in Corporate Giving, 98
School Fund Raiser, 66
Schuettinger, Robert L., 98
Schumacher, Jon L., 91, 106, 126
Section 504 Resources Manual, 44, 52
Seeto, William, 38
Seitel, Fraser P., 149
Selected Bibliography on Grantsmanship, 23, 125
Selected Information Resources on Scholarships, Fellowships, Grants and Loans, 23, 45, 144
Self-Portrait with Donors: Confessions of an Art Collector, 98, 144
Semple, Lisa Pulling, 50, 113
Semple, Robert F., 102
Sethi, S. Prakash, 97
Setting National Priorities, 80
Seymour, Harold J., 108
Shain, Michael, 84
Shapiro, Benson P., 78, 139
Sharpe, Robert F., 97, 106
Sharron, W. Harvey, Jr., 100, 133
Shaw, Donald R., 85
Sheinkopf, Kenneth G., 52, 116
Sheldon, Bernice E., 49, 111, 137, 147
Shellow, Jill R., 28
Shemel, Sidney, 145
Sheppard, William E., 110
Sidman, Lawrence R., 48, 120
Significant Features of Fiscal Federalism, 45
Simplified Accounting for Non-Accountants, 80
Simplified Guide to Small Computers for Business, 85
Sinclair, James P., 94, 112, 166
Sladek, Frea E., 75, 121
Small Change from Big Bucks, 32
Small College Advancement Program: Managing for Results, 80, 144
Small Theatre Handbook: A Guide to Management and Production, 52, 80, 144
Smith, Constance, 156
Smith, Craig W., 96, 120
Smith, G. Stevenson, 71, 130
Smith, Hayden W., 98
Smith, Mitchell B., 131
Smith, Sharon, 34
Smith, Virginia Carter, 97, 154
Smith, Winton, 75, 128
Social Audit for Management, 98
Social Challenge to Business, 98
Social Costs and Benefits of Business, 99
"Social Goals of the Corporation," 90

Social Sciences Citation Index, 59
Social Strategy and Corporate Structure, 99
Sold Out: A Publicity and Marketing Guide, 144, 150
Soroker, Gerald, 93, 109
Sorrels, Susan G., 116, 144
Source Guide to Government Technology and Financial Assistance, 30
Source Telecomputing Corporation, 57
South Carolina Foundation Directory, 37
South Carolina State Library, 37
Southeastern Council of Foundations, 104
Spear, Paula Reading, 34
Spence, Barbara Barrow, 98
Sperberg, Diana, 51, 143, 149
Spurgeon, Edward D., 127
Srikanth, V., 72, 132
SSA Grants Policy Handbook, 45, 52
Stafford, B., 122
Stalking the Large Green Grant: A Fundraising Manual for Youth Serving Organizations, 52, 116, 144
Stallard, John J., 87
Standard Federal Tax Reports, 129
Standard Periodical Directory, 60
State and Local Grant Awards, 30, 45
State Planning Agency Grants: Guideline Manual, 45, 52
States and Intergovernmental Aids, 45
Statistics of Income 1974-1978: Private Foundations, 104
Steckmest, Francis W., 92
Stein, Eugene L., 75, 121
Steiner, George A., x, 89, 91, 95, 99
Steiner, John F., 89, 91, 95
Stenzel, Anne K., 53, 156
Stephenson, Howard, 49, 147
Stern, Sue, 91, 106, 126
Sternberg, Sam, 32, 96
Sternheim, Karen, 83
Strategic Planning: What Every Manager Must Know, 99
Sturdivant, Frederick D., 90
Subscribe Now! Building Arts Audiences through Dynamic Subscription Promotion, 144, 150
Successful Community Fundraising: A Complete How-To Guide, 116
Successful Fundraising: A Handbook of Proven Strategies and Techniques, 52, 116
Successful Fundraising Techniques, 116
Successful Meetings, 80
Successful Public Relations Techniques, 150

Successful Resource Fairs: Guidelines for Planning, 52
Successful Seminars, Conferences and Workshops, 80
Successful Volunteer Organization: Getting Started and Getting Results in Nonprofit, Charitable, Grassroots and Community Groups, 155
Sugarman, Norman A., 129
Sumariwalla, Russy D., 130
Support for the Arts: A Survey of Possible Sources for State University of New York, 116, 144
Survey of Arts Administration Training in the United States and Canada, 4, 30
Survey of Arts Administration Training 1982-83, 145
Survey of Grant-Making Foundations, 30
Survey of United States and Foreign Government Support for Cultural Activities, 45
Swanson, Carl L., 97
Sweeney, Robert D., 115, 143
Symphony Orchestra Program, 45, 145
System Development Corporation, 57
Systems and Procedures Exchange Center, Association of Research Libraries, 108, 109, 136

Taft, Richard J., 108
Taft Basic II, 167
Taft Corporate Directory: Profiles and Analyses of America's Corporate Foundations and Giving Committees, 30, 99, 167
Taft Corporate Information Service, 167
Taft Corporation. *See* Taft Group
Taft Foundation Information System, 167
Taft Foundation Reporter, 66, 167
Taft Group, ix, 30, 65, 66, 73, 81, 89, 91, 98, 99, 108, 111, 113, 115, 116, 117, 125, 137, 149, 166, 167
Taft Trustees of Wealth: A Biographical Directory of Private Foundations and Corporate Foundation Officers, 30, 99, 167
Taranto, Susanne E., 134, 152
Task Force on Corporate Social Performance, 90
Tatum, Liston, 113
Tax Aspects of Charitable Giving, 129
Tax Economics of Charitable Giving, 129
Tax Exempt Organizations, 129

Tax-exempt Charitable Organizations, 129
Tax-exempt News, 66
Tax-exempt Scandal: America's Leftist Foundations, 104
Tax Techniques for Foundations and Other Exempt Organizations, 129
Taxwise Giving, 66
Taylor, Bernard P., 94, 111
Taylor, Eleanor Kendrick, 104
Tedone, David, 149
Teitell, Conrad, 126, 127
Teleconferencing: New Media for Business Meetings, 87
Tenbrunsel, Thomas W., 48, 110, 136
Terminal/Microcomputer Guide and Directory, 85
Terry, George R., 87
Tested Ways to Successful Fundraising, 116
Testimonial Dinner and Industry Luncheon Management Manual, 108
Texas Association of Museums, 51, 143
Texas Foundation Research Center, 37
Theater Market Place, 145
Theatre Management in America: Principle and Practice: Producing for the Commercial, Stock, Resident, College, and Community Theatre, 145
Theatre Profiles/2: An Informational Handbook of Nonprofit Professional Theatres in the United States, 52, 81, 145
Theatre Program: Application Guidelines, 45, 145
Third Sector Press, 167
Thirteen Most Common Fund-Raising Mistakes and How to Avoid Them, 116
This Business of Art, 145
This Business of Music, 145
Thompson, Joan W., 76
Thurston, Ellen, 76, 138
Tips on Charitable Giving, 99
Topinka, James E., 128
Topor, Robert S., 78, 139
Training and Development Organizations Directory, 30
Training Volunteer Leaders: A Handbook to Train Volunteers and Other Leaders of Program Groups, 52, 155
Traub, Jack, 71, 100
Trecker, Harleigh B., 152
Tri-County Community Council of Portland, 37
Troy, Kathryn, 77, 95

Truesch, Paul E., 129
Trustees and the Future of Foundations, 104
Trustees in Fund Raising, 117
Trusteeship and the Management of Foundations, 81
Tunison, Eileen Feretic, 86
Turk, Frederick J., 74, 135
Twentieth Century Fund, 128, 142

UCLA Graduate School of Management, ix
Ulrich's International Periodicals Directory, 60
Umansky, Martin, 50, 140, 148
Understanding and Buying a Small Business Computer, 85
Understanding and Increasing Foundation Support, 104
Understanding Computers: What Managers and Users Need to Know, 85
Uniform Requirements for Assistance to State and Local Governments, 45
United Arts Fundraising, 117, 145
United Arts Fundraising Manual, 53, 117, 145
United Arts Fundraising Policy Book, 117, 145
United for Service, 13, 67
United Nations Centre on Transnational Corporations, 56
U.S. Congress, House, Committee on Government Operations, Intergovernmental Relations and Human Resources Subcommittee, 43, 76
U.S. Department of Commerce, 90
U.S. Department of Education, Office of Vocational and Adult Education, 41, 134, 152
U.S. Department of Health and Human Services, 42, 44, 46, 52, 157
U.S. Department of Health, Education and Welfare, 22, 40, 42, 44, 75
U.S. Department of Health, Education and Welfare, Division of Financial Management Standards and Procedures, 42, 75
U.S. Department of Housing and Urban Development, 39, 41, 74, 118
U.S. Department of Housing and Urban Development, Office of Administration, 41, 74
U.S. Department of Justice, Law Enforcement Assistance Administration, 45, 52
U.S. Department of the Treasury, 25, 41

U.S. Department of the Treasury, Bureau of Government Financial Operations, Division of Government Accounts and Reports, 41
U.S. Department of Transportation, 44, 51, 125
U.S. Environmental Protection Agency, 30, 42, 44, 45, 48
U.S. Environmental Protection Agency, Grants Administration Division, 30, 44, 45
U.S. Executive Office of the President, 39, 40, 41, 42, 43, 44, 45, 74, 77
U.S. Executive Office of the President, Office of Management and Budget, 39, 40, 41, 43, 44, 45, 74, 77
U.S. Executive Office of the President, Office of Management and Budget, Office of Federal Procurement Policy, 41
U.S. General Services Administration, Office of Federal Management Policy, 40, 73
U. S. Government Books, 164
U.S. Government Organization Manual, 164
U.S. Government Printing Office, 163
U.S. Internal Revenue Service, 25, 40, 104
U.S. Library of Congress, 39, 45, 144, 151
U.S. Library of Congress, National Library Service for the Blind and Physically Handicapped, 39, 151
U.S. National Science Foundation, 27, 41
U.S. Office of Education, 72, 132
U.S. Office of Federal Management Policy, 40, 73
U.S. Office of Federal Procurement Policy, 41
U.S. Office of Management and Budget, 39, 40, 41, 43, 44, 45, 74, 77
U.S. Public Health Service, 42, 44
United States Publicity Directory, 150
U.S. Senate Committee on Governmental Affairs, 43, 142
U.S. Senate Committee on Governmental Affairs, Subcommittee on Intergovernmental Relations, 39, 151
U.S. Senate Committee on Labor and Human Resources, 46, 155
U.S. Senate Committee on Labor and Public Welfare, Special Subcommittee on Arts and Humanities, 45

U.S. Social and Rehabilitation Service, 42, 121
U.S. Social Security Administration, Office of Management, Budget and Personnel, 45, 52
United Way International, 17
United Way of America, 17, 59, 62, 67, 71, 72, 96, 130
United Way of America Executive Newsletter, 18, 67
United Way of America International Directory, 18
United Way of America Quarterly Newsletter, 18, 67
United Way of Delaware, 33
United Way of Summit County, Ohio, 36
University Research News, 67
Unrelated Business Income Tax, 129
Up Your Accountability: How to Up Your Serviceability and Funding Credibility by Upping Your Accounting Ability, 81, 117
Urgo, Louis, 50, 103, 123
Using Publicity to Best Advantage, 78, 148
Using Standards to Strengthen Public Relations, 78, 148

Vail, Christopher, 26
Van, Elizabeth A., 23
Vance, Mary A., 23, 156
Van Horn, James, 133
Varney, Jean V., 152
Vastyan, James A., 82
Vecchitto, Daniel W., 113
Velasquez, Manuel G., 90
Vignola, Leonard R., 40, 119
Visual Arts Program: Application Guidelines, 46, 146
Vogt, Jay W., 52
Voluntarism and the Business Community, 155
Voluntarism at the Crossroads, 155
Voluntarism in America: Promoting Individual and Corporate Responsibility, 46, 155
Voluntary Action Center for New York City, 48, 154
Voluntary Action Leadership, 18, 67
Voluntary Action Research, 155
Voluntary Associations in Change and Conflict—A Bibliography, 23, 156
Voluntary Associations: Perspectives on the Literature, 156
Voluntary Non-Profit Sector: An Economic Analysis, 156
Voluntary Organizations, 156

Voluntary Social Services Directory of Organizations and Handbook of Information, 156
Voluntary Support for Public Higher Education, 1977-78, 99, 146
Voluntary Support of Education, 99, 146
Volunteer and Community Agencies, 156
Volunteer Community: Creative Use of Human Resources, 156
Volunteer Gazette, 19, 67
Volunteer Leader, 5
Volunteer Management, 156
Volunteer Services Administration, 5, 67
Volunteer: The National Center for Citizen Involvement, 18, 67, 152, 154, 155
Volunteer Training and Development: A Manual for Community Groups, 53, 156
Volunteer Workers: A Bibliography, 23, 156
Volunteering, 18, 67
Volunteerism: An Emerging Profession, 156
Volunteerism in the Eighties: Fundamental Issues in Voluntary Action, 157
Volunteers in Human Services, 46, 157
Volunteers of America, 18, 67
Volunteers Today, 157
Voros, Gerald J., 150

Waddilove, Lewis E., 97
Walker, John, 98, 144
Wall Street Journal Index, 59
Wallace, Martha R., 102
Walsh, Myles E., 85
Walton, Clarence, 93
Wang, 83
Wanger, Judith, 55
Warner, Irving R., 32, 105
Warnken, Kelly, 55
Warren, Paul B., 119, 134
Warren, Ralph, 47, 72
Warshauer, William, Jr., 74, 168
Washington and the Arts: A Guide and Directory to Federal Programs and Dollars for the Arts, 30, 117, 146
Washington, D.C. Metropolitan Area Foundation Directory, 38
Washington Foundation Journal, 67
Washington International Arts Letter, 24, 29, 67, 96, 124, 140, 141, 167

Wasserman, Paul, 24, 30
Waterhouse, Shirley A., 87
Wattel, Harold L, 155
Wayne, June, 101
Wearly, David A., 133
Webber, Ross A., 73
Weber, Joseph, 132, 152
Weber, Nathan, 152
Webster, Tony, 88
Wehle, Mary M., 74, 135
Weinberg, Charles B., 78, 80, 143
Weiner, Harold, 77, 148
Weiner, Richard, 149
Weisbrod, Burton A., 156
Weithorn, Stanley S., 129
Wertheimer, Stephen, 91, 107, 166
West Virginia Foundation Directory,
     38
Western States Shelter Network, 47,
     108, 134
What Happens in Public Relations,
     150
*What Volunteers Should Know for
     Successful Fundraising*, 117,
     157
Whelan, Donald J., 49
*Where America's Large Foundations
     Make Their Grants*, 31
Where the Money's At, 32
*Where to Get Money for Everything: A
     Complete Guide to Today's
     Money Sources*, 117
*While You're Up, Get Me a Grant: A
     Basic Bibliography on Grants*,
     23, 125
Whitaker, Benjamin Charles George,
     97, 104
Whitcomb, Nike B., 114
White, Anthony G., 23, 138
White, Mike, 95
White, Virginia P., 27, 121, 122, 136,
     166
Why Establish a Private Foundation,
     104
Wiener, Carolyn, 155
Wiley, John, and Sons, 168
Williams, M. Jane, 48, 101, 106
Williams, Martha E., 55
Willmer, Wesley K., 80, 144
Wilson, Betty L., 121
Wilson, Marlene, 153
Wilson, Thomas F., 125

Wilson, William K., 121
*Winning Techniques in Athletic Fund
     Raising*, 117, 146
*Winning the Money Game: A Guide
     to Community-based Library
     Fundraising*, 117, 146
Winston, Martin Bradley, 147
Winterfare (Arts and Business Coun-
     cil), 6
Wiseman, Molly, 34
Wkjei, Erik W., 120
Wolf, Thomas, 143
Wolfe, Joan, 154
Wolfenden Committee, 153
Woman's Day Book of Fund Raising,
     117
Women and Foundations/Corporate
     Philanthropy, 19, 67
*Women and Foundations/Corporate
     Philanthropy Newsletter*, 19,
     67
Women's Action Alliance, 110
*Word Processing Handbook: A Step-
     by-Step Guide to Automating
     Your Office*, 88
Working with Volunteers, 78, 148
World Dictionary of Awards and Prizes,
     31
Worsham, John P., 20
Writing for Public Relations, 150

Yeargain, Eloisa G., 87
Yiannakis, Andrew, 107
Young, Donald R., 81
Young, Joyce, 109, 136
Young Men's Christian Associations
     of the United States, 52, 155
Your First Business Computer, 85
Your Volunteer Program, 157
Youth Project, 111
Yung, Judith, 25

Zallen, Eugenia, 113
Zallen, Harold, 113
Zaltman, Gerald, 76, 138
Zax, Leonard A., 48, 120
Zesch, Lindy, 52, 81, 145
Zurcher, Arnold J., 74, 76, 101, 103